D1238980

THE NEW MIDDLE AGES

BONNIE WHEELER, *Series Editor*

The New Middle Ages is a series dedicated to transdisciplinary studies of medieval cultures, with particular emphasis on recuperating women's history on feminist and gender analyses. This peer-reviewed series includes both scholarly monographs and essay collections.

PUBLISHED BY PALGRAVE:

Women in the Medieval Islamic World: Power, Patronage, and Piety
edited by Gavin R. G. Hambly

The Ethics of Nature in the Middle Ages: On Boccaccio's Poetaphysics
by Gregory B. Stone

Presence and Presentation: Women in the Chinese Literati Tradition
by Sherry J. Mou

The Lost Love Letters of Heloise and Abelard: Perceptions of Dialogue in Twelfth-Century France
by Constant J. Mews

Understanding Scholastic Thought with Foucault
by Philipp W. Rosemann

For Her Good Estate: The Life of Elizabeth de Burgh
by Frances A. Underhill

Constructions of Widowhood and Virginity in the Middle Ages
edited by Cindy L. Carlson and Angela Jane Weisl

Motherhood and Mothering in Anglo-Saxon England
by Mary Dockray-Miller

Listening to Heloise: The Voice of a Twelfth-Century Woman
edited by Bonnie Wheeler

The Postcolonial Middle Ages
edited by Jeffrey Jerome Cohen

Chaucer's Pardoner and Gender Theory: Bodies of Discourse
by Robert S. Sturges

Crossing the Bridge: Comparative Essays on Medieval European and Heian Japanese Women Writers
edited by Barbara Stevenson and Cynthia Ho

Engaging Words: The Culture of Reading in the Later Middle Ages
by Laurel Amtower

Robes and Honor: The Medieval World of Investiture
edited by Stewart Gordon

Representing Rape in Medieval and Early Modern Literature
edited by Elizabeth Robertson and Christine M. Rose

Same Sex Love and Desire Among Women in the Middle Ages
edited by Francesca Canadé Sautman and Pamela Sheingorn

Sight and Embodiment in the Middle Ages: Ocular Desires
by Suzannah Biernoff

Listen, Daughter: The Speculum Virginum and the Formation of Religious Women in the Middle Ages
edited by Constant J. Mews

Science, the Singular, and the Question of Theology
by Richard A. Lee, Jr.

Gender in Debate from the Early Middle Ages to the Renaissance
edited by Thelma S. Fenster and Clare A. Lees

Malory's Morte Darthur: *Remaking Arthurian Tradition*
by Catherine Batt

The Vernacular Spirit: Essays on Medieval Religious Literature
edited by Renate Blumenfeld-Kosinski, Duncan Robertson, and Nancy Warren

Popular Piety and Art in the Late Middle Ages: Image Worship and Idolatry in England 1350–1500
by Kathleen Kamerick

Absent Narratives, Manuscript Textuality, and Literary Structure in Late Medieval England
by Elizabeth Scala

Creating Community with Food and Drink in Merovingian Gaul
by Bonnie Effros

Representation of Early Byzantine Empresses: Image and Empire
by Anne McClanan

Encountering Medieval Textiles and Dress: Objects, Texts, Images
edited by Désirée G. Koslin and Janet Snyder

Eleanor of Aquitaine: Lord and Lady
edited by Bonnie Wheeler and John Carmi Parsons

Isabel La Católica, Queen of Castile: Critical Essays
edited by David A. Boruchoff

Homoeroticism and Chivalry: Discourses of Male Same-Sex Desire in the Fourteenth Century
by Richard Zeikowitz

Portraits of Medieval Women: Family, Marriage, and Politics in England 1225–1350
by Linda E. Mitchell

Eloquent Virgins: From Thecla to Joan of Arc
by Maud Burnett McInerney

The Persistence of Medievalism: Narrative Adventures in Contemporary Culture
by Angela Jane Weisl

Capetian Women
edited by Kathleen Nolan

Joan of Arc and Spirituality
edited by Ann W. Astell and Bonnie Wheeler

The Texture of Society: Medieval Women in the Southern Low Countries
edited by Ellen E. Kittell and Mary A. Suydam

Charlemagne's Mustache: And Other Cultural Clusters of a Dark Age
by Paul Edward Dutton

Troubled Vision: Gender, Sexuality, and Sight in Medieval Text and Image
edited by Emma Campbell and Robert Mills

TROUBLED VISION: GENDER, SEXUALITY, AND SIGHT IN MEDIEVAL TEXT AND IMAGE

Edited by

Emma Campbell and Robert Mills

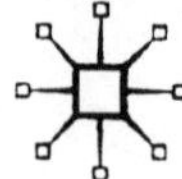

TROUBLED VISION

First published 2004 by
PALGRAVE MACMILLAN™
175 Fifth Avenue, New York, N.Y. 10010 and
Houndmills, Basingstoke, Hampshire, England RG21 6XS
Companies and representatives throughout the world

PALGRAVE MACMILLAN is the global academic imprint of the Palgrave Macmillan division of St. Martin's Press, LLC and of Palgrave Macmillan Ltd. Macmillan® is a registered trademark in the United States, United Kingdom and other countries. Palgrave is a registered trademark in the European Union and other countries.

ISBN 1–4039–6343–6

Library of Congress Cataloging-in-Publication Data is on file at the Library of Congress.

A catalogue record for this book is available from the British Library.

Design by Newgen Imaging Systems (P) Ltd., Chennai, India.

First edition: May 2004
10 9 8 7 6 5 4 3 2 1

Printed in the United States of America.

CONTENTS

ILLUSTRATIONS

ACKNOWLEDGMENTS

The impetus for this collection of essays on the relationship between gender, sexuality, and vision came from a conference organized by the Gender and Medieval Studies Group in London in January 2002 called "Seeing Gender: Perspectives on Medieval Gender and Sexuality." The conference was supported by grants from the British Academy and the Royal Historical Society; we are also grateful to King's College London for hosting the event and to all the participants who made it such a lively and stimulating occasion. In choosing to narrow the focus of this volume to the theme of "troubled vision," we, the editors, were very conscious of the fact that many of the excellent papers presented at the "Seeing Gender" conference could not be included: we would like to acknowledge the authors of these papers all the same, since their conversations on medieval vision have undoubtedly enriched this book. The editors wish to express special thanks to the contributors to *Troubled Vision* for their efficient and thoughtful revisions. Bonnie Wheeler has been extraordinarily helpful from start to finish, displaying enthusiasm for the project throughout and responding with grace and efficiency to our many editorial requests. We are also grateful to the editors at Palgrave Macmillan for their patience in seeing the volume through to completion.

Emma Campbell and Robert Mills
London, June 2003

INTRODUCTION: TROUBLED VISION

Emma Campbell and Robert Mills

Trouble, in its more conventional deployments, betrays a range of negative associations. It communicates a sense of worry or annoyance ("That's the trouble"), a state of being blamed ("She's always getting into trouble"), diagnoses of ill health or malfunction ("She's got heart trouble"), or a more than usual amount of exertion ("I had real trouble finding you"); the word also often designates moments of political and social unrest or cultural disorder ("The trouble spilled out onto the streets"). So when Judith Butler appropriates the term in the context of gender, in her by now classic study *Gender Trouble*, she self-consciously goes against the grain of conventional usage, by suggesting the fruitful and dynamic possibilities of trouble—its place in practices of subversion and moments of rehabilitation.[1] The argument she makes is that gender is a product of discursive repetition, a process that provides the opportunity both for the naturalization of gender, in the context of performative citationality, and for its subversion, in the context of parodic re-presentation.

Arguably, however, Butler's exploitation of the relationship between gender and trouble also offers a rejoinder to long-held associations between femininity and impenetrability in Western thought. Freud's characterization of women as a "dark continent" and Lacan's assertion that woman "n'existe pas" are among the most notorious recent examples of a tendency to demarcate gender identities in terms of their connections with invisibility and inscrutability. These paradigms have been the subjects of discussion and critique in the work of French feminists like Simone de Beauvoir, who, on the opening page of *The Second Sex*, asks the wonderfully tongue-in-cheek question "Are there women, really?"; and Luce Irigaray, who suggests that, within a phallogocentric linguistic economy, women comprise the mysterious *unrepresentable*, the "sex" which is not "one."[2] In turn, one of the motivating factors behind the writing of women's history and the critical reception of women's cultural production in the twentieth century was the desire that woman, as an identity, might at long last "come into the light" and be effectively rendered visible. One of the regrets commonly expressed by writers of medieval women's history in the last fifty years has been that, in the sources, "women are conspicuous by their absence."[3] In shifting the debate from the category of "women" to an understanding of gender as an identity without essence, Butler problematizes this model by suggesting that feminist analyses are themselves frequently indebted to the structures and categories that they wish to critique. Writing women into history, making them visible, potentially endorses a concept of identity that assumes the existence of a unified, naturalized state of femininity that coheres around the term *women*, a state which historians have the capacity to reveal by casting the illuminating beams of their scholarly spotlights upon it. Nonetheless, a deliberate and self-conscious performance of femininity, Butler suggests, say in the context of a contemporary drag show, might well parody and thereby reveal the structures of power that it cites, by exposing the citational mechanisms by which those structures are maintained as normal. In this way, the historical *conditions* by which a particular attribute, concept, or action is gendered male or female might be rendered visible, rather than gendered identities themselves.[4]

What has often gone unobserved in responses to Butler's arguments is the importance of the visual dimension in her proposed sites of subversion. Drag, after all, is a spectacle that typically relies on visualization for its effects—on a person choosing to wear the visual signifiers and perform the "corporeal style" of one gender or another in such a way as to suggest a dissonance between anatomical sex, gender identity, and gender performance. As Butler remarks, drag creates of women "a unified picture," while at the same time implicitly revealing the imitative, contingent structure of gender.[5] The drag artist thus inhabits gender in a way that makes it almost too visible: the essence of gender eludes the spectator insofar as it is revealed to inhere not in physical characteristics but in the spectacle of gendered performance itself. The unified image to which Butler refers thus emerges at a site of disruption where the natural foundation of gender is performatively unhinged; visibility appears at the very moment when the foundations of what is supposedly "seen" are undermined, where performance and essence are at once separated and confused.

The title of this collection insists, after Butler, that the visual encounter is the site of a particular kind of trouble. But the concept of "troubled vision" is not necessarily designed to reproduce Butler's paradigms per se. The definition of performativity in *Gender Trouble* draws implicitly on linguistic analysis; these models of speech act theory and performative enunciation have been articulated more directly in her later work too, most recently in the context of an attempt to consider the relationship between the universal and the particular in modern philosophy and politics.[6] Contributors to the present volume likewise deploy frameworks that are language-based: Foucauldian notions of discourse; Derridean patterns of reading; psychoanalytic concepts of the symbolic; Žižekian narratives of subject formation. Indeed, language could be said to be one of the book's central concerns which, for all its focus on vision, places a great deal of emphasis on the effects of a visual hermeneutic in written narrative—the "text and image" of the subtitle proposes that the two components be thought of together, in their narrative as well as figurative contexts. So by suggesting that the book "troubles" linguistic models, we do not mean to imply that there is a sphere of vision that might be posited as an ontologically prior realm of experience to language and signification—this is not a book about how "medieval people saw their world," beyond what they remembered, imagined, represented, said, and wrote about it. But contributors do advance the notion that vision, while implicated in the production of normative structures and paradigms, might also provide opportunities for troubling forms of engagement with power and might therefore be integrated into a more nuanced understanding of gender performativity in medieval culture. Vision is not simply interpreted here as a prop for power, that which opens the eyes and makes the observer "like God" (to paraphrase the serpent's pronouncements to Eve in Genesis about the consequences of eating from the tree of knowledge).[7] Rather, by continually skirting around its object and never encountering that object directly, vision presents the possibility of a space resistant to normalization and discursive fixing; it follows that modes of discourse that claim the self-evident reality of a particular visual experience (a vision of God, for instance, or a naked, sexed body) might find it necessary to continually, and paradoxically, communicate the meaning of what is being seen, in a mode of representation for which Emma Campbell in this volume has coined the expression "hermeneutic vision."

In this respect the collection is consummately medieval. Suzannah Biernoff, whose book *Sight and Embodiment in the Middle Ages* is one of the most recent contributions to scholarship on premodern visuality, outlines the ways in which vision in the Middle Ages was always mediated by discourses about vision.[8] Assuming no simple correspondence between how people looked and what they looked at—between vision as a mode of interpretation and the visual arts—Biernoff nonetheless shows how medieval theologians and optical theorists attempted to reconcile concepts of a disembodied or distancing gaze amenable to scientific discovery with ideas of vision as an intermediary zone between viewers and their objects. While for thirteenth-century theorists like Roger Bacon a "perspectivist" optical gaze certainly opened up a space for scientific scrutiny by abstracting vision from the flesh, ocular experience was also simultaneously deemed to effect a corporeal mingling of self and other, a process in which one is altered by the things at which one looks. This attempt at synthesis was a product, in part, of a tension between Christian and classical scientific imperatives; its consequence was to implicate the visual dimensions of dispassionate science (what Biernoff terms the "optical gaze") within a logic of fleshly desire ("carnal vision"). As such, medieval theories of vision themselves assume no easy fit between vision, power, agency, and knowledge. Seeing is not so much believing as *feeling*—an itinerant, palpating emotion that is expressed in matter and that, in the words of Bacon, "is a kind of pain."[9] The coincidence of seeing and knowing can only be effected, it follows, by repressing the opacity and unpredictability of human embodiment.

These theories have implications in turn for our understanding of medieval gender. For the belief that vision revolves around an alteration of the viewer's body by its object—the idea that in *acting* the eye could also be *acted on*—potentially troubles the dichotomizing paradigms of modern gender criticism, by attributing stereotypically masculine *and* feminine functions to the mechanism of sight and thereby exhibiting a degree of what Biernoff characterizes as "sexual-symbolic indeterminacy." In this respect, medieval culture produces no simple confirmation of the existence of a predatory masculine gaze or of a reparative, but nonetheless fundamentally restricted, feminine field of vision—two paradigms that have been especially influential in modern feminist commentaries on the maintenance of patriarchal relations through modes of representation like visual art, photography, and film.[10] Commenting on imagery of "wounding" and "penetrating" eyes in medieval courtly love literature, Biernoff writes: "the male gaze is by no means always phallic; and ladies' eyes are not always chaste, reflective orbs or instruments of maternal love. The ocular attributes that, for a modern reader, are so sexually resonant . . . seem repeatedly to be assigned to the wrong sex."[11]

Biernoff's remarks strike a chord with the arguments put forward by Francesca Nicholson and Simon Gaunt, Chapters Three and Four in this volume; for, both of these chapters challenge (in different ways) a common critical assumption that the gaze in lyric poetry secures gender and/or the forms of sexuality that gender is assumed to underwrite. In so doing, however, Gaunt's argument in particular counters Biernoff's assertion that psychoanalytic paradigms of vision reach their historical limits in the medieval period, "where," Biernoff claims, "subject–object relations (mediated by vision) are more indeterminate, and where bodies (or at least *fleshly* bodies) are more fluid."[12] If anything, Chapters Four to Six, by Gaunt, Campbell, and Robert Mills, try to blur the line that Biernoff seeks to (re-)draw between the modern and pre-modern periods in this regard, suggesting that psychoanalytic models are not as rigidly determinist as we have—in some cases—been led to believe and that these models might therefore still usefully contribute to an understanding of the troubling effects of vision in medieval culture.

The failure of vision to articulate a clear division between subject and object nonetheless points to a characteristic intrinsic to the notion of troubled vision. For, if it is the case that vision can have an unsettling effect on subjective boundaries, it also concomitantly perturbs the forms of gender and sexuality that depend upon such distinctions. In a related way, the concept of troubled vision is itself intimately connected to what might be described as a "queer optics": a mode of visuality that assumes no necessary link between vision and gendered agency, and posits no visual encounter as "authentic" or stable in its effects. Troubled vision thus insists upon the potential in any act of visualization for the mobilization of gender and sexuality in ways that can unsettle (as well as confirm) their normative value.

Although not always explicitly acknowledged, the potentially queer effects of vision inform a number of contributions to this book. In addition to the chapters of Nicholson and Gaunt, the essays by Cary Howie and Catherine M. Keen (Chapters Seven and Eight) explore the role of vision or visualization in negotiating between the subject and sexualized object of the gaze. Keen's reading of early Italian verse demonstrates how the modification of the erotic discourse of the lyric to address a personified, feminized city results in often problematically sexualized encounters with the *città-donna* [city-lady]. In his exploration of Iacopone da Todi's poetics, Howie suggests how vision may be implicated in the transformations of gender and sexuality developed in the Italian poet's devotional works. Although neither of these chapters takes queer methodologies as its starting point, it is not difficult to see how, in different ways, the troubling effects of vision in literary representation are in both cases implicated in the destabilizing of (hetero)sexual economy and the forms of gendered agency and identity that such an economy sets up.

Another facet of this exploration of troubled vision as a modality of queer optics is the investigation of attempts to visualize and thereby secure forms of gendered agency and sexual identity. Chapters One, Two, Six, and Nine to Eleven, by Diane Wolfthal, William Burgwinkle, Mills, Anne Simon, Sylvia Huot, and Miranda Griffin, interpret and respond to these attempts in various ways. Simon's contribution, for instance, argues that *Der Ritter vom Turn* (a German translation of the Book of the Knight of the Tower) constructs a narrative space in which the desire and agency of female readers are circumscribed within a masculine disciplinary framework. In this respect, Simon's work presents ideas similar to those recently articulated in Madeline H. Caviness's innovative study *Visualizing Women in the Middle Ages*, which explores the ways in which the work of the fetish in medieval visual culture constructs a circumscribed version of femininity while at the same time excluding "real" women.[13] Huot's close reading of the Old French *Roman de Perceforest* reveals the internal inconsistencies in such a representational regime, exploring how depictions of the feminine can exploit this incoherence to particular ideological effect.

The disciplinary force of scopic regimes in imagining and policing sexuality as well as gender is a theme explored in greater detail in other chapters, such as those of Burgwinkle, Mills, and Wolfthal. Wolfthal considers the ways in which late medieval depictions of same-sex love may have been used to legitimate or to condemn certain forms of sexual desire in particular historical contexts. Mills's argument concerning the sexuality of the virgin identifies points of departure between, on the one hand, Foucauldian notions of the disciplinary gaze and, on the other, psychoanalytic models of the gaze as Other. By so doing, Mills argues that the regulation of virgin sexuality within the narrative framework of early Middle English anchoritic writing both attempts and fails to secure the rigid identities that disciplinary models seek to inscribe. Also exploring the role of vision in the regulation of the sexual body, Burgwinkle's argument concerning the work of Peter Damian raises explicitly an issue that other contributors deal with more indirectly, namely, the relationship between visualization and epistemology. As Burgwinkle suggests, Damian's efforts to contain and treat sodomy appear in the context of his attempt both to visualize and, in an important sense, to produce the sodomite as a recognizable object (and subject) of knowledge. Vision in this account thus constitutes an important part of the taxonomic project in which sexuality is given epistemological—as well as visual—tangibility.

Burgwinkle nonetheless suggests, as do other contributors, that the processes through which gender and sexuality are supposedly rendered visible are often inadequate to the task of representing such categories in clearly delineated form. Griffin's chapter addresses this issue by considering the ways in which the representation of the feminine in modern as well as medieval works constitutes a "blind spot" that simultaneously resists and invites representation. For Griffin, blind spots such as these do not imply an absence of meaning; rather, they are at the very heart of its production, generating a surplus of signification that undermines visibility through its overdetermination. In taking examples from Derrida's commentary on Freud, Griffin's argument can thus be seen to return to questions of epistemology, this time in connection with the production of knowledge of or about the feminine.

As this would suggest, the themes of this collection share concerns with thinkers such as Michel Foucault and Eve Kosofsky Sedgwick as well as

Judith Butler.[14] The interest of both Foucault and Sedgwick in exploring the ways in which sexuality is regulated by means of its definition and classification within discourses that make it an "open secret"—an object of knowledge that is at once effectively suppressed and endlessly discussed—(often in the interests of heterosexual hegemony)—certainly has a pertinence to the issues raised here, especially in the chapters by Wolfthal, Burgwinkle, and Mills. However, the visual dynamics of such an epistemological project are, in these essays, shown to have a more than incidental role not only in producing knowledge but also in troubling or undermining it. As Griffin suggests, this is not simply a matter of challenging the bases of what can be "seen" and understood; it is also a matter of considering how representational mechanisms have an investment in a logic of visibility. What the various contributions to this volume thus invite is a consideration of how troubled vision is located at the very core of representational and epistemological systems, and how it informs the ways in which medieval culture negotiates its relationship to gender and sexuality through these systems.

Such an appreciation is of central importance to an awareness of the way in which modern critical approaches to medieval texts and images also have an investment in producing the Middle Ages as an object of knowledge. Nicholson's essay (Chapter Three) in this volume examines precisely this relationship, demonstrating how modern categories work to reveal or to obscure the more troubling sexual possibilities that might be read into the articulation of desire in Occitan lyrics attributed to the so-called *trobairitz*. In this respect, Nicholson's argument indicates one of the ways in which troubled vision might usefully be brought to bear on the critical categories that make the Middle Ages "visible" to modern eyes. This argument demonstrates how critical readings might themselves be implicated in revealing and suppressing particular modalities of sexual desire by imagining (and reimagining) the sex/gender system upon which such impulses draw, closing down sexual possibilities even as they supposedly bring them to light.

An approach of this sort might, we believe, be developed in relation to the ways in which modern approaches more generally may both trouble and be troubled by vision. This, indeed, is an issue that has implicitly informed recent discussion on the place of vision within the Western critical imaginary. Thus, Martin Jay's book *Downcast Eyes* advances an argument concerning the discourse of antivisuality—or, what he terms "ocularphobia"—which he identifies in modern French thought.[15] Jay argues that thinkers such as Foucault, Lacan, and Derrida have an ambivalence—even an antipathy—toward vision and its role in post-Enlightenment philosophy that leads them to be at once obsessed by vision and unable to countenance it. Describing this in terms of a "denigration" of vision, Jay argues for an almost pathological problematization of vision in modern thought, a problematization that can be related to the idea of "troubling" that we have proposed here. Jay's argument is an important study of the troubling engagement with vision that has been (and continues to be) staged by modern philosophy in the West. However, what remains unclear is the role vision has to play in contemporary theory as a result. Jay's negative assessment of French philosophy's various encounters with vision would seem to imply that this obsession with vision is an illness to be treated; yet he does suggest in conclusion that this malady may nonetheless have beneficial side-effects. As intimated here, we—along with other contributors to this collection—have chosen to explore the productive possibilities that a troubled and troubling relationship to vision might produce. More importantly, we contend, along with Nicholson, that theoretical approaches of all kinds might benefit from retaining a self-consciously problematic relationship to vision in order to exploit its troubling potential.

As Jay points out, the root of the ancient Greek word for theory, *theoria* (meaning "to look at attentively, to behold"), is connected to the word *theatre*. In this way, Greek thought was, according to Jay, abetted by an ocularcentric bias, which maintained a distinction between subject and object so that the latter might be neutrally apprehended by the former.[16] The medieval model of visuality that we have outlined in connection with Biernoff's study possibly provides an alternative to such a perspective and in so doing may even gesture toward a new visual model for theory itself. Bacon's notion of the fusion of subject and object within the visual encounter, his argument that "it receives the species of the thing seen and exerts its own force in the medium as far as the visible object,"[17] suggests that vision does not necessarily have to distance its object and that seeing through the lens of theory therefore might be construed in terms of approximation, intimacy, and reciprocal contact. This view of theory, indeed, has a correlative in medievalist Carolyn Dinshaw's notion of "the touch": a coming together of bodies through time and space that constitutes the ultimate theoretical gesture.[18] Dinshaw develops her epistemology of touch in relation to a model of queer history writing that foregrounds relations of contingency, indeterminacy, and heterogeneity in bringing together past and present. Yet Dinshaw's model of "the queer touch" perhaps overlooks the extent to which vision might provide a mode of engagement with the pre-modern that is itself a coming together of bodies across time, and even, to paraphrase Baconian optics, a form of touching. This theoretical encounter would therefore be both troubling and potentially queer in the sense that vision designates a relationship in which boundaries are blurred, in which subject and object bleed into one another, and in which one always, as it were, "sees through a glass darkly."

The essays collected here attempt such an engagement in a wide variety of ways, presenting a diverse spectrum of approaches to the categories of vision, gender, and sexuality in medieval culture. They shed light on the troubling effects of visual encounters in a range of disciplines, including art history; religious studies; cultural studies; and English, French, German, Italian, and Latin literary studies. As acknowledged above, the volume is also inscribed with difference in relation to the many thinkers and theorists who have inspired individual essays—Leo Bersani, Judith Butler, Joan Copjec, Jacques Derrida, Michel Foucault, Laura Mulvey, Jacques Lacan, Slavoj Žižek, to name but a few—and with respect to the relative attention paid to matters of historical, social, political, and iconographic context. But all essays in the volume share a common commitment to troubling commonly held assumptions about the relationship between gender, sexuality, and vision, whether in its medieval or modern manifestations. If this is a book about building connections between sexual and gender identities and visual frameworks, then it is also a book about dislodging or disrupting some of those connections.

Part One, "Troubled Desires," includes three essays that problematize the categories used to envision and materialize desire in medieval culture. These essays are linked by their appreciation of the extent to which techniques of visualizing desire—for example, painting, confessional writing, or critical classification—might be used to produce and deploy knowledge about sexuality and gender, both in the Middle Ages and today. Although treating material produced in very different cultural contexts, Wolfthal, Burgwinkle, and Nicholson all take up the issue of how cultures attempt to represent, obscure, or elide gender identities and sexual possibilities that have conventionally been conceived as culturally troubling.

Diane Wolfthal, in "Picturing Same-Sex Desire: The Falconer and his Lover in Images by Petrus Christus and the Housebook Master," makes the argument that same-sex desire is occasionally visualized in northern renaissance art, but that the consequences of that visualization are many. Focusing on two previously unidentified (one might say "unseen") images of male–male relationships whose interpretation hinges on the depiction of a falcon, Wolfthal argues that a constellation of visual motifs work in each instance to variously produce and contain the possibility of transgressive sexual relations. But even if visual artifacts of this kind manifest an attempt on the part of artists or patrons to condemn same-sex desire as sinful, they do not necessarily succeed in their aims since, as Wolfthal concludes, her examples "both serve to make the invisible visible."

William Burgwinkle's "Visible and Invisible Bodies and Subjects in Peter Damian" switches from painted depictions of same-sex desire to their representation in the context of the "first comprehensive guidebook to

Christian homophobia." Reading Peter Damian's notorious *Liber gomorrhianus* through its metaphors of sight and seeing, Burgwinkle argues that the assimilation of a visual framework with representations of gender and sexuality in such texts produces, and perhaps even inadvertently advocates, a kind of subjectless subjectivity that uncannily recalls the work of modern queer theorists like Leo Bersani. At the same time, Damian, by remaining beholden to the institutional pleasures of embodying an all-seeing, all-knowing gaze, is finally unable to abandon the notions of selfhood and vision to which he arguably presents an alternative.

Francesca Nicholson's "Seeing Women Troubadours without the '-itz' and '-isms'" likewise considers questions of subjectivity, but from the point of view of modern categories and classifications. Troubling the ways in which contemporary writing on troubadour poetry attempts to "see" and assimilate women poets by deploying a critical vocabulary that produces the categorizing effects of "-isms," Nicholson asks whether it might be possible to articulate a different, more open-ended sense of troubadour gender and desire that relies on semantic troubling rather than visual and discursive fixing.

Part Two, "Troubled Looks," interrogates what is perhaps the thorniest issue in recent feminist accounts of vision: the gender of "the gaze." Examining this issue from a perspective informed by psychoanalytic criticism, but in what may be seen as a critique of certain feminist paradigms that envisage themselves as coming out of a psychoanalytic framework (for instance, Laura Mulvey's hypothesis of the "male gaze"), essays by Gaunt, Campbell, and Mills all suggest ways in which the gaze might be theorized as a source of disruption rather than simply a location for repressive patriarchal identifications.

While many critics have focused on the dynamics of *looking at* sexual objects in courtly love lyrics, Simon Gaunt, in "The Look of Love: The Gender of the Gaze in Troubadour Lyric," considers what happens when the gaze itself becomes the object of desire and the effects this has on the sex–gender system of troubadour poetry. Examining the lyrics of Bernart de Ventadorn through the lens of Lacanian formulations of the gaze, Gaunt notes a degree of congruence between Lacan's conception of the gaze's alignment with the Other—the inscrutable, inaccessible space in which desire is realized—and troubadour poetry presenting the gaze as a mortifying abyss. The consequences are, Gaunt says, gender troubling: "The gaze must . . . be located elsewhere, which is to say nowhere, in a space that escapes and confounds gender by subsuming the feminine and the masculine."

Emma Campbell's "Sacrificial Spectacle and Interpassive Vision in the Anglo-Norman Life of Saint Faith," considers the politics of ocularity in the medieval saints' life from the point of view of "interpassivity": a concept developed by Slavoj Žižek that relies upon Lacanian paradigms of decentered subjectivity. Campbell deploys Žižek's formulation as a way of exploring the dynamics of witness in accounts of martyrdom and the implications of such dynamics for notions of the gendered gaze in hagiography. Reading the visual encounters between witness and saint in Simon of Walsingham's *Vie de Sainte Fey* as the setting for an ideological maneuver in which the faith of the reader/listener is reinforced, Campbell argues that a consideration of what she terms "hermeneutic vision" in hagiographic texts draws attention to figures other than the saint with whom readers or listeners were encouraged to identify. This in turn, she suggests, complicates perceptions of these narratives as the vehicles of an appropriating male gaze.

Robert Mills, in "Seeing Face to Face: Troubled Looks in the Katherine Group," makes the point that texts written for thirteenth-century female anchorites are centrally concerned with vision and that the saints' lives produced in these contexts might be usefully explored in relation to their didactic counterparts: treatises such as *Hali Meiðhad* and *Sawles Warde*, which, like martyrdom narratives, articulate the viewpoint of the virgin, have largely been ignored by critics exploring the dynamics of the "virginal gaze." Mills juxtaposes his analysis of the texts with the film critic Joan Copjec's account, in her book *Read My Desire*, of the various trajectories of the gaze in modern criticism: Copjec disagrees with feminist film theory about the nature of its psychoanalytic heritage. Mills suggests that Copjec's promotion of a rigorously Lacanian approach to vision helps foreground the ideological stake of anchoritic writing in producing a desire for face-to-face encounter with God that is fantasized as possible but nonetheless continually deferred. This, he argues, might in turn trouble perceptions of a neat correlation between vision and identity in early Middle English anchoritic writings.

While all of the essays in *Troubled Vision* pay close attention to the issue of representation as it impacts on constructions of gender and sexuality, the essays in Part Three, "Troubled Representations," argue that the figuration of gender and sexuality produces disruptions in medieval texts by virtue of their metaphorical status, and that this disruption is often mirrored by a frequently problematic modern critical engagement with these narratives. These essays suggest that eroticism is particularly conducive to a troubling presentation of gender and that the discourse of sex, when combined with devotional or political motifs, potentially undermines its perceptual stability.

Cary Howie's "Vision Beyond Measure: The Threshold of Iacopone's Bedroom" offers a challenging account of medieval visionary literature in terms of what he calls its "spatial optics." Focusing especially on the poetry of Iacopone da Todi, medieval Italy's most outrageous vernacular devotional poet, Howie explores how sensation, and more particularly vision, participates in transcendence and how this participation is often presented through spatial imagery. He suggests that modern scholars sometimes find the eroticism of this imagery troubling, but that Iacopone's descriptions of mystical marriage have the capacity to open up new sensory—and trans-sensory—possibilities that produce gender itself as an effect of and participant in space.

Like Howie, Catherine M. Keen's "Sex and the Medieval City: Viewing the Body Politic from Exile in Early Italian Verse" considers metaphorical representations of gender that, in being divorced from bodily reality, disrupt or trouble the gender to which they supposedly refer. Investigating the overlap between amorous and political themes in early Italian verse expressing desire for the figure of the alluring *città-donna*, the feminized body politic, Keen argues that the corporeality assigned to these figures—their visualization in terms of corporeal metaphors—generates a destabilized understanding of gender by virtue of the political allegories in which the lyrics are simultaneously steeped. Political circumstances lead lyricists to cast their ladies in visually ambiguous situations and their lyrics, as such, "reveal an uneasy awareness that the social realities of urban Italy cannot be comfortably accommodated into the metaphorical discourse of courtliness."

If the essays in Parts Two and Three of this collection explore vision as the corollary of a textual gaze on the one hand and a sexual poetics on the other, the essays in Part Four, "Troubled Reading," draw together the previous two sections in exploring how, in the reading process, issues of vision and representation might be combined. Demonstrating how the perception of text and image might be thought of in its narrative context rather than in terms of single moments of visual encounter, the essays by Anne Simon, Sylvia Huot, and Miranda Griffin suggest that a visual focus troubles texts by producing blind spots, mirroring, or symbolic confusion.

Anne Simon, in "Reading Reading Women: Double-Mirroring the Dame in *Der Ritter vom Turn*," focuses on the interaction between textual and visual techniques in circumscribing female behavior in the German translation of a popular French courtesy text. Basing her analysis on a printed edition of the text illustrated by woodcuts, Simon argues that the iconography of the woodcuts, with its echoes of courtly as well as biblical traditions, is not as unambiguous as may at first sight appear. The text, Simon argues, can be read on several levels, permitting a fluidity of interpretative possibilities that subverts the stated purpose of the text and may leave room for women to read text and image to suit their own ends.

Sylvia Huot's "Visualizing the Feminine in the *Roman de Perceforest:* The Episode of the 'Conte de la Rose' " focuses on an episode in a fourteenth-century French romance in which troubled vision is clearly at issue: two motifs, a rose and a shield, are deployed in the narrative as alternative visual emblems for the autonomous woman, subject to different readings: a beautiful, steadfast, and precious thing; ephemeral, vulnerable to male predation, and as unnatural as a fresh rose in winter; and a powerful dominatrix who is paradoxically also easily manipulated by masculine desire. These images, as Huot points out, serve to promote the ideological message of the text, which aims, among other things, to reinforce heterosexuality and nationhood through a preoccupation with sexual violence. But they also adopt a more "woman-centered perspective," using visual coding to pit an antifeminist reading against one that is more pro-feminine.

A privileged category in deconstructive literary criticism is the blind spot produced by double meaning: it functions as a metaphor for the mystery that no amount of revelation can illumine. Miranda Griffin's "Too Many Women: Reading Freud, Derrida, and *Lancelot*" engages with some of the implications of this for medieval texts by pursuing the tension between gender as visible sign and gender as blind spot in the manuscript tradition of the Prose *Lancelot*. Exploring variations between manuscripts in the light of Derrida's reading of the resistance encountered and constructed by psychoanalysis, Griffin argues that the limits of reading are gendered feminine in both instances: women mark a place of unknowability, where too much meaning rubs up against the impossibility of interpretation. As such the text and its female characters cannot be thought of in singular terms, but are instead troublingly plural, demanding closer scrutiny, yet defying the gaze that seeks a unified corpus.

Sarah Salih's response to the collection (Chapter Twelve) enlarges upon the themes of the volume as a whole by considering the volume's scrutiny of gender and vision in terms of "a medieval which looks back": she pursues, through an illuminating example from *Mandeville's Travels*, the extent to which medieval texts and images have the capacity to offer a backward glance at theory that is itself potentially disruptive.

Notes

1. Judith Butler, *Gender Trouble: Feminism and the Subversion of Identity* (London: Routledge, 1990), esp. the discussion of trouble in the Preface, pp. vii–viii.
2. Simone de Beauvoir, *The Second Sex*, ed. and trans. H.M. Parshley (London: Jonathan Cape, 1953), p. 1; Luce Irigaray, *This Sex Which Is Not One*, trans. Catherine Porter (Ithaca, NY: Cornell University Press, 1985), esp. pp. 23–33.

3. See, for instance, Henrietta Leyser, *Medieval Women: A Social History of Women in England, 450–1500* (London: Weidenfeld and Nicolson, 1995), who makes precisely such a remark in the context of the *Anglo-Saxon Chronicle*, p. 3.
4. Butler, *Gender Trouble*, pp. 134–41.
5. Butler, *Gender Trouble*, p. 137; see also the extended discussion of drag in Judith Butler, *Bodies That Matter: On the Discursive Limits of "Sex"* (London: Routledge, 1993), pp. 121–40, 230–33.
6. Butler, *Bodies That Matter*, esp. pp. 224–30; Judith Butler, *Excitable Speech: A Politics of the Performative* (London: Routledge, 1997); Judith Butler, "Restaging the Universal: Hegemony and the Limits of Formalism," in Judith Butler, Ernesto Laclau, and Slavoj Žižek, *Contingency, Hegemony, Universality: Contemporary Dialogues on the Left* (London: Verso, 2000), pp. 11–43.
7. Gen. 3.4–7.
8. Suzannah Biernoff, *Sight and Embodiment in the Middle Ages* (New York: Palgrave Macmillan, 2002).
9. Roger Bacon, *The Opus Majus of Roger Bacon*, trans. R.B. Burke, 2 vols. (New York: Russell, 1962), 2:445–46 (5.1.4.2), quoted in Biernoff, *Sight and Embodiment*, p. 96.
10. The classic film theoretical account of the "male gaze" is Laura Mulvey's "Visual Pleasure and Narrative Cinema," *Screen* 16.3 (1975): 6–18, reprinted in Mulvey, *Visual and Other Pleasures* (London: Macmillan, 1989), pp. 14–26; an articulation of comparable views with respect to art history can be found in Griselda Pollock, *Vision and Difference: Femininity, Feminism and Histories of Art* (London: Routledge, 1988); on the prospect of a reflexive "female gaze" in modern scopic regimes, see Lorraine Gamman and Margaret Marshement (eds.), *The Female Gaze: Women as Viewers of Popular Culture* (London: Women's Press, 1988).
11. Biernoff, *Sight and Embodiment*, p. 58.
12. Biernoff, *Sight and Embodiment*, p. 1.
13. Madeline H. Caviness, *Visualizing Women in the Middle Ages: Sight, Spectacle, and Scopic Economy* (Philadelphia: University of Pennsylvania Press, 2001), esp. pp. 1–16.
14. Michel Foucault, *Discipline and Punish: The Birth of the Prison*, trans. Alan Sheridan (London: Penguin, 1977); Michel Foucault, *The History of Sexuality*, vol. 1, *An Introduction*, trans. Robert Hurley (London: Penguin, 1978); Eve Kosofsky Sedgwick, *Epistemology of the Closet* (London: Penguin, 1990).
15. Martin Jay, *Downcast Eyes: The Denigration of Vision in Twentieth-Century French Thought* (Berkeley: University of California Press, 1993).
16. Jay, *Downcast Eyes*, pp. 22–25.
17. Bacon, *Opus Majus*, 2:470 (5.1.7.3), quoted in Biernoff, *Sight and Embodiment*, p. 86.
18. Carolyn Dinshaw, *Getting Medieval: Sexualities and Communities, Pre- and Postmodern* (Durham, NC: Duke University Press, 1999).

PART ONE

TROUBLED DESIRES

CHAPTER 1

PICTURING SAME-SEX DESIRE: THE FALCONER AND HIS LOVER IN IMAGES BY PETRUS CHRISTUS AND THE HOUSEBOOK MASTER

Diane Wolfthal

The consequences of visualizing transgressive sexual desires are many. This chapter investigates two previously unrecognized depictions of same-sex desire, Petrus Christus's Goldsmith's Shop *and the Housebook Master's* Falconer, *and considers the responses they might have elicited.*

This chapter will explore two previously unrecognized images of same-sex desire, Petrus Christus's *Couple in a Goldsmith's Shop* and the Housebook Master's *Falconer*, which both employ the falcon as a sign of love (figures 1.1 and 1.8).[1] These works have never been satisfactorily explained. Much has been written about the *Goldsmith's Shop*, a canonical work within the field of northern renaissance art, but the literature is characterized by uncertainty, debate, and contradiction, precisely because no one has been able to make sense of the mysterious male couple depicted in the mirror in the right foreground (figure 1.2). The *Falconer* is less well known, but the few studies that discuss the print dismiss it too easily, thereby misinterpreting it. Both works are part of a complex cultural history of sexuality that is just now being written, which explores the conceptualization of heterosexual and homosexual desire, and shows how they became constructed as opposites in the West, with one defined as the norm and the other as deviance.[2] Furthermore, these images demonstrate that love between men is implicated in the history of marriage, an institution that became the privileged site of heterosexuality. Yet these works also reveal that although some images reinforce the idea of sodomy as sin, others, to quote Jacqueline Murray, "extend beyond a litany of prohibitions and condemnations."[3]

One problem in discussing this topic is how to identify images of same-sex lovers. As Warren Johannson and William A. Percy have observed, homosexuals were difficult to recognize visually because they were generally forced to live in "a state of outward assimilation." Unlike Jews or prostitutes who were required to wear visible signs of identification, men who loved men became "the invisible ones," and were not marked by any outward sign of difference.[4] For this reason they are often difficult to identify in works of art. Furthermore, until the rise of gay studies in the 1980s, art historians were by and large not open to the possibility that art could depict same-sex love. But it is precisely because art historians have until recently failed to consider the possibility of interpretations based on sexuality that it today presents such a potentially fruitful category of analysis. This chapter contributes to the growing number of recent studies that embrace that goal.[5] It will not explore homosexual self-definition, or the acts and practices that accompanied it, but rather will be concerned with the cultural representation of sexual desire between men.

Petrus Christus's *Couple in a Goldsmith's Shop*

The artist and date of the *Goldsmith's Shop* are securely known, since the Latin inscription at the bottom of the painting reads, "Master Petrus Christus made me in the year 1449" (figure 1.1).[6] But the function and nature of the painting are disputed. Some scholars support Peter Schabacker's proposal that it was commissioned by the silver- and goldsmiths' guild of Bruges for public display in their chapel, which was renovated in the same year that the painting was completed.[7] According to this theory, it represents St. Eloy, patron saint of gold- and silversmiths, and served as a vocational painting, much like Roger van der Weyden's *St. Luke Painting the Virgin*.[8] Others, however, have recently questioned the basis on which this theory rests and suggested instead that the panel is a genre painting that served a non-devotional function, perhaps in a shop window or guildhall.[9]

Scholars generally agree, however, that the painting concerns two themes. First, it focuses on the goldsmith and his wares, advertising not only the skill, but also, to use Erwin Panofsky's term, the "social usefulness" of such craftsmen.[10] Hugo van der Velden has recently argued that the painting is purely secular,[11] but, even if the goldsmith is not identified as St. Eloy,

1.1 Petrus Christus, *Couple in a Goldsmith's Shop*, 1449. New York, The Metropolitan Museum of Art, Robert Lehman Collection.

the panel's religious aspects are evident. It displays both secular and sacred objects along the side wall,[12] and draws the viewer's attention to the ring that the goldsmith weighs, which played a critical role in the rituals surrounding the holy sacrament of matrimony.[13]

The focus on marriage, the second theme of the panel, has long been recognized. The idea that the standing man and woman represent a betrothed couple was originally proposed in the early nineteenth century and has been supported by almost all later scholars, including Max Friedländer, Erwin Panofsky, and Peter Schabacker.[14] The painting shows a man and a woman who have entered a goldsmith's shop to purchase a ring, which is being weighed in the foreground; the woman underlines the importance of this action by extending her hand toward the scale. Furthermore, prominently displayed on the counter to the left of the scale is a girdle, commonly presented by the groom to the bride.[15] The man's pose confirms his intimate relationship with the woman; he stands quite close to her, turns his head toward her, and tenderly puts his arm around her, resting his hand on her shoulder. This gesture appears in marriage portraits, such as a relief of Emperor Charles V and Isabella, dated 1526, and also in images of lovers, including an engraving by Master E.S., dated ca. 1450, which shows couples in a garden of love.[16] Other aspects of the painting may also belong to the constellation of motifs that refer to marriage. The man's left hand grasps the hilt of his sword, a gesture that recurs in images of grooms and suitors, and the money on the counter may refer to the economic exchange that marriage entailed.[17]

Noting the presence of the ring and girdle, van der Velden agreed that the paintings should be linked to a wedding,[18] but he questioned whether the man and woman were betrothed, suggesting instead that they represent Mary of Guelders and an escort. Van der Velden identified the woman as Mary because her wedding took place the year that the painting was completed, and because her companion wears the coat of arms of Guelders on a chain around his neck. Van der Velden further argued that if the man were the woman's fiancé, he would stand on the left, but Edwin Hall, in his study of images of betrothals and marriages, demonstrated that the man often appears on the right. For example, a Flemish brooch, dated ca. 1430–40, which may have served in lieu of earnest money, and a German painting of a bridal couple, dated ca. 1470, both show the woman to the left of her fiancé.[19] Furthermore, in the painting by Christus, the man's gesture and the closeness of the couple's stance support the idea that they share an intimate relationship. Van der Velden concluded his article by cautioning scholars to "favor genre over unique, allegorical readings,"[20] yet he cites no other examples of a woman and her escort. By contrast, representations of engaged and married couples are numerous. In short, the preponderance of evidence and scholarly opinion supports the conclusion that the man and woman are readying themselves for marriage.

A second couple appears in the painting, but they have never been adequately explained. Represented in a much smaller scale at the margins of the composition, the two men are depicted as reflections in a mirror (figure 1.2). The mirror serves to expand the space of the painting, since it shows the street outside the shop, and also recalls the convex looking glasses that were employed as security devices so that shopkeepers could detect approaching thieves.[21] But Schabacker proposed that the mirror also fulfilled a symbolic function; he argued that since cracks and water spots mar

1.2 Petrus Christus, *Couple in a Goldsmith's Shop*, 1449 (detail). New York, The Metropolitan Museum of Art, Robert Lehman Collection.

its surface, the painter is criticizing the couple reflected in it.[22] Although most scholars accept this theory, van der Velden again disagrees. He questions whether the mirror is spotted,[23] but one spot is clearly visible, just to the right of the two men (figure 1.2). He further ridicules the idea that such objects served as symbols, but the falcon resting on the perched glove of the man in the mirror demands an explanation, since such birds were not paraded through city streets, but rather reserved for the hunt, which took place in the countryside.[24]

Schabacker justly interprets the round mirror as a symbol of the world.[25] Spotted and cracked, and reflecting the street outside the shop,[26] it constructs the imperfect, sinful state of earthly existence. Scholars generally accept the idea that the men reflected in the mirror are linked conceptually to the betrothed couple, and this is supported by visual evidence. The figure on the left in each pair is dressed in brighter and warmer colors, and wears a larger, more ornate headdress than his or her companion. Furthermore, the man on the right in each couple turns his head slightly toward his partner.

Scholars generally agree that these two pairs, which echo each other, were designed in opposition, that the men in the mirror represent a negative model that contrasts with the ideal bridal couple.[27] Moralizing through contrast—or, as Meyer Schapiro puts it, through "paired carriers of opposed meaning"—was common in the visual culture of northern Europe.[28] Crucifixions and Last Judgments frequently construct oppositions by showing the virtuous on the heraldic right side and sinners on the heraldic left.[29] Such contrasts were employed in representations of lovers as well. Images of youthful, handsome couples, for example, often show on the reverse the same pair depicted as corpses.[30] In short, the small size of the men, and their marginalized location in a cracked mirror situated in the lower heraldic left corner of the composition, support the idea that they are being denigrated through the use of contrast, a common rhetorical device.

If most scholars accept the idea that the men in the mirror are designed to contrast with the bridal couple, they disagree as to what the nature of the difference is. The function of the pair has always rested on the meaning of the falcon. Panofsky described the falcon as a "time-honored symbol of the leisure class" and following him, Joel M. Upton emphasized the courtly aspect of the male couple.[31] Indeed falconry was an exclusively aristocratic activity, but the bridal couple is equally noble, according to Margaret Scott, who points to resemblances between their clothing and that of Isabella of Portugal, the duchess of Burgundy, and members of her court.[32] The woman wears an expensive pearl-studded headdress and gold brocade gown and her fiancé is dressed in a velvet doublet, fur-trimmed jacket, elaborate gold necklace, and, pinned to his chaperon, a luxurious brooch composed of four pearls surrounding a ruby, which is attached to a pendant drop. Such attire is far from the more sober and modest garments of bourgeois craftsmen, such as the goldsmith depicted in the painting. Furthermore, hanging from the fiancé's chain is the coat of arms of

Guelders, which connects him to that court.[33] What distinguishes the bridal couple from the pair in the mirror, then, is not their class.

Schabacker offers a second proposal, that the falcon symbolizes "pride and rapaciousness."[34] This argument is unconvincing as well. If the two couples are constructed as opposites, as most scholars believe, then Schabacker's theory would be valid only if the bridal couple showed modesty and humility, attributes that are contradicted by their aristocratic bearing and expensive dress.

My interpretation, like Panofsky's and Schabacker's, hinges on the meaning of the falcon, and links it to the two central themes of the painting, that is, marriage and the social usefulness of goldsmiths. Since the time of Ovid, the hunt has served as a metaphor for pursuits of a sexual nature.[35] This metaphor was not employed solely to refer to heterosexual activities. John Boswell observed that the hunt figures prominently in homoerotic poetry, and Italian fifteenth-century chivalric literature similarly linked leisure activities—such as hunting—with same-sex desire.[36] In particular, in medieval and early modern art and literature the *falcon* was a common symbol of love, according to Mira Friedman, who concludes, "scenes of hunting, falcons, and falconry were allegories of Love, whether Love as sin or the highest courtly ideal."[37] Beate Schmolke-Hasselmann notes that in the courtly love genre the falcon represented the male lover in general and his genitals in particular.[38] Michael Camille devotes a section of a recent book on *The Medieval Art of Love* to images of the falcon, terming the bird the "pre-eminent" erotic symbol.[39] He suggests that falcons became signs of love through their association with the aristocracy, and because of the way they were trained, with the handler gradually forging an intimate relationship with the bird, which he treated with great sensitivity and patience, much like the ideal lover.[40]

Three aspects of images of falcons are noteworthy. First, they fail to follow a single iconographical pattern, but rather engage the falcon in diverse and imaginative ways.[41] Second, images of the falconer, shown with or without a companion, are often constructed as analogous and interchangeable with depictions of lovers. For example, a Flemish casket, dated ca. 1400, shows two comparable motifs: a falconer and his lady to the left, and a couple embracing to the right (figure 1.3).[42] A third feature of falconry imagery is that the falconer and his companion are generally shown in a much more restrained manner than the couples with whom they are juxtaposed. Note how the casket shows on the right a couple locked in a passionate embrace, who kiss ardently (figure 1.3). The lady nestles in her lover's arms, sits in his lap, and is encompassed by his body, while trees to either side bend their trunks and arch their leaves to form a frame that bonds the pair together. By contrast, the falconer and his lady on the left

1.3 "Talbot" casket, Flanders, ca. 1400. London, British Museum.

do not even touch and the only tree in the composition stands between them, its straight trunk and foliage serving to divide the two figures. Nor are these images exceptional; Friedman discusses a series of other examples in which the falconer and his companion are portrayed as equivalent to couples whose lovemaking is more explicitly depicted.[43] In short, the image of the two men in the mirror is consistent with other representations of the falcon (figure 1.2). The falcon functions to signal the erotic nature of the couple's relationship, whose sexuality is not explicitly depicted; that the specifics of the iconography are unique is not unusual for images of falcons.

The reticence of this image parallels not only the discreet character of heterosexual falconers in northern art (figure 1.3) but also the brevity of legal records of sodomy cases in Bruges. Marc Boone concludes that in opposition to Italian practice, Netherlandish scribes were reluctant to describe the crime in detail and preferred to proceed as quickly as possible to other types of cases.[44] In fact, throughout Europe sodomy was often described as unspeakable [*nefandissima*], and referred to only with great reticence.[45]

If northern European images of falcons make clear that the couple in the mirror represents same-sex desire, then Italian renaissance depictions elucidate their relationship to the main figures, the man and woman purchasing a wedding ring. My interpretation rests on the research of

Joseph Manca, who began by pointing to Marco Zoppo's drawing, which reveals the nature of two standing men, by showing them with putti whose play alludes to anal penetration (figure 1.4). Manca then explored similar figures depicted in religious works.[46] One includes an unmistakable sign of lovemaking, the chin-chuck gesture, but this is lacking in other works (figure 1.5). These instead show men apart from the rest of the scene, who stand close to each other, one slightly behind the other; at times one man

1.4 Marco Zoppo, *Playing Putti*, mid-fifteenth century, drawing. London, British Museum.

1.5 Ercole de' Roberti, *Four Miracles of St. Vincent Ferreri*, 1470s (detail). Vatican State, Vatican Museums, Pinacoteca. Scala Art Resource, New York.

turns his head toward his companion. All these features appear in Christus's painting as well (figure 1.2). Although his panel does not include cavorting putti, the chin-chuck gesture, or linked arms, as do the Italian works, it does display a motif that was omitted in the Italian images, but was commonly employed in northern art as a sign of love: the falcon.

Manca discusses one work that is particularly relevant to a discussion of the *Goldsmith's Shop*, Michelangelo's *Holy Family (Doni Tondo)*, ca. 1503–04 (figure 1.6). This painting shows in the foreground a large representation of the Holy Family, and in the background, to either side, nude youths. To the right, a young man stands between the legs of a companion who embraces him across the chest while a third nude pulls his drapery. To the left, two youths lounge in close proximity to each other. Although a series of alternative interpretations for these figures has been proposed, the theory that they represent the sin of sodomy in contradistinction to the purity of the Holy Family has gradually gained currency not only among scholars whose publications focus on gay studies, but also among authors of major critical monographs on Michelangelo, such as Charles de Tolnay and

1.6 Michelangelo, *Holy Family (Doni Tondo)*, ca. 1503–04. Florence, Uffizi. Alinari Art Resource, New York.

William E. Wallace.[47] For this reason, it seems plausible to accept the idea that the nude youths in Michelangelo's *Holy Family*, like the same-sex couples in the other paintings studied by Manca (figure 1.5), represent the sin of sodomy and the "decadent world of paganism," to use Manca's term, and that they function as a foil for the holy figures who, by contrast, symbolize the new Christian era and the path to salvation.[48]

Critical for our discussion is the fact that Angelo Doni commissioned Michelangelo's painting on the occasion of his marriage to Maddalena

Strozzi in late 1503 or 1504.[49] The image, then, contrasts the sin of sodomy with the holy sacrament of marriage through the visual distinction between the homoerotic youths and the ideal marriage of Joseph and Mary in an image produced to honor the Doni–Strozzi wedding. Like the *Goldsmith's Shop*, same-sex desire is employed as a foil for marriage.

Recent publications show that homosexuality and heterosexuality were at times contrasted. Elizabeth B. Keiser notes that the late fourteenth-century Middle English text *Cleanness* constructs heterosexual and homosexual acts as binary opposites, the one clean, natural, and procreative, the other filthy, against nature, and sterile. She concludes: "*Cleanness*'s legitimation of heterosexual desire is linked to, and to a degree depends logically upon, a rhetoric of intolerance against men who take each other for lovers."[50] Similarly, several sixteenth-century poems produced at the French court contrast heterosexual and same-sex desire; one posits a choice between a "Bonne Dame" [Good Lady] and "un jeune fils aux blonds cheveux" [a young man/son with blond hair].[51]

More specifically, sodomy was linked to *marriage*. A sixteenth-century poem produced at the French court condemns marriages that are enacted as a subterfuge to permit homosexual coupling. In fact, the poet concludes that the real marriages are the same-sex relationships: "Un homme à l'autre se marie / et la femme à l'autre s'aillie" [One man marries another / and women similarly mate]. This statement implies, as Joseph Cady justly observes, that same-sex attraction can produce an enduring relationship much like heterosexual marriage. The poet, however, condemns such alternative arrangements.[52] Artists, too, envisioned love between men as analogous to marriage. A drawing by Marco Zoppo, dated in the mid-fifteenth century, shows a man placing a ring on another man's finger, while a third figure stands between them (figure 1.7). Since this drawing appears in the same codex as others that are clearly homoerotic, such as the drawing by Zoppo mentioned earlier (figure 1.4), this image is generally interpreted as a witty parody of traditional marriage. Indeed its composition is similar to those of conventional wedding scenes, which often show a priest standing between the couple as the groom presents a ring to the bride.[53] Jeffrey Richards has noted another link between marriage and homosexuality, the medieval belief that same-sex desire arose in the absence of marriage.[54] San Bernardino of Siena, for example, preached that men who failed to marry would become sodomites. He cautioned:

> Woe to him who doesn't take a wife when he has the time and a legitimate reason! For remaining single they become sodomites. And take this as a general rule. When you see a man the right age and in good health who doesn't take a wife, take it as a bad sign about him, if he hasn't already been practicing chastity for spiritual reasons.[55]

1.7 Marco Zoppo, *Ring Exchange*, mid-fifteenth century, drawing. London, British Museum.

As we have seen, San Bernardino was not alone in believing that men choose either marriage or sexual relationships with other men, and for this reason homosexual attraction presents an obstacle to marriage. His sermons served to reinforce negative thinking about same-sex desire and Christus's couple functions in a similar manner. Shown in small scale in the open space of the street, depicted at the margins of the painting and on the side most often associated with sin, and reflected in a spotted and cracked mirror, the men form a striking contrast with the bridal couple. Christus opposes the sin of sodomy to the holy sacrament of matrimony. The groom-to-be who stands beside a woman, surrounded by markers of heterosexuality, represents the "proper" model of masculinity, whereas the marginalized couple portrays a sinful choice that is condemned.[56] Furthermore, in both Michelangelo's *Holy Family* and the *Couple in a Goldsmith's Shop*, this criticism of same-sex desire appears within the context of marriage, which supports Michel Foucault's thesis that in premodern times, sexual practices were regulated by a system of alliance that turned largely on the family.[57]

Sodomy was a critical issue in fifteenth-century Bruges. Marc Boone notes that, between the years 1385 and 1515, executions of sodomites in Bruges comprised 15 percent of all bodily punishments—a statistic that places Bruges among the "most important centres for the repression of sodomy."[58] Furthermore, no segment of society remained untouched by this persecution; convicted sodomites included men and women, young and old, citizens and foreigners, those from marginal groups who frequented bathhouses and taverns, and those from the upper echelons of society, such as Jan of Uutkerke, who was Duke Philip's godson and the son of the duke's chamberlain. Citing one case in which the chancellor himself, even during the siege of Neuss, took time to personally intercede in a case of sodomy, Boone concludes that the repression of those who engaged in homosexual acts was one of the ways in which the state sought to control its citizens and consolidate its power. Contemporary documents—and none survive from the hand of those convicted of the crime—view homosexual acts as a "vil et detestable criesme contre nature" [vile and detestable crime against nature], to cite one pamphlet. The standard contemporary law code, Philip Wielant's *Practijke criminele*, called for the capital punishment of those convicted of sodomy, and viewed the crime as an offense against both divine and public order.[59] Jan Praet, an Early Netherlandish poet, and Dirk Potter, who composed a discourse on love, also severely condemned same-sex desire.[60] Boone concludes that during the fifteenth century, "fears of sodomy had taken hold of the collective imagination in Bruges."[61]

In particular, several important sodomy trials were prosecuted in the 1440s, the decade in which Christus produced the *Goldsmith's Shop*. Jan of Uutkerke was arrested in 1441, and in the year in which the painting was completed, 1449, Goswijn De Wilde, a high-ranking Burgundian official, was executed for the offence. Moreover, within Christus's own circles, a painter, Jacob de Jonghe, was burned at the stake for having a sexual relationship with a saddler, Jehan Caudron.[62]

The *Goldsmith's Shop* is a relatively large work, over three feet high,[63] and scholars generally assume that it was publicly displayed. If so, it is likely to have contributed to the demonization of homosexuals in Bruges.[64] By constructing the two men as small, marginalized, and depicted in the lower heraldic left corner within a cracked and spotted mirror, Christus may well have reinforced prejudice against homosexuals.[65] He also devised a strategy for their containment. Although the compositional line from the woman's face through her left arm to the goldsmith's hand brings attention to the male lovers, Christus encapsulates them within the mirror, portrays them as mere reflections, and situates them outside the goldsmith's shop. Christus constructs same-sex desire as the antithesis of marriage and therefore a threat to the social order. This interpretation reinforces the two themes of the painting: the social usefulness of goldsmiths—they help fortify marriage—and marriage itself. Displayed in a guildhall or on an altar, the panel was designed to function as a celebration of the social contribution of goldsmiths, who as upholders of "family values" sell rings and other objects used in wedding rituals. Christus's painting is a large work, which has a religious context, and was produced and publicly displayed in a center of sodomy persecution. For these reasons, we should not be surprised that it constructs marriage as the norm, and homosexuality as deviance.[66] The *Goldsmith's Shop* is breathtaking in its rich color, close attention to detail, complex construction of space, subtle treatment of light, and the mood of stillness and tranquility, which is broken only by the cracked mirror. But the panel's beauty should not blind us to the fact that it is implicated in the repression of homosexuals.[67]

The Housebook Master's *Falconer*

By contrast, no criticism is expressed in another Early Netherlandish image of same-sex desire, the Housebook Master's *Falconer*, a drypoint dated ca. 1485 (figure 1.8).[68] Although Max Lehrs called the print *The Falconer and His Companion*, which leaves open the nature of the couple's relationship, most later publications preferred the title *The Falconer and His Attendant*, which views the men's relationship primarily in socioeconomic terms.[69] But in an Italian Tarot card, the falconer and his servant lack the physical intimacy seen in the Housebook Master's image and their social status is sharply differentiated (figure 1.9).[70] The Tarot card focuses on the aristocratic falconer, who stands in the center foreground, occupies more space than his servant, and wears more expensive clothing. But the Housebook Master does not differentiate the class of the two figures, nor does he construct one as subservient to the other. Rather, the two men stand arm-in-arm, one holding a stick used to beat the prey out into the open, the other with the leashes of three hunting dogs wrapped around his arm and a falcon perched on his gloved hand.

1.8 Housebook Master, *Falconer*, ca. 1485, drypoint. Amsterdam, Rijksmuseum.

1.9 Master of the E-series Tarocchi, *Falconer*, ca. 1465, engraving. Washington, National Gallery of Art, Rosenwald Collection.

It is not only the falcon, however, that suggests that this is an image of same-sex desire. The man on the right wears a wreath in his hair, which, like the falcon, was a standard symbol of love.[71] In addition, his companion fingers the young man's jacket suggestively with his left hand. Furthermore, a large phallic dagger rests between his thighs. This couple is close to the Italian images of sodomites studied by Joseph Manca, which often depict men with arms entwined and a sword between the legs (figure 1.5). This last motif is a common marker of sexuality in images of heterosexual lovers by Albrecht Dürer, Israhel van Meckenem, and others.[72]

One final motif refers to love. Lehrs termed the feather held in the falconer's hand a lure,[73] but it does not resemble other contemporary lures, which consist of a fan of feathers attached to a string so that when pulled the illusion of flight is created.[74] Jan Piet Filedt Kok deemed the feather "mysterious," but offered no explanation.[75] The feather may refer to the hunt, but it is also the attribute of Lascivia in an engraving by Heinrich Aldegrever, dated 1549 (figure 1.10).[76] But rather than the fluffy, curved plume held by the woman in Aldegrever's print, the falconer's feather is straight and stiff, which better suits its phallic context.

This precious print, less than five inches high, has been repeatedly connected to a courtly milieu. It belongs to a group of drypoints that all show courtly themes, date in the 1480s, and were kept together as a set into the nineteenth century. These prints were not made for public consumption. Rather, the Housebook Master chose the technique of drypoint, which produces many fewer impressions than woodcut or engraving. David Landau and Peter Parshall estimate that such prints were issued in "tiny editions" of no more than a dozen copies, perhaps even a smaller number in this case, since the plate may have been made of tin, which yields fewer impressions than the more usual copper. This suggests that the Master's clients "had nothing to do with a mass market. . .and may have been as exclusive as that of any court painter at the time."[77]

Other evidence points to courtly patronage. The *Falconer* shows an unusually fine technique, which produced delicate and subtle tonal effects. Furthermore, other works by the artist are connected to the court. He drew the frontispiece for a romance, which was translated by a court poet for the Elector Palatine, Philip the Sincere, at Heidelberg, and his Housebook is intimately connected to the court of Emperor Frederick III.[78] Furthermore, the falconer's costume, like so many in the works produced during his so-called court period, shows the height of fashionable elegance: elongated shoes, tight hose, and slashed sleeves. The subject is also typical of this group of works since it is exclusively aristocratic.[79] In short, the *Falconer*'s technique, style, subject, size, and the Master's connection to courtly patrons, suggest that the print was produced for an aristocratic audience.

1.10 Heinrich Aldegrever, *Lascivia*, 1549, engraving. © Kupferstichkabinett. Staatliche Museen zu Berlin—Preußischer Kulterbesitz.

Keith Moxey has concluded that the Housebook Master's drypoints during this period represent a visual response to courtly ideals.[80] The couple in the mirror, who are dressed and act like noblemen, are members of a group that Jeffrey Richards has asserted were strongly associated with sodomy throughout the Middle Ages.[81] We must conclude, in this instance then, that same-sex love was consonant with the courtly ideal.

It is interesting to compare Filedt Kok's treatment of this print to his readings of the Housebook Master's images of heterosexual lovers, who also often wear wreaths, carry hunting sticks, and are accompanied by falcons and hunting dogs. Filedt Kok, writing of the *Departure for the Hunt* (figure 1.11), concludes, "wreaths of leaves suggest that two of the participants are betrothed" and notes that "the hunt was long associated with the notion of courtly love."[82] Similarly, a drawing showing a wreathed young

1.11 Housebook Master, *Departure for the Hunt*, ca. 1485–90, drypoint. Amsterdam, Rijksmuseum.

man with a falcon who walks beside a woman is unequivocally titled *Standing Lovers with Falcon Seen from Behind* (figure 1.12).[83] The falconer under discussion looks much like the Housebook Master's images of heterosexual lovers, yet Filedt Kok calls the print *Falconer and His Attendant* rather than *Falconer and His Lover.* Although he notes the presence of the "engagement wreath," he fails to explain it, even though no woman appears in the print. Similarly, he remarks that there is "something mysterious" about the "assertive" way in which one man touches the other man's jacket, but he offers no solution to the puzzle.[84] He also neglects to

1.12 Housebook Master, *Standing Lovers with Falcon Seen from Behind*, ca. 1485, drawing. Leipzig, Museum der bildenden Künste.

mention the man's dagger, although a similarly placed dagger in the *Young Man and Death* is described as "looking suspiciously like a phallic symbol."[85] But there is considerable evidence for supposing that the falconer and his companion are lovers: the presence of the falcon, the feather, the wreath, the linked arms, the gesture of familiarity, and the dagger between the legs. Filedt Kok's reticence is understandable considering that he was writing at a time when little had been published in the area of gay studies. His treatment is typical of the general state of scholarship prior to 1986, the year that James Saslow's *Ganymede in the Renaissance* was published.[86]

Unlike the *Couple in the Goldsmith's Shop*, the *Falconer* does not condemn the homosexual couple, but rather leaves the door open for a positive interpretation of same-sex desire. In fact, by showing this couple in much the same way as heterosexual lovers, the artist constructs love between men as an equivalent option.[87] Three factors help to explain the positive attitude expressed in this work. First, the *Falconer* is small, less than five inches high, and so designed for private viewing. Second, the work shows a purely secular subject. Third, those who purchased this print were probably members of the court, and so may well have possessed greater freedom to enjoy homoerotic works than other art patrons.

Seeing the Invisible

Fifteenth-century Netherlandish images of homosexual desire include not only Christus's *Goldsmith's Shop* and the Housebook Master's *Falconer* but also a miniature visualizing Jupiter's yearnings for a youthful Ganymede in a manuscript of Augustine's *City of God*, and illuminations of beautiful youths and embracing monks that Michael Camille has recently explored within the context of the Duc de Berry's love for young men. A wide range of subjects, functions, contexts, and viewpoints characterizes this group of images.[88] The patron or patrons who commissioned the *Goldsmith's Shop* may well have had a particular meaning in mind for the painting. But patrons cannot control audience response. When other viewers saw the work, they brought their own concerns and attitudes to bear upon their understanding of the image. We lack accounts of contemporary responses to the works that we have discussed in this chapter, but since Early Netherlandish society was far from uniform in its feelings toward same-sex desire, viewers may well have had a range of reactions. Undoubtedly many understood and supported the condemnation of the male couple. Others may not have understood the message, because they were unfamiliar with the coded meaning of the falcon. Still others may have ignored the intended message and instead reveled in the visualization of male lovers within a public image. Some may have viewed the men framed within the mirror as a positive marker of homosexual identity. Indeed, unlike other contemporary images of same-sex desire, the painting, on some level, invites us to identify with the male lovers. We, the observers, are situated in the same location and perform the same action as the male couple: we stand outside the goldsmith's shop and look in. But what the fifteenth-century viewer saw was not simply a goldsmith's shop, or a couple buying a wedding ring, but also male lovers strolling through the city streets, displaying a falcon, an emblem of love. In this respect the panel resembles the Housebook Master's print: both serve to make the invisible visible.

Notes

1. This essay is based on a paper that was first presented at the College Art Association convention in February 2001 and later revised for the "Seeing Gender" conference in January 2002. I would like to thank Emma Campbell, Robert Mills, and Anne Roberts for organizing these sessions. I am also extremely grateful to the editors and to Maryan Ainsworth, Marc Boone, Joan Cadden, Anne Derbes, Robert L.A. Clark, Simon Gaunt, Craig Harbison, Martha Howell, Lynn Jacobs, Carol Purtle, Nanette Salomon, James Saslow, and Juliann Vitullo for their many helpful comments. In this essay, the term "falconer" is used to refer to the person holding the bird of prey.
2. For a summary of the arguments against adopting the word "homosexual" to refer to the time before the nineteenth century, see Abigail Solomon-Godeau, *Male Trouble: A Crisis in Representation* (London: Thames and Hudson, 1997), pp. 26–32.
3. Jacqueline Murray, "Twice Marginal and Twice Invisible: Lesbians in the Middle Ages," in *Handbook of Medieval Sexuality*, ed. Vern L. Bullough and James Brundage (New York: Garland, 1996), p. 208 [191–222].
4. Warren Johansson and William A. Percy, "Homosexuality," in *Handbook of Medieval Sexuality*, ed. Vern L. Bullough and James A. Brundage (New York: Garland, 1996), pp. 176–78 [155–89].
5. For recent relevant studies on medieval and early modern images of homosexuals, see Michael Camille, " 'For Our Devotion and Pleasure': The Sexual Objects of Jean, Duc de Berry," *Art History* 24 (2001): 169–91; Michael Camille, *The Medieval Art of Love: Objects and Subjects of Desire* (New York: Harry N. Abrams, 1998), pp. 138–40; Craig Harbison, "The Sexuality of Christ in the Early Sixteenth Century in Germany," in *A Tribute to Robert A. Koch: Studies in the Northern Renaissance*, ed. John Oliver Hand (Princeton: Department of Art and Archaeology, 1994), pp. 69–81; Robert Mills, "Ecce Homo," in *Gender and Holiness: Men, Women and Saints in Late Medieval Europe*, ed. Samantha J.E. Riches and Sarah Salih (London: Routledge, 2002), pp. 152–73; Robert Mills, " 'Whatever You Do Is a Delight to Me!': Masculinity, Masochism, and Queer Play in Representations of Male Martyrdom," *Exemplaria* 13.1 (2001): 1–37; James Saslow, *Pictures and Passions: A History of Homosexuality in the Visual Arts* (New York: Viking, 1999), esp. pp. 76–78, 92–95; and J. Schenk, "Homoseksualiteit in de Nederlandse beeldende kunst voor 1800," *Spiegel Historiael* 17 (1982): 576–83. For other works, see n65.

6. "m petr[us] xpi me fecit a 1449." See Della C. Sperling, "Petrus Christus," in *From Van Eyck to Bruegel: Early Netherlandish Painting in the Metropolitan Museum*, ed. Maryan W. Ainsworth and Keith Christiansen (New York: Metropolitan Museum of Art, 1998), p. 150 [150–53].
7. Peter Schabacker, "Petrus Christus' 'Saint Eloy': Problems of Provenance, Sources and Meaning," *Art Quarterly* 35 (1972): 107–108 [103–18]. See also Maryan W. Ainsworth, "St. Eligius," in *Petrus Christus: Renaissance Master of Bruges*, ed. Maryan W. Ainsworth and Max P.J. Martens (New York: Metropolitan Museum of Art, 1994), p. 96 [96–101].
8. F. Werner, "Eligius (Alo', Loy) von Noyon," in *Lexikon der christlichen Ikonographie*, ed. Englebert Kirshbaum et al., 8 vols. (Rome: Herder, 1968–76), 6: cols. 122–27; Erwin Panofsky, *Early Netherlandish Painting: Its Origin and Character* (Cambridge, MA: Harvard University Press, 1953), p. 490, n2.
9. Guy Bauman, "Early Flemish Portraits 1425–1525," *Metropolitan Museum of Art Bulletin* 43.4 (1986): 11 [44–64]; Lorne Campbell, review of *Petrus Christus* exhibition at Metropolitan Museum of Art, New York, in *Burlington Magazine* 136 (1994): 641 [639–41]; Martha Wolff, "The South Netherlands, Fifteenth and Sixteenth Centuries," in *The Robert Lehman Collection*, vol. 2: *Fifteenth to Eighteenth Century European Paintings: France, Central Europe, The Netherlands, and Great Britain*, ed. Charles Sterling et al. (New York: Metropolitan Museum of Art, 1998), pp. 65, 67, 69, 71 [61–124]; and Hugo van der Velden, who terms it the "epitome of secular painting," in "Defrocking St. Eloy: Petrus Christus's 'Vocational Portrait of a Goldsmith,'" *Simiolus* 26 (1998): 242–76.
10. Panofsky, *Early Netherlandish Painting*, p. 490, n2.
11. Van der Velden, "Defrocking St. Eloy," esp. pp. 261, 268.
12. Jos Kolderweij, in his review of Ainsworth and Martens, *Petrus Christus: Renaissance Master*, in *Simiolus* 23 (1995): 271 [268–73], convincingly argues that the object with the pelican on the lid is a reliquary.
13. Rings functioned in both the betrothal and wedding rituals: see Edwin Hall, *The Arnolfini Betrothal: Medieval Marriage and the Enigma of Van Eyck's Double Portrait* (Berkeley: University of California Press, 1994), pp. 15, 34, 62–64.
14. For a summary of these views, see van der Velden, "Defrocking St. Eloy," p. 250. In addition to those quoted by van der Velden (Schäffer, Weale, Friedländer, Panofsky, and Schabacker), see also Bauman, "Early Flemish Portraits," p. 11; Joel Upton, *Petrus Christus: His Place in Fifteenth-Century Flemish Painting* (University Park: Pennsylvania State University Press, 1990), p. 34; Ainsworth, "St Eligius," p. 96; and Wolff, "The South Netherlands," p. 70.
15. See Wolff, "The South Netherlands," p. 70; Ronald W. Lightbown, *Mediaeval European Jewelry* (London: Victoria and Albert Museum, 1992), pp. 306, 382.
16. Gustav Glück, "Bildnisse aus dem Hause Habsburg: I. Kaiserin Isabella," *Jahrbuch der Kunsthistorischen Sammlungen in Wien*, n.s. 7 (1933): 189, fig. 150, 191 [183–200]; Keith Moxey, "Chivalry and the Housebook Master (Master

of the Amsterdam Cabinet)," in *Livelier than Life: The Master of the Amsterdam Cabinet or the Housebook Master, ca. 1470–1500*, exh. cat., ed. Jan Piet Filedt Kok (Amsterdam: Rijksprentenkabinet/Rijksmuseum, 1985), pp. 65–78. For this gesture, see also Marcantonio Raimondi's *Apollo, Hyacinth, and Amor*, 1506, in Bruce R. Smith, *Homosexual Desire in Shakespeare's England* (Chicago: University of Chicago Press, 1991), p. 2, and two versions of Paris Bordon, *Pair of Lovers*, ca. 1540–50, in Jill Dunkerton, Susan Foister, and Nicholas Penny, *Dürer to Veronese: Sixteenth-Century Painting in the National Gallery* (New Haven: Yale University Press, 1999), pp. 102–103, figs. 115–116.

17. For the sword as phallus see Diane Wolfthal, *Images of Rape: The "Heroic" Tradition and Its Alternatives* (Cambridge, UK: Cambridge University Press, 1999), pp. 61, 81, 83; for the gesture of grasping the hilt of the sword in a marital context, see Margaret Scott, *The History of Dress Series: Late Gothic Europe 1400–1500* (London: Mills and Boon, 1980), p. 33, fig. 13; Raimond van Marle, *Iconographie de l'art profane au Moyen Âge et à la Renaissance*, 2 vols. (The Hague: Martinus Nijhoff, 1931), 1:457, fig. 452; Hall, *Arnolfini Betrothal*, pl. 9. For earnest money, see Wolff, "The South Netherlands," p. 70, and Hall, *Arnolfini Betrothal*, pp. 15, 61.
18. Van der Velden, "Defrocking St. Eloy," p. 262.
19. Hall, *Arnolfini Betrothal*, pp. 44, 10, fig. 3, 62, fig. 26, 43, fig. 20. See also Jan Piet Filedt Kok, "Catalogue," in *Livelier than Life*, ed. Filedt Kok, p. 155, fig. 58c [89–284]; Camille, *Medieval Art of Love*, p. 160, fig. 146.
20. Van der Velden, "Defrocking St. Eloy," p. 268.
21. Heinrich Schwartz, "The Mirror in Art," *Art Quarterly* 15 (1952): 103 [97–118].
22. M.J.H. Madou, "Het gebruik van de spiegel in de Middeleeuwen," in *Oog in oog met de Spiegel*, ed. Nico J. Brederoo (Amsterdam: Aramith, 1988), pp. 57–61 [38–65]; Schwartz, "The Mirror in Art," p. 103; Julien Chapuis, "Early Netherlandish Painting: Shifting Perspectives," in *From Van Eyck to Bruegel: Early Netherlandish Painting in the Metropolitan Museum*, ed. Maryan W. Ainsworth and Keith Christiansen (New York: Metropolitan Museum of Art, 1998), p. 17 [3–21]; Schabacker, "Petrus Christus' 'Saint Eloy,'" pp. 103–118.
23. Van der Velden, "Defrocking St. Eloy," p. 250.
24. Mira Friedman, "The Falcon and the Hunt: Symbolic Love Imagery in Medieval and Renaissance Art," in *Poetics of Love in the Middle Ages*, ed. Moshe Lazar and Norris J. Lacy (Fairfax: George Mason University Press, 1989), p. 162 [157–75].
25. Schabacker, "Petrus Christus' 'Saint Eloy,'" p. 112.
26. They stand in the street, which was often viewed as a dangerous place that is open to sin, especially sins of a sexual nature. See Wolfthal, *Images of Rape*, pp. 185–89.
27. Schabacker, "Petrus Christus' 'Saint Eloy,'" pp. 111–112; Peter Schabacker, *Petrus Christus* (Utrecht: Haentjens, Dekker and Gumbert, 1974), p. 90. Again van der Velden disagrees: see "Defrocking St. Eloy," p. 243.

28. Meyer Schapiro, *Words and Pictures: On the Literal and the Symbolic in the Illustration of a Text* (The Hague: Mouton, 1973), p. 40.
29. See Ruth Mellinkoff, *Outcasts: Signs of Otherness in Northern European Art of the Late Middle Ages*, 2 vols. (Berkeley: University of California Press, 1993), esp. 1:209–27.
30. Filedt Kok, "Catalogue," p. 155, fig. 58c; Stephen K. Scher (ed.), *Europe in Torment: 1450–1550* (Providence: Brown University and Rhode Island School of Design, 1974), pp. 107–109.
31. Panofsky, *Early Netherlandish Painting*, p. 490, n2; Upton, *Petrus Christus*, p. 34.
32. Scott, *Late Gothic Painting*, pp. 146, 148. Bauman also terms them aristocratic: see "Early Flemish Portraits," pp. 11–12. For images of Isabella, see Micheline Sonkes, *Dessins du XVe siècle: Groupe Van der Weyden* (Brussels: Centre National de Recherches "Primitifs Flamands," 1969), p. 110 and pl. XXIIIb.
33. H. Clifford Smith, " 'The Legend of S. Eloy and S. Goddeberta' by Petrus Christus," *Burlington Magazine* 35 (1914): 331 [326–35].
34. Schabacker, "Petrus Christus' 'Saint Eloy,' " p. 112; Schabacker, *Petrus Christus*, p. 91. Sperling, "Petrus Christus," p. 153 and Ainsworth, "St Elegius," p. 98 agree.
35. Wolfthal, *Images of Rape*, pp. 12–14, 26, 34–35, 21, 28, 32, 44, 182.
36. John Boswell, *Christianity, Social Tolerance, and Homosexuality: Gay People in Western Europe from the Beginning of the Christian Era to the Fourteenth Century* (Chicago: University of Chicago Press, 1980), p. 253; Juliann Vitullo, *The Chivalric Epic in Medieval Italy* (Gainesville: University of Florida Press, 2000), pp. 79–80.
37. Friedman, "The Falcon and the Hunt," p. 169.
38. Beate Schmolke-Hasselmann, "Accipiter et chirotheca: Die Artus des Andreas Capellanus—eine Liebesallegorie?," *Germanisch-romanische Monatschrift* 63 (1982): 387–417 (esp. 392–96).
39. Camille, *Medieval Art of Love*, pp. 94–99; see also pp. 78 and 104.
40. Camille, *Medieval Art of Love*, pp. 95–98.
41. See, for example, Camille, *Medieval Art of Love*, figs. 64 and 80 and n42.
42. Camille, *Medieval Art of Love*, p. 97, fig. 82. See also, for example, Mira Friedman, "Sünde, Sünder und die Darstellungen der Laster in dem Bildern zur 'Bible Moralisée,' " *Wiener Jahrbuch für Kunstgeschichte* 37 (1984): 162, 165–66; 253, fig. 6; 254, figs. 11–12; 260, fig. 33 [157–71].
43. Friedman, "The Falcon and the Hunt," p. 160.
44. Marc Boone, "State Power and Illicit Sexuality: The Persecution of Sodomy in Late Medieval Bruges," *Journal of Medieval History* 22 (1996): 143–44 [135–53].
45. Jacques Chiffoleau, "Dire l'indicible. Remarques sur la catégorie du 'nefandum' du XIIe au XVe siècle," *Annales: Économies, sociétés, civilisations* 45.2 (1990): 289–324.
46. Joseph Manca, "Sacred vs. Profane: Images of Sexual Vice in Renaissance Art," *Studies in Iconography* 13 (1990): 145–90; Joseph Manca, *The Art of Ercole de' Roberti* (Cambridge: Cambridge University Press, 1992), p. 96.

47. Charles de Tolnay, *Michelangelo: Sculptor, Painter, Architect* (Princeton: Princeton University Press, 1975), p. 19; Manca, "Sacred vs. Profane," 155–57, 187–88, n29; Saslow, *Pictures and Passions*, p. 97; William E. Wallace, *Michelangelo: The Complete Sculpture, Painting, Architecture* (Hong Kong: Hugh Lauter Levin, 1998), p. 137. Howard Hibbard, *Michelangelo*, 2nd edn. (New York: Harper and Row, 1974), cites this explanation along with another, p. 318.
48. Manca, "Sacred vs. Profane," p. 156.
49. Hibbard, *Michelangelo*, p. 67.
50. Elizabeth B. Keiser, *Courtly Desire and Medieval Homophobia* (New Haven: Yale University Press, 1997), pp. 2–5, 133.
51. See Joseph Cady, "The 'Masculine Love' of the 'Princes of Sodom' 'Practicing the Art of Ganymede' at Henri III's Court: The Homosexuality of Henri III and His *Mignons* in Pierre de L'Estoile's *Mémoires-Journaux*," in *Desire and Discipline: Sex and Sexuality in the Premodern West,* ed. Jacqueline Murray and Konrad Eisenbichler (Toronto: University of Toronto Press, 1996), p. 126 [123–54].
52. See Cady, "The 'Masculine Love' of the 'Princes of Sodom,' " p. 127. For this phenomenon elsewhere, see Bernd-Ulrich Hergemöller, "Homosexuelles Alltagsleben im Mittelalter," *Zeitschrift für Sexualforschung* 5 (1992): 117–118.
53. Lilian Armstrong first proposed this in *The Paintings and Drawings of Marco Zoppo* (New York: Garland Publishing, 1976), pp. 252, 313–314, 420. Later scholars have supported her proposal: see Betty Rosasco, "Albrecht Dürer's 'Death of Orpheus': Its Critical Fortunes and a New Interpretation of Its Meaning," *Idea: Jahrbuch der Hamburger Kunsthalle* 3 (1984): 33 [19–41]; Hugo Chapman, *Padua in the 1450s: Marc Zoppo and His Contemporaries* (London: British Museum, 1998), p. 38.
54. Jeffrey Richards, *Sex, Dissidence and Damnation: Minority Groups in the Middle Ages* (London: Routledge, 1995), p. 138.
55. Michael J. Rocke, "Sodomites in Fifteenth-century Tuscany: The Views of Bernardino of Siena," in *The Pursuit of Sodomy: Male Homosexuality in Renaissance and Enlightenment Europe*, ed. Kent Gerad and Gert Hekma (New York: Haworth Press, 1989), p. 18 [7–31]. Also see his *Forbidden Friendships: Homosexuality and Male Culture in Renaissance Florence* (Oxford: Oxford University Press, 1996).
56. If the panel does represent St. Eloy, then the contrast is even stronger, with the groom-to-be at the saint's side and within the sacred space of his shop.
57. Michel Foucault, *The History of Sexuality*, vol. 1, *An Introduction*, trans. Robert Hurley (London: Penguin, 1978).
58. Boone, "State Power and Illicit Sexuality," p. 135. The following paragraph is a summary of his article.
59. Boone, "State Power and Illicit Sexuality," pp. 138–39.
60. See Frits Pieter van Oostrom, *Court and Culture: Dutch Literature 1350–1450*, trans. Arnold J. Pomerans (Berkeley: University of California Press, 1992), pp. 222, 232; Boone, "State Power and Illicit Sexuality," p. 142.
61. Boone, "State Power and Illicit Sexuality," p. 147.

62. Boone, "State Power and Illicit Sexuality," p. 152. Saddlers belonged to the same guild as painters, see Schabacker, "Petrus Christus' 'Saint Eloy,' " p. 107. A letter of 1475 from the Bruges *ecoutête* (the "schout", or local bailiff) to the duke and chancellor mentions the trial, which is said to have taken place some 25 years earlier. (General Archives, Chambers of accounts, Acquits de Lille, portefeuille no. 369, the old archives of the ducal chamber of accounts.) This information was kindly communicated to me via E-mail by Marc Boone in 2000.
63. It measures 38½ × 33½ in. (98 × 85 cm).
64. The term "demonization" may seem too strong to some, but see Johannson and Percy, "Homosexuality," p. 172, and Hergemöller, "Homosexuelles Alltagsleben," p. 111.
65. Although they differ iconographically, a few other fifteenth-century northern European works construct similar negative views of homosexuality. A *Bible moralisée* condemns embracing monks; Albrecht Dürer visualizes vicious attacks on Orpheus and Hercules, who are portrayed as pedophiles that frighten innocent infants; and an illumination in a Swiss chronicle shows sodomites burning at the stake. See Camille, "For Our Devotion and Pleasure," pp. 169–91; James Saslow, "The Middle Ages and Negative Imagery," *The Advocate* (January 21, 1986): 56–58; Saslow, *Pictures and Passions*, p. 77, 92; Edgar Wind, " 'Hercules' and 'Orpheus': Two Mock-Heroic Designs by Dürer," *Journal of the Warburg Institute* 2 (1938–39): 214–217 [206–18]. Colin Eisler, noting Dürer's close relationship with Willibald Pirckheimer, has suggested that the two were lovers; see his review of Jane Campbell Hutchison, *Albrecht Dürer: A Biography*, in *Renaissance Quarterly* 45 (1992): 165 [163–66]. Sixteenth-century Netherlandish art also represented same-sex desire. Bosch is probably referring to sexual acts when he shows a man inserting a flower into another man's rear end, a print by Theodor de Brij depicts dogs attacking homosexuals in the New World, and those by Frans Hoogenberg show the arrest and execution of monks condemned for sodomy in Bruges. See Saslow, *Pictures and Passions*, p. 78, and J. Schenk, "Homoseksualiteit in de Nederlandse beeldende kunst voor 1800," *Spiegel Historiael* 17 (1982): 579–80 [576–83]. See also an illumination of Jupiter and Ganymede in *The City of God*, Philadelphia Museum of Art, '45-65-1, fol. 33r.
66. See, for example, Jonathan Goldberg, *Sodometries: Renaissance Texts/Modern Sexualities* (Stanford: Stanford University Press, 1992).
67. For a parallel example, see Wolfthal, *Images of Rape*, p. 2.
68. Filedt Kok, "Catalogue," p. 167, cat. no. 70.
69. Max Lehrs, "Die deutsche und niederländische Kupferstich des fünfzehten Jahhunderts in der kleineren Sammlungen," *Repertorium für Kunstwissenschaft* 15 (1892): 122 [110–46], no. 64: "der Falkonier" and "sein Begleiter"; Max Lehrs, *Geschichte und Kritischer Katalog des Deutschen, Niederländerischen und Französischen Kupferstichs im XV. Jahrhundert*, 10 vols. (Vienna: Gesellschaft für Vervielfältigende Kunst, 1932), 8:140, no. 75: "der Begleiter" and "der

Genosse"; Max Lehrs, *The Master of the Amsterdam Cabinet* (Paris: International Chalcographical Society, 1893–94), p. 70; Max Lehrs, "Der deutsche und niederländische Kupferstich des fünfzehnten Jahrhunderts in den kleineren Sammlungen," *Repertorium für Kunstwissenschaft* 15 (1892): 122 [110–46]; Jane Campbell Hutchison, *The Master of the Housebook* (New York: Collector's Edition, 1972), p. 60; Filedt Kok, "Catalogue," p. 167. Alfred Stange called the print "The Falconer with the Aristocratic Lord" (*Die Falkner mit dem vornehmen Herren*): see Stange, *Das Hausbuchmeister* (Baden-Baden: Heitz, 1958), pp. 15, 39. Fabrizio Augustoni returns to Lehr's title in *Catalogo completo delle incisioni del Maestro del Libro di Casa* (Milan: Salamon and Agustoni, 1972), p. xxx ("Der Falkenier und sein Begleiter").

70. For this print, see Jay A. Levenson, Konrad Oberhuber, and Jacqueline L. Sheehan, *Early Italian Engravings from the National Gallery of Art* (Washington: National Gallery, 1973), p. 94, cat. no. 17. For another print that shows the gentleman and his servant out falconing, see Arthur M. Hind, *Early Italian Engraving* (New York: Knoedler, 1938), II, A.III. 22, a1. Here the gentleman rides on horseback while his servant walks, again a clear class distinction.
71. For the wreath, see Friedman, "The Falcon and the Hunt," pp. 162–63, 167; Filedt Kok, "Catalogue," p. 277.
72. See Filedt Kok, "Catalogue," p. 156, fig. 58f and p. 175, fig. 75c; Wolfthal, *Images of Rape*, p. 185, fig. 112.
73. Lehrs, *Geschichte und Kritischer Katalog*, 8:149.
74. Jonathan J.G. Alexander, *The Master of Mary of Burgundy: A Book of Hours for Engelbert of Nassau* (New York: Georges Braziller, 1970), cat. nos. 41–58, fol. 55v. Alexander notes that Emperor Frederick II described the same sort of lure. See also Heinz Peters, "Falke, Falkenjagd, Falkner, und Falkenbuch," in *Reallexikon zur Deutschen Kunstgeschichte*, ed. Otto Schmitt et al. (Munich: Alfred Druckmüller, 1937–), 6:1279, 1281–82, 1314 [1251–1366].
75. Filedt Kok, "Catalogue," p. 167.
76. Guy de Tervarent, *Attributs et symboles dans l'art profane, 1450–1600: dictionnaire d'un langage perdu*, 3 vols. (Geneva: Droz, 1958–64), 2:309; F.W.H. Hollstein, *German Engravings, Etchings, and Woodcuts ca. 1400–1700* (Amsterdam: Menno Hertzberger, 1954–), 1:56, B.109.
77. David Landau and Peter Parshall, *The Renaissance Print: 1470–1550* (New Haven: Yale University Press, 1994), pp. 5 and 378, n109.
78. Jane Campbell Hutchison, "The Housebook," in *Livelier than Life*, ed. Jan Piet Filedt Kok, pp. 218–20, 245 [218–45].
79. See, for example, van Marle, *Iconographie de l'art profane*, 1:26–30 and Smith, "The Legend of S. Eloy and S. Goddeberta," p. 335.
80. Moxey, "Chivalry and the Housebook Master," p. 75.
81. Richards, *Sex, Dissidence and Damnation*, p. 137.
82. Filedt Kok, "Catalogue," p. 169.
83. Filedt Kok, "Catalogue," p. 252.
84. Filedt Kok, "Catalogue," p. 167.

85. Filedt Kok, "Catalogue," p. 154.
86. James Saslow, *Ganymede in the Renaissance: Homosexuality in Art and Society* (New Haven: Yale University Press, 1986).
87. This is not the only northern work to show this attitude. Dürer's *Bathhouse*, a woodcut dated ca. 1496, also refrains from condemning same-sex desire; see Saslow, *Pictures and Passions*, p. 94.
88. See Ganymede miniature mentioned in n65 and Camille, "For Our Devotion and Pleasure," pp. 169–91.

CHAPTER 2

VISIBLE AND INVISIBLE BODIES AND SUBJECTS IN PETER DAMIAN

William Burgwinkle

This chapter argues that Peter Damian's Liber gomorrhianus *(1049) may be an attack on sodomites within the eleventh-century clergy, but his panoptical gaze, his concern with discipline and subjectivization, sameness, community, and identity-less desire, also establish him as an early queer theorist.*

Peter Damian is not the first figure that comes to mind when compiling a list of medieval queer theorists. Though he is often cited as a key figure in the formulation of the sin of sodomy and as an innovator in disciplinary discourse, he is not usually considered an advocate for what I would call, following Foucault, a queer aesthetics of the self.[1] Yet when grated against Leo Bersani's *Homos*, specifically against Bersani's reading of André Gide, Peter emerges as an important theorist of male communities whose views resonate uncannily with Foucauldian concerns about the power and fantasy of control through sight and the disciplinary effects of being seen.[2] The Peter Damian in question is, of course, the author of the by now infamous *Liber gomorrhianus* [*Book of Gomorrah*], probably the first comprehensive guidebook to Christian homophobia, but also of the *De laude flagellorum* [*In Praise of Flagellation*], a work of incredible daring which he wrote in the last years of his life. Both works were written in a defensive mode, as justification for his own versions of the Law and as public denunciations of those who had other ideas. It would not, in fact, be inaccurate to call them angry texts, Peter himself having confessed that anger was the one vice he could never truly extirpate.[3] The *Gomorrhianus* was written as an open letter to Pope Leo IX in 1049, and the *Flagellorum* around 1070. In the former, Peter asks the pope to instigate an extensive crackdown on the cancer then devouring the Church:

> A certain abominable and most shameful vice has developed, and unless it be prevented as soon as possible by the severest punishment, it is certain that the sword of divine fury will be unsheathed, leading in its unchecked violence to the destruction of many.[4]

In the latter, he denounces the presumption of those who would forego flagellation as a penitential practice:

> Tell me, you who in your arrogance mock at Christ's passion, you who, in refusing to be stripped and scourged with Him, deride His nakedness and all His torments as foolish and vain things like the illusions that come to us in sleep, what will you do when you see Him who was stripped in public and hung on the Cross. . .more glorious than all things, *visible or invisible*? What, I say, will you do when you behold Him for whose shame you have nothing but scorn, seated on the fiery throne of the tribunal of Heaven, and judging the whole human race in the dreadful judgment of His justice? By what rash boldness or presumption do you hope to share in His glory, whose shame and injuries you scorned to bear?[5]

The *Book of Gomorrah* is a paradoxical text in which vision plays a major role. Peter claims the ability to see what cannot be seen [*omnia visibilia et invisibilia*], to see what others must wait until death to see, even to see what the sinner cannot see in himself. Arrogating to himself such powers is an act of overweening presumption: he challenges implicitly the authority of the Pope, implying that he has been soft on sodomites and dictating appropriate punishment. In the process, he sends a warning to his enemies, those who would hide from him their "true" selves. Peter's X-ray vision is the arbiter of truth; it can penetrate even into the confessional, the most secret and inviolable of spaces, but it thereby risks being marked by the very qualities he elsewhere condemns as sodomitical. A brief summary of the points to which he returns again and again should give a taste of his argument:

- — There are four acts that count as sodomy: masturbation, mutual masturbation, interfemoral intercourse (that is, between the thighs), and anal intercourse.
- — There are serious inconsistencies in the ways Penitentials recommend dealing with those who confess such sins and this is

compounded by the fact that there are confessors who are themselves sodomites.

— The Church is in crisis over this issue of sodomites within the clergy and risks imminent destruction, either from rot within or from an act of divine retribution.

The text is remarkable both for what it leaves out—almost any mention of gender, for example—as for its curious rhetoric. In the middle of a personal letter, in which Pope Leo is addressed as "you," Peter quite suddenly launches into a confrontational soliloquy, in which he addresses the sodomite directly, such that it is not entirely clear how much overlap there might be between one addressee and the other. The first apostrophe, "But now we meet face to face, you sodomite, whoever you may be" (18) is followed by a whole string of similar epithets: "my good sodomite" (21), "miserable" or "unhappy soul" (35).[6] The tricky "whoever you may be" [*quisquis es*] implies that Peter holds the sodomite in his gaze, has his attention, knows his tricks better than he knows them himself; and that the sodomite, in an Althusserian moment of *prise de conscience* will somehow recognize himself in this call.[7] But whom, actually, does Peter see? Or, rather, what takes shape as a result of his vision? Peter's appropriation of the panoptical seat of vision, the fantasy point from which all can be seen and controlled, is a clear recuperation of the confessional, with Peter as interrogator and no one and everyone as its penitent.[8] But since confession itself has now been polluted by sodomites on either side of the curtain, Peter sets himself up performatively as the public confessor to whom all must now turn. The imaginary sodomite to whom he addresses his harangue is thus the silent subject *for whom* Peter speaks and whom he judges. This overtly sadistic and solipsistic scenario has Peter identifying with the gaze of the Other.[9] From this vantage, he casts the drama, writes the dialogue, directs the action, and enjoys the privileged view afforded of his own work at play.

Peter's ultimate aim is a whole-scale purge of the clergy, both monastic and regular, a surgical intervention to cut from the mystical body of Christ "the befouling cancer of sodomy" (6), but he first needs some sodomites to cut. He must therefore induce someone to identify himself as such, to answer his call, by providing the category within which that recognition can occur. The subject can only truly know that he belongs to this category through identifying with others who have previously self-identified in the same way. In other words, Peter creates a category by claiming to have seen into the heart of his penitents, but he assumes that his subjects must already know of this category before he has defined it. Their prior bonding with other like-minded individuals is seen as a process of spontaneous auto-identification that both defines them and, from the viewpoint of the outsider, imprisons them within their own imaginary community. Once again, vision is allied with power and the imaginary: Peter can "see" the truth of the subject through that subject's identificatory affiliations, while the subject can only attain subjectivity through this now maligned process of identification. Given that Peter sees himself as allied with the Law, but a Lawgiver who can stand above the Law, he can only imagine the sodomite as someone who equally stands outside one Law while being subject to another. This ability to evade the Law's gaze while remaining within it (thus creating a community within a community that can remain invisible to all but Peter) is what he finds most galling. Peter clearly wants to see his ideal Christian community as occupying a similarly privileged position, that is to say remaining within the Law but also outside it, maintaining itself through extra-linguistic identificatory bonds that conform to his prescriptions.

Religiosity and Law

Though Peter knows that in writing the *Gomorrhianus* he risks being seen as an "informer and delator" of his brothers' crimes (49) [*proditorem delatoremque fraterni criminis* (326:1)] he argues that he is simply doing his duty. How, he asks disingenuously, could he claim to love his neighbor if he were to allow him to die brutally from a festering wound without attempting a cure through the "surgery of [his] words" (50)?[10] Peter is obviously used to recuperating, performing, and rewriting the Law, just as he did in rewriting the rules of Saint Benedict for his monastic order at Fonte Avellana; and the God whose word he sees himself enacting is vengeful, controlling, possessive, and angry, exemplified in the citation from Deuteronomy: "My sword shall feed on flesh" (Deut. 32.42). Peter claims that God so detested sodomy that he returned repeatedly to condemn it, warning that the sodomites and those who approve of them would be struck with the "sword of divine fury" (citing Romans 1.32). As agent of this Lawgiver, Peter sets out to regulate masculine desire—not by banishing it from the community, as if one could, but by channeling it, creating performative categories through which it could be expressed, and redefining the transgressive routes through which it might travel. Unsurprisingly, these routes are corporeal and theatrical: they focus almost exclusively on the individual hermit, subject to what Peter insistently calls "the discipline," an extreme regime of physical penance that includes deprivation of food and comfort and the practice of self-flagellation.

In spite of these innovations, Peter still presents himself as a theologian working within a doctrinal mode, his arguments based on traditional and authoritative texts.[11] Even his most orthodox defenders, however, must acknowledge that he is often guilty of adapting those citations to his own ends. Thus he strays frequently from the doctrinal to the imagistic mode in an attempt to produce a more shocking, and therefore more memorable effect on the reader.[12] Indeed, while setting out biblical injunctions against sodomy, he dips frequently into the semantic field of disease and contagion, to the sensual and visual abject. Sodomy is not an act, it is a "deadly wound reeking in the very body of Holy Church," which "slays modesty, strangles chastity, and slaughters virginity with a knife dipped in the filthiest poison" (14). Like gonorrhea and leprosy, it "defiles all things, sullies all things, pollutes all things. . .allows nothing to be pure, nothing to be spotless, nothing to be clean" (26, 37). Sodomy should induce physical retching, not just moral condemnation. It "corrupts"; it "pollutes" (27); it reeks and sickens.[13]

Gendered Bodies

The body in Peter's writings is an effect of his vision and it flits uneasily from male to female, collective to singular, institutional to private. The "mother of all churches . . . bathed in the utter brilliance that Truth imparts" (5) is also the polluted body that harbors the deadly and reeking wound of sodomy (14). Thus, in violating the body of the Church, the sodomite violates the collective body, the identity from which he has now been banished, his mother and his former self. As in Alain de Lille's *Planctu*, written a century later, the sodomitical act is seen as an attack on the collective body of males, which is, nonetheless, referred to as feminine—Mother Nature and Mother Church. This is, in fact, one of the few allusions to women one finds in the *Gomorrhianus*, other than a brief discussion on the relative wickedness of raping nuns and goddaughters as opposed to animals or other males. Femininity acts then both as a wall that demarcates the male collective from the outside, a sort of womb that gives structure to the community but which has no place within, and as the devouring she-monster which attacks that wall and rapes the men within, the very embodiment of sodomy itself:

> This utterly diseased Queen of Sodom renders him who obeys the laws of her tyranny infamous to men and odious to God. She mobilizes him in the militia of the evil spirit and forces him to fight unspeakable wars against God. She detaches the unhappy soul from the company of the angels and, depriving it of its excellence, takes it captive under her domineering yoke. She strips her knights of the armor of virtue, exposing them to be pierced by the spears of every vice. She humiliates her slave in the church and condemns him in court; she defiles him in secret and dishonors him in public; she gnaws at this conscience like a worm and consumes his flesh like fire. (31)[14]

The underside of this devouring femininity—sodomy as woman—can be seen in the gender-switching imagery used to characterize the sodomite, once he has been infected:

> Truly the daughter of my people has suffered a grievous injury, because a soul that had been the daughter of Holy Church has been cruelly wounded by the enemy of the human race with the shaft of impurity. She who had once been mildly and gently nourished on the milk of sacred wisdom at the court of the eternal king, is now viciously infected with the poison of lust and lies *rigid and distended* in the sulphurous ashes of Gomorrah. (33)[15]

Peter essentially erases femininity by incorporating it within the masculine, as in his allusion to the rigid and distended phallus of the raped, she-male victim, but he also "heterosexualizes" the rape. The allegorical figure of Sodomy is not satisfied just to invade the particular subject; she attempts as well to "destroy the walls of our heavenly fatherland and... rebuild the defenses of Sodom that were razed by fire" (30–31). This figure of the phallic female is then counterbalanced by that of the maternal male. Listen to how Peter, in one of his sermons, colonizes the female womb by placing it within the male body of the faithful:

> We must consider, dearly beloved, what a dignity is ours, and what a likeness there is between us and Mary. Mary conceived Christ in her bodily womb, and we bear Him about in the womb of our mind. Mary fed Christ when she gave milk from her breasts to His tender lips; and we feed Him with the varied delights of our good works.[16]

Men may well conceive and breastfeed but their gender bending stops at sexual acts: these are always a corruptive force, extirpable only through violence. Just as his fictional hermit, virtuous if naive (41), is condemned for having imagined that inner corruption (desire) could be eliminated through masturbation—mistakenly assuming that "whenever he is excited by passion. . .he should eject semen by handling his organ, just as if he were blowing his nose" (41)[17]—so the Church hierarchy is wrong in thinking that it can simply rid the faithful of sodomy through penance, an act of simple blood-letting, without cutting off completely, even murdering, the offending party. Peter is insistent that if even one member of the collective is corrupted, then "the whole body together with the soul is afterwards tortured forever in a dreadful holocaust" (47).[18] Furthermore, the sodomite is incestuous since, when he preys on other members of the community, he preys on his own spiritual "sons."[19]

The Sodomite Within

Up to this point, we could think that Damian conceives of sexual identities entirely in terms of acts: the sodomite is someone who performs any of the four acts outlined in the first section of the *Gomorrhianus*. Yet he implies throughout the rest of his discussion that sodomites are sodomites before and after the acts have been completed, during confession, and when they associate with others of their kind. He assumes that such men are recognizable to one another while escaping the notice of most, and that they can therefore more easily dissolve within the larger community and infiltrate even the highest echelons of power. They are thus, like Peter, gifted with a sort of added vision, an ability to read the soul of their fellow monks, and to force recognition. But, unlike Peter, they are assimilated to Satan, who, having been barred from creation, must now insinuate himself, through illicit entry, into the body of Christ. Unable because of his blindness to "recognize the entrance that is obviously right before him or even that the door is Christ" (16)—as he himself says: "I am the door" (John 10.9, 13)—the sodomite within holy orders, like his namesake, attempts "violently to break in on angels." He forces entry through "some impassible obstacle of the wall" rather than through "the obvious gateway" (14).[20] Then, "since they are unable to cross the threshold in straightforward fashion, they wander about in circles, dizzied by the maddening rotation" (14).[21] This rape imagery, extending even to the rape of Christ himself, is itself dizzying: the sodomite, blinded to the truth, sees it instead in the soul of his brethren, while Peter maintains that he sees both the truth and its counterfeit, the sodomite soul.

Elsewhere, however, Peter suggests that not all sodomites have such powers of vision. Some are actually unable to recognize themselves for what they are: "if sodomites of themselves are unable to discern their own identity, they may at least be enlightened by those with whom they are assigned to a common confinement for prayer" (28).[22] This startling statement suggests that the sodomite might only come to know himself as such once he has been told as much by others facing the same accusation and punishment. Peter's slip here is not negligible: if the sinner does not recognize himself as a sinner, has he sinned? The solution he proposes is performative: call the sinner a sinner and he is a sinner. Subject him to ritualistic penance in the form of community ostracism and he will soon embrace that identity. Thus, specific recommendations are given on punishment: public flogging, loss of tonsure, besmirching with spit, confinement in prison, iron chains, and a diet of barley bread suitable only for a horse or mule. These will then be followed by a less conspicuous regime guaranteed to cement this identity:

> a further six months living in a small segregated courtyard in the custody of a spiritual elder, kept busy with manual labor and prayer, subjected to vigils and prayers, forced to walk at all times in the company of two spiritual brothers, never again allowed to associate with young men for purposes of improper conversation or advice. (29)[23]

One could say that isolating the sodomite with other men in a confined space might send a mixed message, however Peter seems to think that sexual relations are likely to occur only between younger and older members of the community, or between two younger members. This is one of the most intriguing implications of his prescribed penance: there is no way to extirpate the possibility of sexual attraction between men other than to choose, somewhat arbitrarily, that it can only occur under preordained conditions and can only be contained by the penance he proffers. As Foucault might say, this disciplinary practice is then eroticized, both as it defines erotic pathways and points toward transgressive possibilities.

Community as Queer Utopia

Now, with all this talk about bodies, it seems appropriate to discuss the relation of religiosity to corporality—how the saintly bodies that are produced from within "the discipline" form a community. Let us begin by looking at what Leo Bersani has to say about sadomasochism:

> Societies defined by those structures (*of dominance and submission*) both disguise and reroute the satisfactions, but their superficially self-preservative subterfuges can hardly liberate them from the aegis of the death drive. S/M lifts a social repression in laying bare the reality behind the subterfuges, but in its open embrace of the structures themselves and its undisguised appetite for the ecstasy they promise, it is fully complicit with a culture of death.[24]

Though I am a bit hesitant to relate Peter Damian too explicitly to sadism or masochism, since it subsumes him within a formation that he predates, I do think that "Damianism" has much in common with its later cousins. Peter's open defense and praise of flagellation does lay bare structures of dominance and submission that lie at the heart of Christianity but, to use Bersani's terms, this is not a simple unveiling or deconstruction of these structures but rather an open embrace of the death drive. According to Freud, this death drive is always fused with eroticism, and Lacan agrees to a point, arguing that this drive, like all (erotic) drives strives toward an excess of *jouissance*, where pleasure becomes pain. Peter's advocacy of an explicit identification with the tortured Christ, and his claim that such discipline is the best way to purge the passions, take leave of the self, and cleave more insistently to the collective and mystical body, resonates quite interestingly with Foucault's notion of embodied discourse, "spiritual corporality."[25] This identification is taken to the limit in the act of self-flagellation, but this is just one part of the practices of corporeal "discipline" that Peter advocated for all his monks, and which closely resembles the penance cited earlier prescribed for sodomites: strict fasting and deprivation, almost total silence, and the isolation of monks, in pairs, within cells, in which one party was designated as superior and the other as submissive. The following citation shows us Peter at his most exultant, advocating a self-disciplinary regime that anticipates Foucault's age of reason:

> How blessed, how wonderful a sight! *When the celestial Judge looks forth from heaven and man abases himself in atonement for his sins!* There the accused, *sitting in judgment in the tribunal of his inmost being, holds three-fold office: in his heart he appoints himself as judge, in his body he appears as defendant, while with his hands he rejoices to assume the role of executioner;* as though the holy penitent would say to God: "Lord, it is not necessary to command your official to punish me, nor is it to your advantage to strike fear into me with the retribution of a just trial. *I have laid hands upon myself, have taken revenge and offered myself in place of my sins. . ." The angels. . .delight to announce this event to God, although the unseen Judge has already beheld the selfsame deed with pleasure.* This is the victim which is made a living sacrifice, borne aloft by angels and offered to God. And thus the victim of the human body is invisibly joined to that unique sacrifice which was offered on the altar of the cross; thus is every sacrifice gathered into a single treasure, both that which each member and that which the head of all the elect has offered.[26]

What at first looks like a call to masochism, submission to the Oedipal father, is equally a celebration of the sadistic, as Peter ecstatically identifies with the unseen Judge's delight, or *jouissance*—the *invisibilis Judex* and *Deo gaudentes*—at the narcissistic spectacle of His own sacrifice reenacted. God's ultimate pleasure, according to this fantasy, is in seeing himself be seen suffering; and man is counseled to provide him that pleasure. The circular and self-enclosed *jouissance* of God thus looks much like Peter's own, both scopophilic and uncannily sodomitical. The self-punishing monk who finds within himself the judge, defendant, victim, and executioner is led to a state of imaginary wholeness that is then further fueled by the identification with the sacrificed Christ. This call to doubling, even quadrupling, within the self resonates with Peter's own attempts to instill that same sense of doubleness in the sodomite, through his claim to "see" a hidden self of the sinner that he, in fact, instantiates. A similar call to banish lack occurs in this probably ironical fantasy of sexual wholeness:

> Tell us, you unmanly and effeminate man, what do you seek in another male that you do not find in yourself? What difference in sex, what varied features of the body? What tenderness, what softness of sensual charm? What smooth and delightful face? Male virility, I say, should terrify you, and you should shudder at the sight of manly limbs. For it is the function of the natural appetite that each should seek outside himself what he cannot find within

> his own capacity. *Therefore if the touch of the masculine flesh delights you, lay your hands upon yourself and be assured that whatever you do not find in yourself, you seek in vain in the body of another.* (35)[27]

What begins as a condemnation of sodomy as imaginary and narcissistic sounds, in the end, like a call to masturbation.

Leo Bersani theorizes in *Homos* that effacement of lack might be the key to an understanding of same-sex desire and the foundation of a queer community. Arguing against Lacan's dictum that lack is always at the base of desire, Bersani postulates, "desire in homo-ness is desire to repeat, to expand, to intensify *the same.*" Rather than aiming to fill lack through the incorporation of difference, queer desire, "the desire in others *of what we already are* is, on the contrary, a self-effacing narcissism, a narcissism constitutive of community in that it tolerates psychological difference because of its very indifference to psychological difference." Such a community, based on a willed elision of all signs of difference, is a self-abnegating congregation in which "the narcissistic subject seeks a self-replicating reflection in which s/he is neither known nor not known"; where "individual selves are points along a transversal network of being in which otherness is tolerated as the non-threatening margin of, or supplement to, a seductive sameness."[28]

This notion of "self-effacing narcissism" applies equally well (a) to Peter Damien's conception of the sodomites' extralinguistic, identificatory bonds within the community; (b) to his own utopian vision of an eremitical collective, in which interchangeable dominant and submissive monks play out before one another their conscious imitation of Christ's sacrificial drama; and (c) to God's own desire to watch eternally a "self-replicating reflection" of his own suffering enacted before him. In each case, the protagonist is, in Bersani's terms, a homo; and all three anticipate elements of Foucault's S/M utopian fantasy in which identities are abandoned in favor of a truly egalitarian and reversible regime of bodily pleasures.

Georges Bataille saw the sexual as a form of "self-shattering" self-debasement, in which "the melancholy of the post-Oedipal superego's moral masochism is wholly alien, and in which, so to speak, the self is exuberantly discarded."[29] Peter Damian would probably subscribe to the letter of that argument, if not the context. His sodomite in the *Gomorrhianus*, once bitten by the poisonous serpent of sin, "is deprived of all moral sense, his memory fails, and the mind's vision is darkened. Unmindful of God, he also forgets his own identity" (31). Both Peter and Bataille dismiss the idea that community could be founded on sex, as "this disease" sodomy "erodes the foundations of faith, saps the vitality of hope, *dissolves the bond of love*" (31); but could a sense of community be based on the "self-shattering" that follows it? This is a question that interests Peter: he fully approves of "self-shattering" when it results from "the discipline," that is to say when it depends *completely* upon the moral masochism of the post-Oedipal super-ego. But he denounces it when it follows upon sexual debasement and humiliation, precisely because it suggests the possibility of independence from the community. Peter tries to harness the two by eroticizing, however subtly, the discipline, linking the loss of self to a theatricalization of dominance and submission, all performed for a controlling gaze. Indeed, an ideal reading of the *Gomorrhianus* should itself function as an act of flagellation: a verbal laceration, self-imposed yet sent from the Other, a call that we answer and which serves to eliminate the self and instantiate the subject through a regime of scopophilic abjection.

What most galls Peter, however, and it comes out repeatedly in his characterization of the imaginary sodomites around him, is that they do not play along with his script. Sodomites do not disintegrate through debasement; they stay undercover. They do not even confess, except to one another. They do not merge into an identity-less mystical body: instead they form an alternative body within the community from within which they defy his and God's Law. These subjects militate, converse, and conspire; aim at high Church offices and get them; in essence, operate a ring of successful double agents who get on with it, forming what today might be dismissively referred to as a "gay mafia." Peter has in mind a very much "queerer" community, in which denunciation and scapegoating of sodomites is essential since, in Judith Butler's words, "the act of renouncing homosexuality. . .paradoxically strengthens homosexuality, but it strengthens [it]. . .*as* the power of renunciation."[30] Peter's renunciation of sodomy allows for the creation of a "same-sexual" frame of mind, a category that exalts sameness rather than difference, and celebrates "a culture of death." Like Bersani's version of Gide, Peter is working toward unidentifiable and unlocatable same-sex relations that eliminate from "sex" *the necessity of any relation whatsoever.*[31] Sex thus becomes, to quote Bersani, a "gliding into an impersonal sameness ontologically incompatible with analyzable egos," a "self-divestiture enacted as a willful pursuit of abjection, a casting away not only of possessions but also of the attributes that constitute the self as a valuable property."[32] This pursuit of abjection is key to Peter Damian's own radical penitential mode and the one he prescribes for his monks:

> I often beheld, by an immediate perception of my mind, Christ hanging from the Cross, fastened with nails, and thirstily received His dripping blood in my mouth.[33]

Or when he counsels his charges to:

> begin an unremitting struggle against the flesh, always standing armed against the dangerous disease of passion. . .If the sly tempter puts before your eyes an enticing vision of the flesh, address your thoughts at once to the tombs of

> the dead and take careful note of what you find there that pleases the touch or delights the eye. (46)[34]

Once again, vision predominates in this fantasy as the "sly tempter" places flesh before our eyes, flesh that we, quite understandably in this formulation, see as death. Touching and seeing, united here in fantasy, allow us to take pleasure in this contemplation, as eroticism is conjoined with the embrace of death. (After all, whatever can it be in the tombs of the dead that he thinks might please and delight?) But we must not forget that the vision is not ours: like Peter's accusation of sodomy, it is "put before our eyes," the immediate prelude to an act of interpellation in which we declare ourselves subjects. Thus, though it is to the religious impulse to "overcome the isolated discontinuity of being [flesh, desubjectivizing sex] with a sense of continuity [in death]" that Peter appeals,[35] he can only suggest that end through the evocation of the sexual, the supplement of his own *jouissance*:

> When any holy soul is truly joined to its Redeemer by love, then it is united with Him as if on the bridal couch in a bond of intimate delight.[36]

Where Peter Damian's queer utopia finally parts ways with the sexless continuum of Gide or Foucault is in his reliance on institutions. Not for him the pleasure of dissolution he counsels to others. He is not able to give up selfhood (as his hundreds of texts testify) or the power of vision, any more than his God is. He takes his pleasure in embodying the gaze, seeing, and listening, from the exalted position of father/confessor/reformer of the Law. Peter needs the nameless sodomites he sees through the confessional curtain so as to secure that fantasy. The corporeal *jouissance* he preaches—self-flagellation and nonverbal communication, in very close quarters—might, from one perspective, gesture toward the impossibility of the sexual relation, queer or straight. But it also holds out the promise of an alternative that he, and many since, have found alluring: subjectless bodies, sexless pleasure, a truly mimetic community in which someone is *always* watching.

Notes

1. Peter (1007–72) was a prolific writer and preacher whose career included high church office (as a papal ambassador) and involvement in contemporary politics (writing on such burning issues as the Investiture controversy and the role of simony). His first work was the *Vita Romualdi*, dated to 1042, followed by several volumes of letters, sermons, and some fifty-three letters and treatises. An inveterate reformer, he has been seen by scholars as both a very stern and saintly figure and an unhappy neurotic who acted out in his writings his

personal sufferings and grievances. See Lester Little, "The Personal Development of Peter Damian," in *Order and Innovation in the Middle Ages: Essays in Honor of Joseph R. Strayer*, ed. William C. Jordan, Bruce McNab, and Teofilo F. Ruiz (Princeton: Princeton University Press, 1976), pp. 317–41.

2. See Michel Foucault, *Surveiller et punir: naissance de la prison* (Paris: Gallimard, 1975) and the essays collected in *Foucault Live: Interviews 1961–1984*, ed. Sylvère Lotringer, trans. Lysa Hochroth and John Johnston (New York: Semiotext(e), 1989).
3. In his *De frenanda ira*, Peter admitted that he was always prone to explosions of anger but learned to curb these outbursts through reason (*Opusculum* 40.9; PL 145:658d). As Little notes, he said much the same thing about the effects of sexual temptation: Little, "Personal Development," p. 335. The abbreviation PL refers throughout to the *Patrilogiae Cursus Completus: Series Latina*, 217 vols., ed. Jacques-Paul Migne (Paris, 1844–64).
4. Peter Damian, *Letters 31–60*, trans. Otto J. Blum, The Fathers of the Church: Mediaeval Continuation 2 (Washington: Catholic University of America Press, 1990), p. 6. Subsequent references to this translation of the Latin text of the *Liber gomorrhianus* are provided in parentheses in the text. The Latin text itself is taken from *Die Briefe des Petrus Damiani*, ed. Kurt Reindel, 4 vols. (Munich: Monumenta Germaniae Historica, 1983), 1:284–330; subsequent references to the Latin are provided by page and line number. The Latin of the passage quoted here is: "Quoddam autem nefandissimum et ignominiosum valde vitium in nostris partibus inholevit, cui nisi districtae animadversionis manus quantocius obviet, certum est, quod divini furoris gladius in multorum perniciem immaniter crassaturus impendent" (*Die Briefe*, 287:1–4).
5. "Dic ergo, quisquis es qui Christi passionem superbus irrides, qui, cum eo nudari flagellarique despiciens, nuditatem ejus et cuncta supplicia tanquam nugas ac naenias et quaedam somniorum deliramenta subsannas; quid facies cum eum, qui publice nudatus est et in cruce suspensus. . .et super omnia visibilia et invisibilia ineffabiliter gloriosum? Quis, inquam, facies, cum eum, cujus nunc ignominiam despicis, aspexeris in igneo tribunalis exceis solio praesidentem, et omne genus humanum rescto acquitatis examine terribiliter judicantem?. . .Qua fronte, qua praesumptionis audacia illius gloriam participare sperabis, cujus portare contumeliam et ignominiam despexisti?" (*Opusculum* 43.4; PL 145:682–83), cited in *Peter Damian: Selected Writings on the Spiritual Life*, trans. Patricia McNulty (London: Faber and Faber, 1959), p. 38.
6. "Nunc autem ad te, papa beatissime" (*Die Briefe*, 329:6); "Sed iam te ore ad os quisquis es, sodomita, convenio" (*Die Briefe*, 298:8); "Ego, ego te, infelix anima" (*Die Briefe*, 311:20); "Ecce, o bone vir sodomita" (*Die Briefe*, 301:20); "O miserabilis anima" (*Die Briefe*, 314:1).
7. Mark Jordan calls attention to this same technique in his excellent discussion of this text in *The Invention of Sodomy* (Chicago: University of Chicago Press, 1997), pp. 45–66. Other important recent reevaluations of Peter include David Lorenzo Boyd, "Disrupting the Norm: Sodomy, Culture and the Male

Body in Peter Damian's *Liber Gomorrhianus*," *Essays in Medieval Studies* 11 (1994): 63–73; Conrad Leyser, "Cities of the Plain: The Rhetoric of Sodomy in Peter Damian's 'Book of Gomorrah,'" *Romanic Review* 86.2 (1995): 191–211; and Larry Scanlon, "Unmanned Men and Eunuchs of God: Peter Damian's *Liber Gomorrhianus* and the Sexual Politics of Papal Reform," *New Medieval Literatures* 2 (1998): 37–64.

8. Foucault, *Surveiller*, chap. 3.
9. According to Lacan, "the masochist prefers to experience the pain of experience in his own body, the sadist rejects this pain and forces the Other to bear it." Jacques Lacan, "Kant avec Sade," in *Écrits* (Paris: Seuil, 1966), p. 778 [765–90], cited in Dylan Evans, *An Introductory Dictionary of Lacanian Psychoanalysis* (London: Routledge, 1996), p. 168.
10. "Qualiter enim proximum meum sicut meipsum diligo, si vulnus, quo eum non ambigo crudeliter mori, neglegenter fero in eius corde crassari, videns ergo vulnera mentium, curare neglegam sectione verborum" (*Die Briefe*, 326:17–20).
11. For biblical sources see Damian, *Letters 31–60*, ed. Blum; Owen J. Blum, *St. Peter Damian: His Teaching on the Spiritual Life* (Washington: Catholic University of America Press, 1947).
12. See Harvey Whitestone, *Arguments and Icons: Divergent Modes of Religiosity* (Oxford: Oxford University Press, 2000) on the differences between doctrinal and the imagistic modes of transmitting ritual.
13. The Latin text for these three citations is as follows: "quid rogo, dixisset, si loetale hoc vulnus in ipso corpore sanctae ecclesiae foetere conspiceret" (*Die Briefe*, 294:13–14); "Hoc est enim, quod sobrietatem violat, pudicitiam necat, castitatem iugulat, virginitatem spurcissime contagionis mucrone trucidat" (*Die Briefe*, 310:2–3); "Omnia foedat, omnia maculat, omnia polluit et quantum ad se nichil putum, nichil a sordibus alienum, nichil mundum esse permittit" (*Die Briefe*, 310:3–5); "ubi non de corruptis sed de pollutis exorsum est" (*Die Briefe*, 307:4–5).
14. "Haec pestilentissima sodomorum regina suae tyrannidis legibus obsequentem hominibus turpem Deo reddit odibilem. Adversus Deum nefanda bella conserere, nequissimi spiritus imperat militiam baiulare, ab angelorum consortio separat et infelicem animam sub propriae dominationis iugo a sua nobilitate captivat. Virtutum armis suos milites exuit omniumque vitiorum iaculis, ut confodiantur, exponit. In ecclesia humiliat, in foro condempnat, foedat in secreto, dehonestat in publico, conscientiam rodit ut vernis, carnem exurit ut ignis, anhelat, ut voluptatem expleat, at contra timet, ne ad medium veniat, ne in publicum exeat, ne hominibus innotescat" (*Die Briefe*, 310:9–17).
15. "Filia quippe populi mei pessima plaga contrita est, quia anima, quae sanctae ecclesiae fuerat filia, ab hoste humani generis telo inmunditiae est crudeliter sauciata et auqe in aula regis aeterni lacte sacri eloquii tenerre ac *molliter* educabatur, nunc veneno libidinis pestilenter infecta in sulphureis Gomorrae cineribus *tumefacta ac rigida* iacere conspicitur" (*Die Briefe*, 312:10–14).
16. "Hinc etiam, dilectissimi, considerandum est quanta sit dignitas nostra, quantaque imbis sit proportio cum Maria. Concepit Maria Christum in

vulva cannis deferimus et nos in visceribus mentis. Reficiebat Maria Christum, cum teneris labris lac exprimeres uberum; reficimus et nos raviis honorum deliciis operum" (*Sermo* 45; PL 144:747b), cited in Blum, *St. Peter Damian*, p. 150.

17. "Hoc ille hermita suo facto probat, qui cum ultis virtutibus cum quodam suo collega deservisset, haec ili per diabolum iniecta cogitatio est, ut quandocumque libidine titillaretur, sic semen detritu genitalis membri egerere deberet, tanquam flegma de naribus proiceret" (*Die Briefe*, 319:3–7).
18. "Cogita, quam miserum sit, quod per unum membrum, cuius nunc voluptas expletur, totum postmodum corpus simul cum anima atrocissimis flammarum incendiis perpetuao cruciatur" (*Die Briefe*, 324:1–3). This follows from the conclusions he draws in his *Liber gratissimus* 25 (PL 145:119c) and his *Dominus vobiscum* 10 (PL 145:239d) that the individual is what it is only through its participation in the universal, as in the metaphor of the micro- and macrocosm (cited in Blum, *St. Peter Damian*, p. 144).
19. "quod uterque iste licet incestuose naturaliter tamen, quia cum muliere peccavit, ille in clericum turpitudinem operans sacrilegium commisit in filium, incestus crimen incurrit, in masculum naturae iura dissolvit" (*Die Briefe*, 296:4–7).
20. "Qui enim non per humilitatis iter, sed per arrogantiae et tumoris anfractus ad Deum accedere gestiunt, patet profecto, quia unde ingressionis aditus pateat, non agnoscunt, vel quia ostium Christus est, sicut ipse dicit: *Ego sum ostium*" (*Die Briefe*, 293:14–17); "*Sodomitae ergo ad angelos conantur violenter irrumpere, cum immundi homines ad Deum temptant per sacri ordinis officia propinquare*" (*Die Briefe*, 293:10–11).
21. "Qui enim indignus ordine ad sacri altaris officium conatur irrumpere, quid aliud quam relicto ianuae limine per immeabilem parietis obicem nititur introire" (*Die Briefe*, 293:27–29). Peter is using citations from the psalms and the Old Testament (for example, Ps 11.9, 14: "the wicked walk in a circle" [In circuitu impii ambulant]; and see *Die Briefe*, 294:3–5) to suggest the non-teleological itinerary of the sodomite.
22. "quatinus si sodomite ex semetipsis nesciunt pensare quod sunt, ab ipsis saltim valeant edoceri, cum quibus sunt communi orationis ergastulo deputati" (*Die Briefe*, 307:7–9).
23. "Post hec aliis sex mensibus sub senioris spiritalis custodia segregata in curticula degens operi manuum et orationi sit intentus, vigiliis et orationibus subiectus et sub custodia semper duorum fratrum spiritalium ambulet, nulla prava locutione vel consilio deinceps iuvenibus coniungendus" (*Die Briefe*, 308:7–11).
24. Leo Bersani, *Homos* (Cambridge, MA: Harvard University Press, 1995), p. 97.
25. For a fuller discussion of this Foucauldian notion as it relates to theology, see Jeremy R. Carrette, "Male Theology in the Bedroom," in his *Foucault and Religion: Spiritual Corporality and Political Spirituality* (London: Routledge, 2000), pp. 63–84.
26. "O quam jucundum! O quam insigne spectaculum! Cum Supernus Judex de coelo prospectat, et homo semetipsum in inferioribus pro suis delictis

mittat! Ubi reus ipse, in pectoris sui tribunalibus praesidens, trifarium tenet officium; in corde se constituit judicem, reum in corpore, manibus se gaudet exhibere tortorem; ac si Deo sanctus poenitens dicat: Non opus est, Domine, ut officio tuo me punire praecipias; ipse mihi manus injicio, ipse de me vindictam capio, vicemque meis peccatis reddo. . .Huic econtra spectaculo assistunt angeli, qui gaudent de peccatore converso; et hoc Deo gaudentes annuntiant, cum jam invisibilis Judex id ipsum per se delectabiliter cernat. Haec est hostia quae viva mactatur, ad Deum per angelos oblata defertur; et *sic* humani corporis victima ili unico sacrificio quod in ara crucis oblatum est, invisibiliter permiscetur; et sic in uno thesauro sacrificium omne reconditur, videlicet et quod unumquodque membrum, et quod caput omnium obtulit electorum" (*Opusculum* 43: *De laude flagellum*; PL 145:679–85), cited in Blum, *St. Peter Damian*, p. 117.

27. "Dic, vir evirate, responde, homo effeminate, quid in viro quaeris, quod in temetipso invenire non possis? Quam diversitatem sexuum, quae varia liniamenta membrorum, quam mollitiem, quam carnalis illecebrae teneritudinem, quam lubrici vultus iocunditatem? Terreat te, quaeso, vigor masculini aspectus, abhorreat mens tua viriles artus. Naturalis quippe appetitus officium est, ut hoc unusquisque extrinsecus quaerat, quod intra suae facultatis claustra reperire non valeat. Si ergo te contrectatio masculine carnis oblectat, verte manus in te et scito, quia quicquid apud te non invenis, in alieno corpore in vacuum quaeris" (*Die Briefe,* 313:13–22).
28. Bersani, *Homos*, pp. 149–50.
29. Leo Bersani, "Is the Rectum a Grave?" in *AIDS: Cultural Analysis, Cultural Activism*, ed. Douglas Crimp (Cambridge, MA: MIT Press, 1988), p. 218 [197–222].
30. Judith Butler, *The Psychic Life of Power* (Stanford: Stanford University Press, 1997), p. 143.
31. Bersani, *Homos*, p. 122.
32. Bersani, *Homos*, pp. 125–26. All of these citations occur in the context of Bersani's discussion of André Gide's *L'Immoraliste* (London: Harrap, 1974).
33. "Saepe cernebam praesentissimo mantis intuitu Christum clavis affixum, in cruce pendentem, avidusque suspiciebam stillantem supposito ore cruore" (*Opusculum* 19; PL 145:432), cited in *Peter Damian: Selected Writings*, trans. McNulty, p. 32.
34. "Statue quoque tibi certamen assiduum adversus carnem, armatus semper assiste contra inportunam libidinis rabiem. Si luxurie flamma in ossibus estuat, portinus illam memoria perpetui ignis extinguat. Si callidus insidiator lubricam carnis speciem obicit, ilico mens ad mortuorum sepulchra oculum dirigat et quid illic suave tactu, quid delectabile visu reperiatur, sollerter attendat" (*Die Briefe*, 323:17–22).
35. Carrette, "Male Theology," p. 72.
36. "Cum ergo sancta quaelibet anima Redemptori suo veraciter in amore conjunctitur, cum ei denique velut in sponsali thalamo per oblectationis intimae glutinum copulatur" (*Epistolae* 4.16; PL 144:333), cited in *Peter Damian: Selected Writings*, trans. McNulty, p. 30.

CHAPTER 3

SEEING WOMEN TROUBADOURS WITHOUT THE "-ITZ" AND "-ISMS"

Francesca Nicholson

Against the critical tendency to "see" and secure the femininity of the women troubadours, this chapter shows how their subjective voice alternates between the feminine and the masculine, sustaining gender hybridity in poetic practice.

Although scholars of Old Occitan have long been aware that there were women composing troubadour poetry in southern France (Occitania) from the thirteenth century onward,[1] the idea of the woman troubadour still troubles them. It is now generally accepted that courtly reverence for the lady did not entail reverence for the female, and that courtly structures are as much about homosocial bonds as they appear to be about heterosexual love. Leaving aside the question of the socioeconomic circumstances that may have given Occitan women the freedom to be poets,[2] how, many scholars have asked themselves, could they compose within such a seemingly masculinist tradition? Critical opinion is thus frequently divided into two camps: those who believe the identity of these women poets to be a fiction created by male troubadours, and those who imagine them as the Virginia Woolfs of their day, creating embryonic feminist poetic practices of their own. In either case there is a problem in seeing the women troubadours as troubadours. My concern in this essay is the latter, and especially latter-day, tendency to over-feminize the women troubadours and to read their poetry as expressive of a steadfast female identity. Readings of this sort, which claim to be gender-conscious, turn gender into a stricture, a normalizing filter through which a group of "troublesome" texts can be reclassified. While spotlighting the overlooked or underestimated feminine aspects of a text, they leave in shadow that which is inassimilable to the feminine, or to a singular category of gender. What remains in shadow under this new vision is just as troubling to it as the unacknowledged presence of women troubadours is to a vision of troubadour culture as a whole.

The full suffix that feminizes the word "trobador" is "-airitz," thus giving "trobairitz," but I have abbreviated this to "-itz" for the purpose of creating a phonetic and in turn semantic approximation with "-ism." "-isms," as I see them, territorialize concepts and reading practices and can as a result territorialize the literature they look at. It should be clear from my opening remarks that the "-isms" of which I am particularly suspicious are those that impart a biological determinism to poetry by women, which see translated in it an experience of womanhood. These "-isms" usually go by the name of essentialism or sentimentalism. The reason for my suspicion is that, rather like the too highly focused vision that leaves shadows in its periphery, an excessive concern with the femininity of these texts reduces the consideration we give to them as troubadour texts, which surely is their overriding characteristic. Such a consonance between male authorship and masculine experience is not sought or even expected in texts attributed to male troubadours; but the minute one strips a female poet of her gender particularity, her very existence risks being doubted. To revisualize the trobairitz as troubadours is not about subsuming one gender into another, as impassioned feminist readers may fear, but about seeing the full span of gendered identities and combinations of desire that poetic invention makes possible.

Given that it only occurs once in an Occitan text, it is surprising that the word "trobairitz" has gained such a strong foothold in our critical vocabulary. This is largely due to the trailblazing anthology of essays on the women troubadours edited by William Paden in 1989 and called *The Voice of the Trobairitz*. In the introduction, Paden writes:

> *Trobairitz* is very rare in medieval Occitan. It does not occur in lyric poetry, in the grammatical treatises, or in the biographies of the trobairitz or troubadours; it seems to be found only once, in the thirteenth-century romance *Flamenca*. The heroine of the romance becomes involved in a clandestine exchange of two-syllable messages with the knight who will become her lover; at one point, when her maid thinks of the perfect response, she congratulates her as a *bona trobairis*, a "good trobairitz" . . . . Despite the rarity of the term, however—which surpasses the rarity of the trobairitz—it fulfills a logical and useful function in contrast with the word "troubadour."[3]

The impetus to contrast the trobairitz with the troubadours, which Paden argues for, has produced a problematic segregation of the two that not even the manuscript transmission of the poetry lends credence to; there are no separate *chansonniers* of poetry by the women troubadours, nor are they demarcated from the male troubadours in extant *chansonniers*.[4] Scholars have done this in good faith, with the intention of revalorizing previously neglected texts, and editions of the corpus of the women troubadours (which varies according to the number of anonymous poems admitted to it) by Matilda Bruckner, Laurie Shepard, Sarah White, and by Angelica Rieger, are indisputably valuable.[5] But the danger of the term "trobairitz" is that it sets up expectations for a gendered poetic practice that aligns with the supposed biological identity of the author. It is as though the only axes along which we can plot our readings of this corpus of poetry are feminine voice or subject matter, and female authors, and indeed much of the early scholarship on the women troubadours follows precisely this pattern. Examples of such readings are the articles by Pierre Bec and Antoine Tavera who are both on the trail of feminine lyricism,[6] or Joan Ferrante and Sophie Marnette in their efforts to identify a female rhetoric.[7] These critics all take the feminine identity of the woman troubadour, where supported by an external referent such as a rubric, as a textual anchor and as the originary principle of their poetry. As with the justification for adopting the "trobairitz" designation in the earlier quote by Paden, the trobairitz is always contrasted with the troubadour and treated as an isolated phenomenon in courtly lyric. While the corpus of the women troubadours is unarguably small, this in itself does not justify the perception of exclusionary or mutually resistant poetic practices determined by the sex of the poet. The substantial number of *tensos* (courtly debates) between interlocutors of different genders, as well as the laudatory descriptions of women troubadours in the *vidas* and *razos* (Occitan prose biographies of the troubadours or commentaries of their songs), all point to a more heterogeneous and collaborative poetic tradition than many critics have allowed themselves to see.[8] By not taking identity a priori and instead observing the various identity-formations that arise from troubadour poetry (and in this I encompass male and female troubadours), it becomes possible to make the case for ungendered poetic practices, or practitioners who deploy both genders in a playful, pliable fashion.

"Identity" is such an overused term in all types of discourse that it has become dilated, shapeless, and weary. Though I cannot avoid using it altogether, I would like to sharpen its contours by associating it with the process of *identification* in psychoanalysis. There are two stages or types of identification: primary identification, which occurs at the mirror-stage when the ego appropriates the image of itself as ideal; and secondary identification, which is the ego's attempt to appropriate an ideal other than itself. Secondary identification may be said to be at work in the creation of troubadour identity. The troubadour seeks to acquire identity in relation to the beloved of whom he or she sings, since without that object of love there is no song, and at the same time seeks identification with other troubadours. Clearly the troubadour cannot identify with the beloved, since that would nullify the subject position altogether, but that subject position is largely beholden to having an object of desire. Similarly the troubadour desires to be a troubadour without desiring other troubadours as such, as in the Lacanian model of secondary identification, where the ego ideal is constituted by the father although the ego does not desire the father.[9] These patterns of identification can be traced for both male and female troubadours, and even though sexuated identities can emerge following identification processes, the important thing is that they do not preexist, far less determine, those processes.[10] Moreover, the relation between the subject and its identity/identification is shown to be a troubled one, or one where the connections are interrupted and re-formed according to the impulses of desire. The troubadour poem, as the symbolic domain in which identification occurs, thus plays out a multiplicity of identification possibilities through the malleability of the poetic "I," the ego in search of identification.

To illustrate this point I would like to take two poems. The first is attributed to "Na Bieris de Roman" [Lady Bieris de Roman] in the rubric preceding it:

Na Maria, pretz e fina valors
e.l gioi e.l sen e la fina beutatz
e l'acuglir e.l pretz e las onors
e.l gent parlar e l'avinen solatz
e la douz cara e la gaia acundansa
e.l ducz esgart e l'amoros semblan,
qe son en vos, don non avetz egansa,
me fan traire vas vos ses cor truan.

Per qe vos *prec*, si.us platz, qe fin'amors
e gausiment et doutz umilitatz
me puosca far ab vos tan de socors,
qe *mi donetz*, bella dompna, si.us platz,
so don plus *ai d'aver gioi esperansa*,
car en vos *ai mon cor e mon talan*
e per vos *ai tut so c'ai d'alegransa*
e per vos *vauc mantas ves sospiran*.

E car beutas e valors vos enansa[11]
sobra tutas, c'una no.us es denan,
vos *prec*, se.us plas, per so qe.us es onransa,
qe non ametz entendidor truan.

Bella dompna, cui pretz e gioi enansa,
e gient parlar, a vos *mas coblas man*,
car en vos es gauss'[12] e alegransa
et tut lo ben c'om en dona deman.[13]

[Lady Maria, the virtue and pure worth
and joy and wisdom and pure beauty
and welcoming disposition and virtue and honor
and noble speech and charming company
and the sweet face and cheerful manner
and the sweet gaze and loving appearance,
which are in you, and in which you have no equal,
draw me towards you without a deceitful heart.

For this I beg you, if it please you, that pure love
and delight and sweet humility
may be of assistance to me with you,
so that you will give me, lovely lady, if it please you,
that which I most hope to enjoy,
for in you I have my heart and my desire
and for you I have whatever happiness I have
and for you I often go about sighing.

Because beauty and worth exalt you
above all [women], so that none is superior to you,
I beseech you, if it pleases you, for the honor it will bring you
not to love a false suitor.

Lovely lady, whom virtue and joy elevates,
and noble speech, to you I send my verses,
for in you is gaiety and happiness
and all the good which one/a man asks for in a lady.]

The critical controversy surrounding this poem is, very bluntly, whether or not the first person subject, assumed to be feminine, is a lesbian because she expresses desire for another woman. Angelica Rieger's article "Was Bieiris de Romans Lesbian?" again in Paden's volume of essays, *The Voice of the Trobairitz*, begins by considering the possibilities of homosexuality in the Middle Ages, both for men and women, and in male troubadour poetry.[14] She discards the possibility that the author of this poem is not a woman but a man, which previous readers have put forward as a way of wriggling out of the lesbian question, and proceeds to examine the various expressions of female-to-female tenderness in the poem and by comparison with other texts such as *ensenhamens* or poems by other women troubadours. Although in the end Rieger does not wholly corroborate the lesbian hypothesis, she sticks to the idea that this poem does involve feminine identities and that there is an expression of tenderness, be it amicable or erotic, which subtends it.

In my view Rieger jumps the gun in her analysis of this poem. She launches into discussing the attributes of desire that the poem suggests without examining the identities implicated in that matrix of desire. Because the poem possesses the thematic traits we have come to expect for courtly lyric, with the topos of the lady in all her perfection and the suppliant "I" representing the lover, Rieger questions only the quality of the emotion, rather than the articulation of each subject position created by the poem. Although on the face of it this poem appears to be primarily a description of the poet's beloved, I want to look at the subjectivity of the poet that emerges very subtly and almost imperceptibly in the course of this description. I would like to call these emergences "instances of subjectivity," and I have drawn attention to them by italicizing them in the text of the poem.

As is typical of the Occitan language, verbs do not need subject pronouns before them, and the verbs connected to the first person subject in this poem are "prec" [I beg or beseech] (once in stanza 2, l. 9 and once in stanza 3, l. 19); "ai" [I have] (three times in stanza 2, ll. 13, 14, and 15); "vauc" [I go] (once in l. 16); and "man" [I send] (once in l. 22). Na Maria, by contrast, is the subject of only three verbs: "avetz" [you have] (l. 8); "donetz" [you give] (l. 12); and "ametz" [you love] (l. 20). Agency in the form of active verbs is definitely on the side of the first person subject. But having said this, the verbs of the first person subject are dependent on the second identity represented by Na Maria in the poem, since "prec" has the object "vos," two of the "ai" examples as well as "vauc" are preceded by "en vos" [in you], or "per vos" [for you], and "man" is preceded by "a vos" [to you]. "Prec" is qualified further by "si.us platz" [if it pleases you] each time it is uttered. The subjectivity of the first person is also articulated by means of object pronouns—"me fan traire" [draw me] (l. 8), "me puosca far" [it may do me] (l. 11), "mi donetz" [you give me] (l. 12)—and one possessive adjective—"mas coblas" [my verses] (l. 22). These features confound the possibility of positing a "singular" identity for the first person subject, or for that matter the addressee, and we are confronted instead with meshed identities or identities in process. It is also important to observe that there are no gender markings for the first person subject in this poem, and that Na Maria's only characterization by gender (apart from her name) is in the address "Bella dompna" in lines 12 and 21. With all the artifice that the term "dompna" connotes, as a construct from the masculine term "dominus," her femininity is almost as equivocal as that of the first person subject. Although "dompna" or "domna" is translated as "lady," the gender of the term is not straightforwardly feminine. Semantically, as Sarah Kay has pointed out, the gender of the "domna" is mixed, "partaking of both masculine and feminine," since she is the beloved who is addressed as a feudal lord.[15] The "domna" designation is a highly conventionalized element of troubadour poetry, but in a poem such as Bieiris's where identity is seen to be a network rather than a unit, the gender equivocations that underlie this conventional term resurface as it is applied to Na Maria. If the first person subject cannot express its identity except in relation to Na Maria, her characterization as "domna" produces a fundamentally ambivalent point of reference.

I now wish to look at the potential identifications for the first person subject. In line 8 the first person subject claims not to have a deceitful heart—"cor truan." This may allude to fickle troubadours who are inconstant in their affections and sing to more than one lady. The recurrence of "truan" in line 20 as the adjective for "entendidor" [suitor] surely forces us to read these lines side by side and think not only about hearts and suitors but of potential falsehood. Where is the guarantee that the first person subject is not "truan" when there has been no overt declaration of identity? Where is the identity of the first person subject if it is so imbricated in the love object? It is perhaps at this point that we can ask whether a feminine voice is identifying with the first person subject and beginning to expose it as a masquerade, an identity-assumption that exists only within the poem, and hence the warning not to love false admirers may refer not to others but to the first person subject itself. Is the "I" who sends these verses to Na Maria subsequently the same "I" who has spoken previously? The last line in this stanza raises further doubts as to the identification assumed by the first person subject: "lo ben c'om en dona deman" is not the good that "I" asks for in a lady but which "one" or "a man" looks for in a lady, the "om" being ambiguously impersonal or masculine. Throughout the poem the first person subject has appeared to assume the position customarily occupied by a lover, thus creating expectations as to that first person identity and the desire it expresses. When it avoids declaring its identification with "om" at the end of the poem—in other words, when it does not unite the "cor" with the speaking self—the subject throws into question the parameters of identification that were set up by those expectations, rather than by what the first person subject actually declared about itself. Tension is thereby maintained between a feminine identity suggested by the rubric, the courtly dyad of desire, and the absence of stable, gendered correlates in the text.

A poem that is frequently juxtaposed by critics to *Na Maria, pretz e fina valors* is the *salut d'amor* by Azalais d'Altier, *Tanz salutz e tantas amors*—indeed Angelica Rieger brings it into her article on Bieiris de Roman as evidence of non-homoerotic relations between women. Despite the difference in terms between my analysis and Rieger's, this poem works equally well as a second example in my readings of identification in the poetry of the women troubadours. This is a much longer text than Bieiris's poem, therefore I have selected quotations from it.[16]

Azalais's song also addresses a lady. Like Bieiris, Azalais begins by an enumeration, this time not of the lady's qualities but of the greetings, compliments, and praises that are to be lavished upon the lady. In effect, Azalais is acting as an intermediary between the lover and the lady, as she declares in the lines:

> vos tramet N'Azalais d'Altier,
> a vos, donna, cui ilh volria
> mais vezer qe ren q'el mon sia (ll. 6–8)
>
> [N'Azalais d'Altier sends [these greetings etc.]
> to you, lady, whom she/he? would like
> to see more than anything else in the world.]

"Ilh" is a crucial pronoun, for it reveals who the desiring subject is, but the pronoun is ambivalent. Both Rieger, and Bruckner, Shepard, and White translate it as "she," thus imputing desire to Azalais; however, grammatically, "ilh" (and its orthographic variant "ill") can be either a feminine pronoun or a masculine one.[17] Because Azalais and the lover whom she purports to represent in ambassadorial fashion are both referred to in the third person, the pronoun could be attached to either or both. Such pronoun confusion heralds the commingling of the identities of Azalais and the lover, and the potential commingling of desire. Azalais's desires have not been planted by the lady, but by the words of the lover about his lady:

> per lo ben qu'el me n'a dich
> ai tant inz en mon cor escrich
> vostre semblant que, si.us vezia,
> entre milh vos conoisseria. (ll. 11–14)
>
> [for the good of which he has spoken to me
> I have inscribed so deeply in my heart
> your face that, if I saw you,
> I would know you among thousands.]

After this, Azalais piles on the ardor, which, in a change from the earlier lines, is all expressed in the first person:

Et dic vos ben aitan en ver
qez anc donna senes vezer
non amei tan d'amor coral,
et dic vos ben, si Deus mi sal,
quez el mon non es nulla res
q'eu penses qez a vos plagues
qes eu non fezes volentiera
senes mant e senes priguiera,
ez ai, donna, trop gran desire
quez eu vos vis e.us pogues dire
tot mon cor e tot mon voler
e pogues lo vostre saber. (ll. 15–26)

[And I tell you so in truth
that never before have I loved a lady without seeing her
with such heartfelt love,
and I tell you, God save me,
that there's nothing in the world
if I thought it might please you
that I would not do willingly
without hearing a command or a request,
for I have, lady, too great a desire
to see you so that I can tell you
all my heart and all my will
and know yours.]

Interpreting this declaration of love again rests on the subject position that Azalais may be occupying. Preceding it is the condition of Azalais's subject position as messenger, and in a way mouthpiece, for the lady's male lover. To what extent is she therefore at liberty to speak from her own subject position? We might compare her insistence upon truthfulness and sincerity with Bieiris swearing that she does not have a "cor truan." This absence of a deceitful heart or identity-core does not, however, necessarily remove the possibility of outward masquerade. In pressing her own suit, is she not jeopardizing the embassy with which she has been entrusted on behalf of the male lover? Or is she using the first person subject in a changeable way, identifying sometimes with the Azalais announced in the third person in line 6, sometimes with the lover who has transferred his knowledge and desire for the lady on to Azalais? Identifying Azalais singularly as the experiencing "I" of this part of the poem seems even more out of place when we read the rest of the poem, where she takes up the cause of the lover and his mistreatment at the hands of the lady for a full sixty-three lines: over half of the poem. The "I" of the declaration of love must be either a double subject position (inhabited both by the voice of Azalais and the sentiments of the male lover) or one adopted solely for the purpose of flattering and cajoling the lady to better dispose her to the argument that follows.

The love declaration reemerges toward the end of the poem, this time with a clearer conflation/confusion of Azalais and the lover:

per q'eu vos prec, per gran merze,
qe vos *tot per amor de me,*
li perdones e.l finiscatz
los tortz don vos l'ucasonatz,
Ez *eu faz vos per lui fianza*
qe ja en diz ni en semblanza
non faza nul temps ni non diga
ren per qe.l sias enemiga. (ll. 89–96)

[Therefore I beg you, in great pity,
that you, wholly for love of me,
pardon him and absolve
the wrongs you charge him with,
and I give you my word for him
that never in speech or in looks
shall he do or say
a thing that makes you his enemy.]

I have italicized the parts where the intersubjective position of Azalais and the lover, or Azalais, the lover and the lady, occur. In lines 90–91 the lady is supposed to forgive the lover for the love she bears toward Azalais, and wholly for that reason. In line 93 the three of them are intertwined in the word—*fianza*—that Azalais gives as guarantee. Subject positions and intrasubjective relations are once more mediated and conjoined in the symbolic domain of language, in the word.

What both these poems appear to be saying about troubadour subjectivity, about the "I" who speaks in them, is that the position and the identification of that "I" is changeable: no single identification is claimed, and none is rejected. Clearly there are reasons to believe that the authors of these texts were women, but neither capitalizes on femininity any more than she does on masculinity. Instead she weaves in and out of subjective structures in relation to the other identities present in the text. This troubles not only the notion of essential or self-identical traits in the first person subject, but also the expected trajectories of desire between subjects and objects.

Kelly Oliver has made an important contribution to theories of identity and subjectivity in her book, *Subjectivity without Subjects*, and it is with reference to this that I would like to conclude. She advances the theory that subjectivity need not be oppressive or exclusionary, "violent" as she puts it, but that instead we can conceive of relationships "across difference," relationships "beholden to difference."[18] This formula resonates with the way troubadour identification comes about, through ideals external to oneself, and with the complex articulation of the self through the other. It also resonates with the manner in which female troubadours coexist with male troubadours: though different subjects, they are involved in the same subjectivity. Identity, according to Oliver, need not be a tyrannical exercise involving the abjection of the other. By removing subjects as "identifiers," it becomes possible to speak of subjectivity in the dynamic yet unoppressive way Oliver suggests. For her this is also a matter of vision, as she writes in chapter nine with reference to phenomenological conceptions (particularly those of Maurice Merleau-Ponty) of self, space, and world:

> The use of theories of identity as constructed through the exclusion or abjection of the other is widespread—and not just among feminist theorists. . . . I suggest that these theories are based on a faulty notion of space that views difference as distance and distance as void. . . .This view of space and vision leaves us forever cut off from the world outside ourselves unless we can incorporate it and make it our own. In this view, difference and identity are opposites because space is discrete and not fluid; two things cannot be in the same place at the same time unless they are identical. But, if we replace this model with one of circulation that links vision to the other more proximal senses, we see that there is no inherent gap between us and the world outside.[19]

Closed categories of gender and island-like "-isms" are at variance with this reimagining of identity. If they once served to identify identities in obscurity, they are insufficient to illuminate the vast and intricate network that produced them. This open vista of gender interplay in troubadour culture may well trouble our sense of what constituted that culture, but the view will certainly be exhilarating.

Notes

1. The earliest edition of the women troubadours was Oscar Schultz-Gora, *Die provenzalischen Dichterinnen: Biographien und Texte nebst Anmerkungen und einer Einleitung* (Leipzig: Foch, 1888).
2. One of the concerns of Jennifer Lynne Smith's unpublished Ph.D. dissertation, "Subjects of Desire," has been to examine this widely held but largely unsubstantiated "truism" regarding the women troubadours. She argues

convincingly that socioeconomic factors alone do not account for why women began to write poetry. I am grateful to Simon Gaunt for drawing my attention to this dissertation. See Smith, "Subjects of Desire: Relocating the *domna* in the Lyrics of the Trobairitz" (unpublished Ph.D. thesis, University of Western Australia, 2001).

3. *The Voice of the Trobairitz*, ed. William Paden (Philadelphia: University of Philadelphia Press, 1989), p. 13.
4. Manuscript *H* (Vatican City, Biblioteca Apostolica Vaticana MS Vat. lat. 3207) has a particular concentration of texts by the women troubadours and miniatures of them on fols. 43v–53v, leading some critics to view this as a trobairitz section, or even a micro-*chansonnier* of trobairitz poetry within *H*. These folios nonetheless contain texts by male troubadours interspersed among those of the women troubadours, interpreted idiosyncratically by Elizabeth Wilson Poe as a satirical denigration of the latter because she equates misogyny with anti-trobairitz sentiment. See Poe, *Compilatio: Lyric Texts and Prose Commentaries in Troubadour Manuscript H (Vat. Lat. 3207)* (Lexington: French Forum, 2000), chap. 3.
5. Matilda Bruckner, Laurie Shepard, and Sarah White (eds.), *Songs of the Women Troubadours* (New York: Garland, 2000); Angelica Rieger (ed.), *Trobairitz: Der Beitrag der Frau in der altokzitanischen höfischen Lyrik* (Tübingen: Max Niemeyer, 1991).
6. Pierre Bec, " 'Trobairitz' et chansons de femme: contribution à la connaissance du lyrisme féminin au moyen âge," *Cahiers de Civilisation Médievale* 22.3 (1979): 235–63; Antoine Tavera, "A la recherche des troubadours maudits," *Senefiance* 5 (1978): 135–62.
7. Joan M. Ferrante, "Notes Towards the Study of a Female Rhetoric in the Trobairitz," in *Voice of the Trobairitz*, ed. Paden, pp. 63–72; Sophie Marnette, "L'expression féminine dans la poésie lyrique occitane," *Romance Philology* 51.2 (1997): 170–92. Even though both Marnette and Ferrante aim for impersonal linguistic assessments, they nonetheless equate feminine discourse with the women troubadours and masculine discourse with the male troubadours and present them contrastively, for example Ferrante: "Most of the women use a higher number of negatives than the men" ("Notes," p. 65); Marnette: "Les trobairitz donnent deux fois plus d'ordres à leur amant que ne le font les troubadours" [The *trobairitz* give twice as many orders to their lovers as do the troubadours] ("L'expression," p. 177).
8. Rather than designating them as "troubadours," their competence at the art of making poetry—"trobar"—is what is emphasized in the *vidas* and *razos* of both male and female poets. An example of such a description of a woman troubadour is to be found in the *razo* before the mirror-poem between Bernart Arnaut d'Armagnac and Lombarda, where Lombarda is described as "sabia ben trobar e fazia bellas coblas et amorosas" [she knew how to compose good poetry and made beautiful verses about love]; Rieger (ed.), *Trobairitz*, p. 242.
9. Unlike primary identification, which produces the ideal ego—the *i(a)* or *moi idéal*—secondary identification produces the ego ideal—the *I(A)* or

idéal du moi. The ideal ego subsists to some extent with the ego ideal, although Lacan is at pains to distinguish the two in Seminar XI by means of the "trait unaire" or single stroke, as Alan Sheridan translates it, which constitutes the core of secondary identification: "The single stroke is not in the field of narcissistic identification, to which Freud relates the first form of identification—which, very curiously indeed, he embodies in a sort of function, a sort of primal model which the father assumes anterior even to the libidinous investment on the mother—a mythical stage certainly. The single stroke, in so far as the subject clings to it, is in the field of desire, which cannot in any sense be constituted other than in the reign of the signifier, other than at the level in which there is a relation of the subject to the other. It is the field of the Other that determines the function of the single stroke, in so far as it is from it that a major stage of identification is established in the topography developed by Freud—namely, idealization, the ego ideal"; Jacques Lacan, *The Four Fundamental Concepts of Psychoanalysis*, ed. Jacques-Alain Miller, trans. Alan Sheridan (London: Vintage, 1998), p. 256.

10. More precisely, the assumption of sexual identity is not a direct outcome of secondary identification, but of the castration complex. Both the male subject and the female subject are defined by Lacan in relation to the phallus, and it is the difference in their relation to this object that accounts for sexual difference. See Jacques Lacan, *Encore: le séminaire livre XX*, ed. Jacques-Alain Miller (Paris: Seuil, 1975) and the entry on "sexual difference" in Dylan Evans, *An Introductory Dictionary of Lacanian Psychoanalysis* (London: Routledge, 1996), pp. 178–81.
11. Rieger opts for "onransa" here (which technically is not a verb, as she concedes in the notes) and translates the lines as "Und da Euch Schönheit und Tugendehren vor allen anderen Frauen" [beauty and love honor you above all women]. See Rieger, *Trobairitz*, pp. 505–17.
12. Rieger has "saess'," which she interprets as a condensed form of "sa(g)essa" [wisdom]; *Trobairitz*, p. 509, n23.
13. The text is found in only one manuscript, *T* (Paris, Bibliothèque Nationale MS fonds fr. 15211, fol. 208v). I have chosen the Bruckner, Shepard, and White edition of this poem (see earlier, n5). The translation is also on the whole theirs, with some modifications of my own.
14. Angelica Rieger, "Was Bieris de Romans Lesbian? Women's Relations with Each Other in the World of the Troubadours," in *Voice of the Trobairitz*, ed. Paden, pp. 73–94.
15. Sarah Kay, *Subjectivity in Troubadour Poetry* (Cambridge, UK: Cambridge University Press, 1990), p. 86. As indicated in the *Französisches Etymologisches Wörterbuch*, ed. Walther von Wartburg, 8 vols. (Bonn: Klopp, 1925–83), 3:126, "domna" is derived from the Latin "dominam," meaning "lady, mistress." The lady could also be designated as "midons," which poses greater etymological problems. (Kay considers the terms "domna" and "midons" equivalent designations from the point of view of their gender indeterminacy.) William Paden has questioned the long-held belief that

"midons" is derived from "meus/mi dominus," "my lord," and instead proposes "mihi domus" ("my home"), which is gendered feminine in Latin and has obvious semantic associations with the feminine. In this way, Paden can argue that there is gender consistency between the term's etymology and what it signifies in Occitan. How he arrives at this derivation is plausible, but he does not manage to discredit altogether the masculine root, "meus/mi dominus." See Paden, "The Etymology of *Midons*," in *Studies in Honor of Hans-Erich Keller*, ed. Rupert Pickens (Kalamazoo: Medieval Institute Publications, 1993), pp. 311–35. That "midons" could have derived from a masculine or a feminine noun-phrase in Latin only reinforces the polyvalence of the expression.

16. Again, I have used the Bruckner, Shepard, and White edition and translation (with modifications). Like *Na Maria, pretz e fina valors*, this is an *unicum*, found only in manuscript *V* (Venice, Biblioteca Marciana MS fr. App. cod. XI), fols. 149r and 149v.
17. See Raymond T. Hill and Thomas G. Bergin (eds.), *Anthology of the Provençal Troubadours*, 2nd edn., 2 vols. (New Haven: Yale University Press, 1973), table of personal pronouns at 2:88; and William Paden, *An Introduction to Old Occitan* (New York: MLA, 1998), pp. 296–302 (a more extensive explanation of personal pronouns, although Paden only mentions the gender ambivalence of the dative pronoun "li").
18. Kelly Oliver, *Subjectivity without Subjects: From Abject Fathers to Desiring Mothers* (Lanham: Rowman and Littlefield, 1998), p. xvi.
19. Oliver, *Subjectivity*, pp. 158–59.

PART TWO

TROUBLED LOOKS

CHAPTER 4

THE LOOK OF LOVE: THE GENDER OF THE GAZE IN TROUBADOUR LYRIC

Simon Gaunt

This chapter's Lacanian reading of the gaze in troubadour lyric examines what happens when the gaze itself becomes the object of desire and how this affects the sex-gender system of troubadour poetry.

The gaze is often central to troubadour love lyric. As Jean-Charles Huchet observes of Bernart de Ventadorn, who is perhaps the troubadour to give himself up most completely to the rituals of *fin' amor*:

> Chez Bernard de Ventadorn, plus que chez tout autre troubadour. . .la Dame se donne à voir. Le regard s'y arrête, tourne autour de cet objet qui le captive avant de faire retour sur soi.[1]
>
> [With Bernart de Ventadorn more than with any other troubadour. . .the Lady gives herself up to be seen. The gaze lingers on her, circles around this captivating object before turning back on itself.]

Huchet's remark, though made specifically about Bernart, in fact holds true for the vast majority of troubadours, who frequently evoke the sight of their lady, or the desire to see their lady. A troubadour's lady is often, therefore, construed as the object of a masculine gaze. Needless to say, the importance of sight in the process of falling or being in love in troubadour lyric—indeed in courtly literature generally—clearly owes a good deal to the Ovidian tradition, in which love is said to enter a man's heart through his eyes.[2]

However, in an earlier essay, which is a Lacanian analysis of sacrificial desire in the lyrics of Bernart de Ventadorn, I took issue with Huchet to the extent that I argued in passing that because his focus was exclusively on the lady as object of the troubadour's gaze, he failed to show—and indeed to see the ramifications of—how a *retour sur soi* is effected by the lover's gaze. I suggested that the gaze in troubadour lyric is often evoked as part of a fantasy of being *looked at*, a fantasy that is quite literally vital in that the poet's life seems to depend on his haughty lady's gaze.[3] The present chapter is an attempt to explore further the ramifications of the dynamic of the gaze in troubadour lyric and, as in my previous essay, I shall be using the theoretical models of the gaze offered by Lacanian psychoanalysis. The first section of this chapter will explore this theoretical framework further. In the subsequent three sections, I will consider in turn the dynamics of seeing and being seen in troubadour lyric, the mortifying properties of the gaze, and finally the gender of the gaze.

The Gaze in Troubadour Lyric: Why Lacan?

As already noted, troubadours often evoke the gaze and death together. Here are two examples from Bernart de Ventadorn:[4]

I Per melhs cobrir lo mal pes e.l cossire
chan e deport et ai joi e solatz;
e fatz esfortz car sai chantar ni rire,
car eu me mor e nul semblan no.n fatz;
e per Amor sui si apoderatz,
tot m'a vencut a forsa e a batalha.

II Anc Deus no fetz trebalha ni martire,
ses mal d'amor, qu'eu no sofris en patz;
mas d'aquel sui, si be.m peza, sofrire,
c'Amors mi fai amar lai on li platz;
e dic vos be que s'eu no sui amatz,
ges no reman en la mia nualha.

III Midons sui om et amics e servire,
e no.lh en quer mais autras amistatz
mas c'a celat los seus bels olhs me vire,
que gran be.m fan ades can sui iratz;
e ren lor en laus e merces e gratz,
qu'el mon non ai amic que tan me valha. (XXI, ll. 1–18)

[In order better to conceal my painful thoughts and anxieties I sing and make merry, and am joyful and comfort myself; and I try hard because I know how to sing and laugh, since I die and yet give no sign of this; and I am so controlled by Love, that it has entirely vanquished me by force and in battle.

God never made torment or martyrdom without love-sickness (i.e. except the martyrdom of love-sickness) that I could not suffer in peace; but I will endure this, even if I do suffer, for love makes me love wherever it pleases; and I tell you indeed that if I am not loved, this is absolutely nothing to do with my indolence.

I am my lady's man and friend and servant, and I do not ask for any other type of friendship except that she turn her beautiful eyes toward me, for they do me great good when I suffer; and I praise them, thank them and am grateful to them, for I have no friend in the world who helps me as much.]

III Ab Amor m'er a contendre,
que no m'en posc estener,
qu'en tal loc me fai entendre
don en nul joi non esper
anceis me fari' a pendre
car anc n'aic cor ni voler;
mas eu non ai ges poder
que.m posca d'Amor defendre.

IV Pero Amors sap dissendre
lai on li ven a plazer,
e sap gen guizardo rendre
del maltraih e del doler.
Tan no.m pot mertsar ni vendre
que plus no.m poscha valer,
sol ma domna.m denhes vezer
e mas paraulas entendre. (XXVII, ll. 16–32)

[I have to contend with Love for I cannot avoid this, since he makes me die in a place where I can expect no joy, rather I should hang myself for I never had the heart nor the desire for this; but I do not have the power to defend myself against Love.

But Love knows how to alight wherever it wishes, and how to give a noble reward to compensate for the bad treatment and suffering. It cannot bargain or barter with me to make it worth more [the reward?], as long as my lady deigns to see me and to listen to my words.]

Lyrics such as these show the relevance of Lacan's theory of desire to any analysis of courtly love. For Lacan, "le désir de l'homme c'est le désir de l'Autre" [man's desire is the desire of/for the Other],[5] and it is the ambivalence of this aphorism that makes his account of desire and subjectivity so compelling. Does the subject desire the Other? Or does the subject rather seek to subordinate her or his own desire to the Other's, in order to seek from the Other the recognition the subject needs to fill the gaping hole that lies at the core of the self?[6]

What then exactly does Lacan mean by the Other? He often works hard to ensure that the term is deliberately ambiguous, referring to the "problématique de l'Autre," for example, rather than offering a clear definition:

> la problématique de l'Autre, qui est bien cet Autre absolu, cet inconscient fermé, cette femme impénetrable, ou bien derrière celle-ci, la figure de la mort, qui est le dernier Autre absolu.[7]
>
> [the problem of the Other, which is indeed that absolute Other, the inaccessible unconscious, an inscrutable woman, or even, behind her, the figure of death, the ultimate absolute Other.]

The Other then is that place in the psyche that eludes the subject's control, in other words the unconscious—which for Lacan is language itself. But the Other may also be identified with "an inscrutable woman" (which is clearly pertinent to any discussion of troubadour lyric) and "the figure of death," as well as, elsewhere, God.[8]

The gaze is crucial to Lacan's explanation of subjectivity and the function therein of the Other because the subject is shored up by the Other's gaze.[9] In other words, the subject will sacrifice her or his desire in order to be seen by the Other, so that she or he may construe her or his self as whole, as ontologically coherent. Put simply: if I am seen by the Other (or by the others who may occupy the position of the Other in my psyche, for instance "an inscrutable woman," or the "figure of death," and so on), and if the Other reflects an image of me that is whole, unproblematic, and beyond question, then I must be more than a self-induced illusion, more than a figment of my own imagination. But, of course, for the Other to confer wholeness on the subject in this way, the Other in itself must lack nothing: as L.O. Aranye Fradenburg puts it, "We imagine the Other as full, so that the Other can explain and potentially supplement our lack."[10] However, for Lacan the supposed integrity of the Other is nothing but illusion, a projection of our needy imagination, which is why he introduces the notion of the barred Other, with which he seeks to indicate that the Other's wholeness is in fact always illusory, always a product of our own need for coherence.[11] Since the subject's illusion of integrity is sustained by the illusion that the Other lacks nothing, when we realize this is not the case, we are necessarily traumatized.

Despite the beguiling simplicity of some of Lacan's formulations about the gaze, it is in fact one of his most complex theoretical models, as is well illustrated by his attention to anamorphosis, of which his two main examples are famously courtly love and Holbein's painting, now in the National

Gallery in London, the *Ambassadors*.[12] In Lacan's account of the *Ambassadors*, the gaze is (characteristically) triangular. The subject gazes upon the figures in the painting, who gaze upon the subject; but from another perspective altogether, the anamorphic skull that stretches across the bottom of the painting gazes out obliquely. It is important to realize that the skull's gaze is not the gaze of the real of death. In fact, in Lacan's account the real emerges more from the gap between the two perspectives (that of the realistic image that centers the painting and then that of the anamorphosis). The point here is that the real exists on a plane that resists symbolization absolutely and that the anamorphic skull does not in fact resist symbolization, but rather offers an alternative plane of symbolization; the gap between the two planes of symbolization is the location of the real because it is here that the subject may intuit that there is a sphere outside the symbolic that can never be recuperated into it.[13] The skull gestures and beckons toward this sphere; it does not reside in it. Furthermore, unlike the apparently meaningful gaze of the ambassadors and the empty stare of the skull, the real is characterized by a terrifying indifference to the subject. And we should note that the real by definition may *not be gazed upon*. This point is also illustrated by Lacan's famous optical model, which he presents repeatedly along with the anamorphosis of the *Ambassadors* to expound his theory of the gaze. The optical model is a diagram showing how the use of a concave mirror can create the visual illusion of a vase full of flowers when the "real" object is upside down and the flowers not in the vase. The model thus shows how the symbolic structures an imaginary order that like itself serves to screen the subject from the radical incoherence of the real: as Lacan puts it when describing how the model functions, "C'est dans l'espace de l'Autre que [le sujet] se voit, et le point d'où il se regarde est lui aussi dans cet espace" [The subject sees himself in the Other's space, and the point from which he sees himself is also in this space].[14] In other words, because our gaze is transfixed by the Other, this in turn turns our gaze away from other spaces, spaces where the comforting coherence of the symbolic order fails to sustain itself. Our attempts to derive coherence from the visual constantly deflect our attention from that which we are utterly incapable of seeing.

The object of the gaze and the gaze as object thus have the potential to reassure the subject, but also the potential to terrify, indeed to mortify, when they afford a glimpse of the real. We see this ambivalent potential in the stanzas by Bernart de Ventadorn that I quoted earlier, where the gaze is evoked alongside death. But in Lacan's account the trauma of this is intensified by the way the Other always looks at the subject from a place where the subject cannot see it.[15] We see this in the *Ambassadors*: if the point of Lacan's analysis is that we are eventually—as we move around the room—apparently looked at by the empty eyes of the skull, we cannot actually realize this if we are looking at the ambassadors, that is the painting's ostensible subjects, if, in other words, we continue to align ourselves with the plane of coherence, that is the symbolic plane. Thus anamorphosis always troubles vision. As Lacan also talks about courtly love as anamorphosis, carrying this style of analysis over to the courtly lyric is an obvious analytic step (though not one that Lacan himself takes in quite this way).

This theoretically oriented first section of my essay is not intended to foreground Lacan at the expense of the troubadours. On the contrary, I wish rather to draw attention to the congruence between Lacan's thinking about the gaze and that of the troubadours. Of course in some ways this theoretical congruence is unsurprising in that Lacan thought that courtly love had impacted profoundly on modern Western culture and he used troubadour lyric to expound his ideas about subjectivity and love. Lacan, like many troubadours, calls into question a primarily narcissistic view of the gaze as located at the point where the subject is positioned in order to produce visual cohesion; and like many troubadours, Lacan believes that it is not possible for either the subject or the object fully to *coincide*—as Joan Copjec puts it—with the gaze.[16] This in turn has important implications for the relation between the gaze and gender. In much feminist theory the gaze is represented as quintessentially masculine and as the mainstay of a repressive phallic law: consider, for example, the influential work of Laura Mulvey and Jacqueline Rose.[17] Men look at women; the gaze is rapaciously heterosexual as well as male. Of course both Mulvey and Rose were working in film theory, but both nonetheless suggest that film merely brings out dynamics of the gaze that are endemic to all discursive contexts. However, in a Lacanian approach to desire, as I shall suggest here, the gaze is perhaps characteristically *feminine* and a source of potential disruption rather than the axis that produces a heterosexual, masculine order. My argument here has been informed by the work of writers such as Joan Copjec and Dylan Evans who suggest that Mulvey and Rose misconstrue the psychoanalytic notion of the gaze precisely because—like Huchet and other critics of the troubadours—they fail to see the extent to which the gaze is aligned with the Other, not the subject.[18] Furthermore, as Lacan's thinking progresses (for example in *Encore*) he increasingly feminizes the Other.[19] But because this in itself is a traumatic notion to contemplate—something that is desired but also feared—the gaze is on occasion regendered masculine, as we will see.

I shall concentrate, in the remainder of this chapter, on a corpus of lyrics by two twelfth-century troubadours, Bernart de Ventadorn (active ca. 1147–ca. 1170) and Arnaut de Maruelh (active in and around the last decade of the twelfth century), because both use *senhals* that are particularly

pertinent to the subject of this book: Bel Vezer [Fair Seeing/Sight], and Bel Esgart [Fair Glance/Gaze].[20] A *senhal* is a device troubadours use ostensibly to conceal the identity of their ladies. Rather than using her name, a troubadour will use a *senhal* or code-name and sometimes (though by no means always) a *senhal* will be masculine, for example Bon Vezi [Good Neighbor], or Belhs Semblans [Fair Appearance]. Before returning to what we might make of *senhals* such as Bel Vezer, I should first like to outline further how the gaze is represented in my corpus.

Subjects and Objects: Seeing and Being Seen

For Bernart and Arnaut, the desire to be seen by the object of desire is often as strong as the desire to see her.[21] One effect of this is that subject/object distinctions are troubled:

VII Bela domna,. l vostra cors gens
e.lh vostre belh olh m'an conquis,
e.l doutz esgartz e lo clars vis,
e.l vostre bels ensenhamens,
que, can be m'en pren esmansa,
de beutat no.us trob egansa:
la genser etz c'om posch' el mon chauzir,
e no i vei clar dels olhs ab que.us remir.

VIII Bels Vezers, senes doptansa
sai que vostre pretz enansa. . . (Bernart, III, ll. 49–58)

[Fair lady, your noble body and your beautiful eyes have conquered me, and your fair glance and your glowing face, and your comely behavior, to such an extent that when I take stock I can find no equal to you in beauty; you are the most noble that any man can hope to find, and I am incapable of seeing clearly with the eyes with which I gaze upon you.

Fair Seeing, without doubt I know that your worth grows. . .]

If the subject here retains his subject status by actively gazing and acting upon (by judging) the lady's beauty, he nonetheless represents himself as the object of her gaze, as conquered by it,[22] and he further suggests that his own vision is troubled by the spectacle of her beauty, of which a key component is her gaze (her *belh olh*, her *doutz esgartz*).

The troubling of subject/object relations in the evocation of the gaze is part of the phenomenon that Lacan describes when he talks about the gaze as *objet a*, that is as the *cause* of desire as much as its *object*:[23]

III Meravilh me com posc durar
que no.lh demostre mo talan.

Can eu vei midons ni l'esgar,
li seu bel olh tan be l'estan:
per pauc me tenh car ey vas leis no cor.
Si feira eu, si no fos per paor,
c'anc no vi cors melhs talhatz ni depens
ad ops d'amar sia tan greus ni lens.

...

V S'eu saubes la gen enchantar,
mei enemic foran efan,
que ja us no saubra triar
ni dir re que.ns tornes a dan.
Adoncs sai eu que vira la gensor
e sos belhs olhs e sa frescha color,
e baizera.lh la bocha en totz sens
si que d'un mes i paregra lo sens. (Bernart, XX, ll. 17–24 and 33–40)

[I am amazed that I am able to survive without revealing my desire to her. When I see or gaze upon my lady, her beautiful eyes suit her so well: I can hardly restrain myself from running toward her. And I would do so, were it not for fear, for I have never seen a fairer body represented in a statue or a painting through the dictates of love, however intense or urgent.

...

If I could cast a spell on people I would make my enemies into children so that they could not say or do anything to harm us. And I know that then I would see the noblest of women and her beautiful eyes and fair complexion, and I would kiss her mouth every which way so that the marks would last for a month.]

Once again the lady's eyes are the focus of desire: the poet looks at her primarily, it would seem, in order to see them, and therefore by implication also to be seen. But his desire is first and foremost a desire to register desire, to leave a trace, whether this be in the implicit comparison between his own account of his lady's beauty and statues or paintings of other women, or in the sadistic kissing that will leave visible bruises. Desire here is the precondition to subjectivity; the poet only makes his mark in the symbolic through desire as his lady's body becomes the screen on which he writes, the medium through which he makes his mark; his lady is thus less the object of his desire than its cause.

Of course the troubadour's lady's body is a discursive fabrication that needs, to some extent at least, to be disassociated from the material bodies of the women in the courts for which troubadour lyrics were composed. As such the lady's body as object of the subject's gaze is primarily an image in the poet's mind's eye:

VI Dompna, si no.us vezon mei olh,
be sapchatz que mos cors vos ve;
e no.us dolhatz plus qu'eu me dolh,
qu'eu sai c'om vos destrenh per me.
Mas si.l gelos vos bat de for,
gardatz qu'el no vos bat' al cor.
Si.us fai enoi, e vos lui atretal,
e ja ab vos no gazanh be per mal!

VII Mo Bel Vezer gart Deus d'ir' et de mal,
s'eu sui de lonh, e de pres atretal!

VIII Sol Deus midons e mo Bel Vezer sal,
tot ai can volh, qu'eu no deman ren al. (Bernart, XXIV, ll. 41–52)

[Lady, if my eyes do not see you, know that my heart does; and do not be more pained by this than me, for I know how tormented you are on my account. But, if the jealous man beats your body, do not let him touch your heart. He hurts you, and you hurt him, and do not let him obtain from you kindness in exchange for a harsh act.

May God protect my Fair Seeing from anger and evil, when I am distant and then when I am near by also.

As long as my lady and my Fair Seeing are safe, I have all I want and ask for nothing more.]

VII Domna, Amors m'a dat tant d'ardimen,
quar sap qu'ieu fis vos sui e no.m destuelh,
qu'el cor m'a fag miralh ab que.us remir.

VIII Domna, de Pretz sui en l'aussor capduelh,
mas per semblan mon cor no vos aus dir.

IX Domn', el semblan podetz mon cor chauzir. (Arnaut, IV, ll. 43–48)

[Lady, love has made me so bold, since it knows that I am true to you and never waver in this, that it has made a mirror in my heart in which I can gaze upon you.

Lady, I am at the highest peak of worth, but I do not dare to reveal my heart to you through my expression.

Lady, in my expression you can read my heart.]

In both these lyrics, the subject evokes moments when he physically does not see his lady, but "sees" her nonetheless in his heart. The Bernart lyric specifically theorizes the internal and external worlds as separate domains, both for himself and for his lady, implying on both counts that the physical and the external are subordinate to the psychic and internal. The use of the language of vision here in relation to the poet's internal world enacts precisely the distinction that Lacan makes when he distinguishes between vision or the eye and the gaze.[24] The subject's eye does not see the object, but the object is nonetheless in his field of vision. Bel Vezer, the gaze, is evoked, but is tellingly a separate entity from the subject. Furthermore, the lady [*midons*] and Fair Seeing initially seem to be one and the same, but then appear to be distinct. There are thus apparently three elements in this love story: the poetic subject, his lady, and the gaze, personified by Bel Vezer. The lady's physical presence is *not* essential for her to be seen. We see this clearly in the Arnaut lyric, where the lady is absent and the image of her that the poet carries in his heart is in fact more important. If the poet in his heart gazes upon the mirror with which love has provided him, a mirror of course always returns the gaze of the onlooker and Arnaut thus seems more concerned with his own internal world than with the lady, who is ostensibly shut out of his heart here by the opacity of his poetic expression.[25]

If Looks Could Kill: The Mortifying Properties of the Gaze

The internalization of vision in the lyrics I have just examined resonates strongly, of course, with one of the most famous motifs of the troubadour lyric corpus: the distant love or *amor de lonh*, best known through the small corpus of lyrics by Jaufre Rudel (active ca. 1125–48). Jaufre's most famous lyric can be read as a prayer that he might see his distant lady, and of course that he might be seen by her:[26]

V Ben tenc lo Senhor per verai
per qu'ieu veirai l'amor de lonh;
mas per un ben que m'en eschay
n'ai dos mals, quar tan m'es lonh.
Ai! car me fos lai pelegris,
si que mos fustz e mos tapis
fos pels sieus belhs huelhs remiratz! (IV, ll. 29–35)

[I indeed consider God to be true, which is why I will see my distant love; but for every good thing that befalls me, I seem to suffer two bad things, because of this distance. Alas! If only I could be a pilgrim there, so that my staff and my pilgrim's mat might be gazed upon by her beautiful eyes.]

Jaufre's metaphorical use of the idea of pilgrimage here elevates and deifies the distant lady. Only by being seen by this Other can he be whole. The religious metaphor is taken up strongly in his thirteenth-century *vida* (or fictional biography), in which he falls in love with the countess of Tripoli "ses vezer" [without seeing her], and takes the cross [*el se croset*], "per voluntat de leis vezer" [because of his desire to see her], which culminates in his dying: "e lauzet Dieu, que l'avia la vida sostenguda tro qu'el l'agues vista; et enaissi el mori entre sos bratz" [and he praised God, who had kept him alive until he had seen her; and thus he died in her arms]. The *amor de lonh* material is thus suggestive for any consideration of the gaze in troubadour lyric. The gaze here is clearly the object of desire: to see his lady—and therefore to be seen by her—is Jaufre's sole aim. And yet when he does see her and is seen by her, this kills him.

The mortifying properties of the gaze also emerge in Bernart's lyrics:

VIII Can vei vostras faissos
e.ls bels olhs amoros,
be.m meravilh de vos
com etz de mal respos.
E sembla.m trassios,
can om par francs e bos
e pois es orgolhos
lai on es poderos.

IX Bel Vezer, si no fos
mos enans totz en vos,
laissat agra chansos
per mal dels enoyos. (Bernart, XVII, ll. 56–67)

[When I see your face and your beautiful, amorous eyes, I am amazed that your response is so hostile. And it seems to me like treachery when one seems generous and good to be then proud when one is powerful.

Bel Vezer, if my well-being did not depend entirely on you, I would have given up singing entirely because of the kill-joys.]

VI Li seu belh olh traïdor,
que m'esgardavon tan gen,
s'attressi gardon alhor,
mout i fan gran falhimen;
mas d'aitan m'an mout onrat
que, s'eron mil ajostat,
plus gardon lai on eu so,
c'a totz aicels d'eviro. (Bernart, XXV, ll. 41–48)

[Her treacherous eyes, which gazed upon me so sweetly, would commit a great outrage if they were to look elsewhere in this way; but they have honored me greatly to such an extent that if a thousand men were assembled here, they would look more towards me than all those around.]

III Anc non agui de me poder
ni no fui meus de l'or' en sai
que.m laisset en sos olhs vezer

en un miralh que mout me plai.
miralhs, pus me mirei en te,
m'an mort li sospir de preon,
c'aissi.m perdei com perdet se
lo bels Narcisus en la fon. (XXXI, ll. 17–24)

[I never had any power over myself, nor was I my own from the moment she allowed me to look into her eyes, into a mirror that pleases me greatly. Mirror, since I gazed upon you deep sighs have killed me, for I lost myself just as the fair Narcissus lost himself in the fountain.]

In the first two quotations, the treacherous potential of the lady's gaze is brought to the fore and even if, in the second quotation, the subject insists that she only has eyes for him, this is asserted in the context of the possibility of her on the contrary having a roving eye, or, even more traumatically, of her gaze in fact being indifferent to him, of it being unable to distinguish him from other men.[27] The first quotation also evokes the gaze in relation to power, which is an issue as well in Bernart's most famous lyric, "Can vei," from which the final stanza quoted is taken. Here, the lady's gaze exercises power over the lover and leads him to lose power over himself. That the gaze is then crucial to self-definition is underlined by the mirror motif and by the evocation of Narcissus: the lover is locked into a reciprocal, but fatal gaze with the image he sees in the perilous mirror. In Lacanian terms, the imaginary, the symbolic, and the real interact poignantly in this stanza: the surface of the mirror—the symbolic—structures the imaginary—the beguiling image the lover perceives—but fails to conceal completely the mortifying properties of the real. What this in turn suggests is that the gaze (like the lady) is also what Lacan calls the Thing.[28] The Thing, which Lacan defines obscurely as that which suffers from the signified in the real,[29] is the terrifying spectacle just perceptible from the symbolic that enables the subject to glimpse the real that is concealed by and in the symbolic and the imaginary. The anamorphic skull at the bottom of the *Ambassadors* offers an example of just such a terrifying spectacle, one which returns the subject's gaze with mortifying indifference. The lady in the courtly lyric is also, for Lacan, a good example of the Thing: the poetic subject looks to her so that she might turn her gaze upon him, but receives no acknowledgment in return and it is this duel perspective on and of the lady that explains why Lacan talks of courtly love as anamorphosis. The implicit conflation of the gaze and the Thing as Lacan moves through his seminars serves to suggest the horror that the subject feels on realizing that the Other's gaze is in fact the barred Other's gaze, on realizing, in other words, that the Other does not have the power to confer wholeness and completeness on the subject, that the Other like the subject is lacking. To put this in less stridently Lacanian terms, the gaze as object of desire becomes the Thing when a troubadour realizes that there is in fact nothing out there to gaze back at him, that the Other is quite literally a figment of his imagination, that all he contemplates in his lady's eyes is an abyss.[30]

The Gender of the Gaze

What are we then to make of the *senhals* Bel Vezer or Bel Esgart? We have seen that the gaze is indeed the object of desire in Bernart and Arnaut's lyrics and also that this troubles subject/object distinctions in that it is not always clear whose gaze is at stake. In part the *senhals* reinforce the troubling power of this imagery. If it is not always clear that the *senhals* designate the poet's lady—in at least one instance in Bernart's corpus Bel Vezer explicitly designates a male friend,[31] and in others the referent is unclear—this very ambivalence highlights the ambiguity of the gaze in these lyrics, suggesting that the *senhals* function in a manner not dissimilar from anamorphoses such as the skull in Holbein's the *Ambassadors*, in that they call into question the fixity and solidity of the symbolic order. It is interesting, in this respect, that these *senhals* are masculine. Of course *senhals* often are. Yet at same time in the context of Lacanian theory, it is striking, though unsurprising, that the feminine Other is not identical with any embodied woman and that frequently she is masculinized. "Woman does not exist," Lacan tells us in *Encore*,[32] by which I take him to mean that the cultural ideal of woman is a fantasy that structures the symbolic order. We may take Bernart's use of masculine *senhals* as a further indication that the troubadour love lyric is a homosocial discourse that marginalizes women.[33] But the dynamic of the gaze means that something more than homosocial desire is at stake in the *senhal* Bel Vezer. If woman is man's Other here and woman the subject of the gaze, then it follows that man's subjectivity derives from his wish to construe himself as the object of the Other's gaze. The troubadour lyric is then a discourse in which only women can truly be the subject of the gaze, but in which also they may see only one thing (a man) and then only as he wishes to be seen. But when—as he inevitably will regardless of whether he contemplates the *domna* in his lyric or a "real" lady—a troubadour fails to see what he looks for in a lady's eyes—that is a gaze directed at himself, focused on recognition—and sees instead an abyss of non-recognition and indifference, this is truly mortifying. The gaze must then—urgently and desperately—be located elsewhere, which is to say nowhere, in a space that escapes and confounds gender by subsuming the feminine and the masculine. The *senhals* Bel Vezer and Bel Esgart perhaps therefore encapsulate perfectly the gaze's troubling power. As Lacan said: "Dans l'amour. . .*Jamais tu ne me regardes là où je te vois.*"[34]

Notes

All translations throughout are my own.

1. Jean-Charles Huchet, *L'Amour discourtois: la "fin'amor" chez les premiers troubadours* (Toulouse: Privat, 1987), p. 183.
2. Obvious examples of this convention abound in courtly romance, for instance see Chrétien de Troyes, *Cligès*, ed. Charles Méla and Olivier Collet (Paris: Le Livre de Poche, 1994), ll. 688–704, and Chrétien de Troyes, *Le Chevalier au lion*, ed. David Hult (Paris: Le Livre de Poche, 1994), ll. 2017–26.
3. Simon Gaunt, "A Martyr to Love: Sacrificial Desire in the Poetry of Bernart de Ventadorn," *Journal of Medieval and Early Modern Studies* 31 (2001): 491–94 [477–506].
4. I will cite Bernart de Ventadorn from *Bernard de Ventadour: Chansons d'amour*, ed. Moshé Lazar (Paris: Klincksiek, 1966).
5. Lacan repeats the aphorism frequently, but for an example see Jacques Lacan, *Les Quatre Concepts fondamentaux de la psychanalyse: le séminaire livre XI* (Paris: Seuil, 1973), p. 261.
6. For good expositions see Slavoj Žižek, *The Sublime Object of Ideology* (London: Verso, 1989), pp. 105–28 and *Enjoy Your Symptom! Jacques Lacan in Hollywood and Out* (London: Routledge, 1992), pp. 55–60.
7. Jacques Lacan, *La Relation d'objet: le séminaire livre IV* (Paris: Seuil, 1994), p. 431.
8. Lacan, *Quatre Concepts*, p. 306.
9. For Lacan's main analysis of the gaze, see part 2 of his *Quatre Concepts*, "Du regard comme objet petit a," pp. 79–135. That the gaze, for Lacan, is located primarily in the field of the Other is articulated clearly on several occasions. For example: "N'y a-t-il pas de la satisfaction à être sous ce regard dont je parlais tout à l'heure. . .ce regard qui nous cerne, ce qui fait d'abord de nous des êtres regardés, mais sans qu'on nous le montre" [Is there not some satisfaction to be had from being subjected to the gaze of which I spoke earlier. . .the gaze that delimits us and which makes of us first and foremost watched beings, but without our being made aware of this], p. 87. Consider also: "Le regard se voit. . .Ce regard que je rencontre. . .est, non point un regard vu, mais un regard par moi imaginé au champ de l'Autre" [The gaze may be seen. . .This gaze which I encounter is not a gaze truly seen, but rather a gaze imagined by me in the field of the Other], p. 98. And further: "Au niveau scopique, nous ne sommes plus au niveau de la demande, mais du désir, du désir de l'Autre" [With the scopic, we are no longer on the level of demand, but on the level of desire, that is to say the desire of the Other], p. 119. Lacan's account of the gaze insists throughout (for example p. 91) on

a distinction between *vision* and *regard* (vision and gaze), that is to say on a distinction between mere sight and the fantasmic, thereby invisible, gaze of the *omnivoyeur* (p. 87).

10. L.O. Aranye Fradenburg, *Sacrifice Your Love: Psychoanalysis, Historicism, Chaucer* (Minneapolis: Minnesota University Press, 2002), p. 5.
11. See, for example, Jacques Lacan, "Subversion du sujet et dialectique du désir," in *Ecrits*, 2nd edn., 2 vols. (Paris: Seuil, 1971), 2:151–91, where he remarks that the formula he uses to indicate the subject's relation to the Other—S(Ⱥ)—is the "signifiant d'un manque dans l'Autre" [the signifier of a lack in the Other], p. 180, and, even more more bluntly, that the subject being deprived of enjoyment would be "la faute de l'Autre s'il existait: l'Autre n'existant pas, il ne me reste qu'à prendre la faute sur le Je" [the Other's fault, if it existed: but since the Other does not exist, I can only lay the blame on myself], p. 182. See also, for a pertinent account of the gaze as the gaze of the barred Other in Lacan, Joan Copjec, *Read My Desire: Lacan Against the Historicists* (Cambridge, MA: MIT Press, 1994), p. 36: "The subject instituted by the Lacanian gaze does not come into being as the realization of a possibility opened up by the law of the Other. It is rather an impossibility that is crucial to the constitution of the subject—the impossibility, precisely, of any ultimate confirmation from the Other." See further, Fradenburg, *Sacrifice Your Love*, p. 30.
12. See Lacan, "L'Amour courtois en anamorphe," in *L'Ethique de la psychanalyse: le séminaire livre VII* (Paris: Seuil, 1986), pp. 167–84; and "L'Anamorphose," in *Quatre Concepts*, pp. 92–104.
13. See Lacan, *Quatre Concepts*, p. 101, where he evokes the power of painting to evoke "une dimension qui n'a rien à voir avec la vision comme telle" [a dimension that has nothing whatsoever to do with vision as such]. Indeed, every painting, for Lacan, is "un piège à regard" [a trap for the gaze], p. 102, while the painter is the source of "quelque chose qui peut passer dans le réel" [the source of something that may pass into the real], p. 128. Earlier in *Les Quatre Concepts*, the real has been defined as "ce qui revient toujours à la même place" [that which always returns to the same place], p. 59, and as that which "se soit présenté sous la forme de ce qu'il y a en lui d'*inassimilable*" (original emphasis) [has presented itself in the form of that which is *not in the least susceptible to assimilation*], p. 65.
14. See Lacan, *Quatre Concepts*, p. 162.
15. Lacan, *Quatre Concepts*, p. 118.
16. Copjec, *Read my Desire*, p. 36.
17. Laura Mulvey, "Visual Pleasure and Narrative Cinema," in *Visual and Other Pleasures* (London: Macmillan, 1989), pp. 14–26; Jacqueline Rose, *Sexuality in the Field of Vision* (London: Verso, 1986). For Mulvey, woman is "image," man "bearer of the look" (p. 19); for Rose "women are meant to *look* perfect, presenting a seamless image to the world so that a man, in that confrontation with difference, can avoid any apprehension of lack" (p. 232).

18. See Copjec, "The Orthopsychic Subject: Film Theory and the Reception of Lacan," in *Read my Desire*, pp. 15–38, and Dylan Evans, *An Introductory Dictionary of Lacanian Psychoanalysis* (London: Routledge, 1996), pp. 72–73. For a further concise, but useful summary see Margaret Olin, "Gaze," in *Critical Terms for Art History*, ed. Robert S. Nelson and Richard Shiff (Chicago: Chicago University Press, 1996), pp. 208–19.
19. Jacques Lacan, *Encore: le séminaire livre XX* (Paris: Seuil, 1975), p. 52: "L'Autre, dans mon langage, cela ne peut donc être que l'Autre sexe" [The Other, in my terminology, can be nothing other than the Other sex].
20. Bernart de Ventadorn uses the *senhal* Bel Vezer in: III, l. 57; VII, l. 50; IX, ll. 41 and 43; XVI, ll. 49 and 54; XVII, l. 64; XXIII, l. 60; XXIV, l. 49. Bernart also uses the *senhal* Dous-Esgar in XXX, l. 50. Arnaut de Maruelh is cited from *Les Poésies lyriques du troubadour Arnaut de Mareuil*, ed. R.C. Johnston (Geneva: Slatkine Reprints, 1973; orig. 1935); he uses the *senhal* Bel Vezer in XIX, l. 20 and Bel Esgar in I, l. 41.
21. For the troubadours' tendency to construe themselves as objects of the lady's desire, see Sarah Kay, *Subjectivity in Troubadour Poetry* (Cambridge, UK: Cambridge University Press, 1990), pp. 96–99.
22. This type of contradiction captivates Bernart and courtly writers more generally. See Sarah Kay, *Courtly Contradictions: The Emergence of the Literary Object in the Twelfth Century* (Stanford: Stanford University Press, 2001), and on Bernart in particular pp. 3–8. Also, for a stimulating use of Lacan's notion of the gaze in reading medieval romance, see pp. 269–83.
23. For the gaze as *objet a*, see Lacan, *Quatre Concepts*, pp. 79–135. Here Lacan often speaks of the gaze as the object of desire and later he explains: "Comprenez que l'objet du désir, c'est la cause du désir" [Understand that the object of desire is also the cause of desire], p. 270.
24. See earlier n9.
25. On the gender politics of this lyric see further Simon Gaunt, *Gender and Genre in Medieval French Literature* (Cambridge, UK: Cambridge University Press, 1995), pp. 131–32.
26. Cited from *Il canzoniere di Jaufre Rudel*, ed. Giorgio Chiarini (Rome: Japadre Editore, 1985).
27. See Fradenburg, *Sacrifice Your Love*, p. 30, which talks of the barred Other's "roving gaze."
28. On the Thing, see Lacan, *L'Ethique*, pp. 27–102; on the courtly Lady as the Thing, see p. 193.
29. See Lacan, *L'Ethique*, pp. 142 and 150: "ce qui du réel pâtit du signifiant," by which I take Lacan to mean that the Thing marks the point at which the symbolic (the signifier) comes into contact with the real.
30. See Slavoj Žižek, "Courtly love, or, Woman as Thing," in *The Metastases of Enjoyment: Six Essays on Women and Causality* (London: Verso, 1994), pp. 89–112.
31. See XXIII, l. 60, where the *senhal* is preceded by the masculine honorific *En*.
32. Lacan, *Encore*, p. 14: "il n'y a pas *la* femme."

33. See, among other things, Rouben C. Cholakian, *The Troubadour Lyric: A Psychocritical Reading* (Manchester: Manchester University Press, 1990); Gaunt, *Gender and Genre*, pp. 135–47.
34. "In love. . .*you never look at me from a place where I can see you*." Lacan, *Quatre Concepts*, p. 118.

CHAPTER 5

SACRIFICIAL SPECTACLE AND INTERPASSIVE VISION IN THE ANGLO-NORMAN LIFE OF SAINT FAITH

Emma Campbell

Focusing on the Anglo-Norman Life of St. Faith, this chapter explores how what Campbell terms (after Žižek) "interpassive vision" might be used to theorize modes of response to saints' lives. This notion of interpassive vision is deployed as a means of complicating the claim that these narratives are vehicles for male voyeurism.

The importance of vision in saints' lives has been a widely recognized, if not always explicitly discussed, element of a genre that both represents and invites particular kinds of "visual" response. This is perhaps especially the case in accounts of martyrdom, where the martyr's suffering not only bears witness to his or her belief in the divine, but also articulates a demand to be seen and recognized as such.[1] Partly because of this emphasis on spectacle, the treatment of vision in saints' lives has received a certain amount of attention from feminist scholars, most notably in relation to the lives of female martyrs. In this criticism, the gaze is often considered to be complicit with patriarchal hegemony, performing an intrusive appropriation or even violation of the body of the female saint through a voyeuristic engagement with the depiction of her assault at the hands of male attackers. Thus, in making an argument for seeing female saints' lives as thinly veiled narratives of rape, Kathryn Gravdal claims, "hagiography affords a sanctioned space in which eroticism can flourish and in which male voyeurism becomes licit, if not advocated."[2] Although arguing for the metonymic function of virginity and the unrepresentability of rape in female saints' lives, Kathleen Coyne Kelly also asserts that "these tales of near-rape skew the narrative focus toward the virgin's body in a way that invites readers and listeners to situate themselves as voyeurs or victims (depending on their subject position)."[3] Brigitte Cazelles similarly focuses upon the violence of the visual encounter in what she refers to as the female saint's "trial by disclosure," arguing that "martyrs, virgins, married heroines, innocent as well as repentant hermits all undergo the ordeal of disrobing; and each of them achieves holiness as a result of circumstances that involve voyeuristic incarnation."[4]

Considering vision as a mode of relationship to the saint that may involve sexualized or gendered positions provides a useful way into thinking about how the politics of ocularity might operate in hagiographic texts of this kind. More to the point, it helps to focus attention upon the possible investment of the reader or listener in the visual economy of texts that seem to invite a complex engagement with sacrificial spectacle and the forms of witness that such spectacle encourages. However, what is overlooked by feminist arguments such as these is the precise status of the object of the voyeuristic encounter and the relationship that this object bears to the visualization of the sexual body.[5] What does it mean, for instance, to speak of voyeurism in these texts in terms of "mental spectacle" or "linguistic contemplation"?[6] For, as this would suggest, if it is indeed possible to speak of "seeing" the body in the text, this is by no means an unproblematic or unmediated spectacle, being filtered (as it inevitably is) through layers of textual description. The crucial question here is thus not whether the female body is subject to a gaze that objectifies and denudes it of agency but, instead, the more basic question of whether the female body is *seen* at all.

This chapter attempts to develop the valuable work on medieval hagiography begun by feminist scholars within the broader framework of a reflection on the role that vision plays—or can play—in Old French hagiography. Rather than assume that visual participation in the text is always already rigidly gendered and/or sexualized, it is one of the contentions of this essay that the specular dimension of accounts of martyrdom can work against the materialization of sex and gender. The question then becomes not just how saints' lives help to reinforce a conservative sexual agenda but also how they work to obscure the positions on which that agenda might rely.[7] This reflection on vision responds to the themes of this volume in two, related ways. First, I will consider what might be at stake in the narrative deployment of a specifically visual mode of encounter in scenes of martyrdom, suggesting how the function of vision might rely upon or produce various kinds of "trouble." Second, I will develop this analysis by focusing on the role of the spectator in this process and the forms that a textually mediated "visual" engagement with the text (and the saint) might take. It will be in this latter section that the relevance of the notion of "interpassivity" mentioned in my title will be fully discussed.

Sacrificial Spectacle and Hermeneutic Vision

The Anglo-Norman *Vie de Sainte Fey* by Simon of Walsingham is a poem written in Bury before 1216, probably between 1210 and 1216. The text is part of the Campsey manuscript (London, British Library MS Additional 70513), a relatively well-known late thirteenth-century collection used for refectory reading in the nunnery of Campsey Abbey near Woodbridge, Suffolk in the fourteenth century. (The manuscript contains a note to this effect at the top of fol. 265v.)[8] It is worth pointing out that the Life of St. Faith is one of the only items included in the collection that is not accompanied by an image of the saint in a portrait initial at the beginning of her life story.[9] What this means is that, unlike some of the saints' lives that it appears alongside, the visual dimension of the text is entirely mediated through narrative: the imaginative visualization of both the saint and the events that take place around her is a matter of purely *textual* reconstruction.

The section of the saint's life relating her *passio* describes how, in the age of the Roman emperors Maximian and Diocletian, a beautiful maiden called Fey (Faith) lived in the town of Agen. Having received both her name and her faith (which are effectively the same thing) from Christ, the maiden maintains an unwavering devotion to Christianity. This causes trouble when Decius, a pagan provost, comes to Agen in a fury of anti-Christian, persecuting zeal; Fey is arrested, questioned, and tortured after denouncing the pagan faith. As she is enduring these sufferings, a Christian called Capraise who is fleeing Agen sees Fey's martyrdom from a vantage-point just outside the town. What he sees persuades Capraise to return to face his pagan persecutors, just as Fey has done. Capraise is then tortured and manages to convert two brothers, who similarly vow to sacrifice themselves for Christ. All four of the saints (including Fey) are then taken to the temple and decapitated, upon which their souls proceed to heaven.

As a prelude to discussing the importance of vision to Capraise's response to Fey's martyrdom, I would like to suggest how visualization of the saint is troubled from the very beginning of the text. Simon's description of the saint in the prologue to the poem interweaves physical and conceptual motifs in such a way as to frustrate any attempt simply to see her as a beautiful female body. There is in these initial passages a dense interweaving of metaphoric and symbolic meanings that find coherence through their association with the concept of faith [*fei*]. The stress in the opening lines of the poem is upon the connection of faith, and the Christian subject's commitment to it, to a particular form of symbolic enclosure.[10] Simon addresses his audience as "vous que en Deu creez / e en la fei estes fermeez" [you who believe in God and who are enclosed in faith], reminding them that their salvation depends upon precisely this enclosure in "ferme fei" [firm faith] (Fey, 1–7). Playing upon the polysemy of the word *fei*, Simon then tells his listeners that this envelopment is facilitated by hearing of faith (meaning—ostensibly—both the form of belief and the saint that represents it): "cum vus plus de fei orrez / en fei plus fermé en serrez" [the more you hear of faith, the more you shall be enclosed in faith] (Fey, 15–16). The semantic slippage between faith as a belief that encloses and secures the Christian subject and faith as it is embodied in the saint is clearly deliberate; indeed, this double meaning is further developed in the description of the relationship between the saint's name and her Life, which, Simon explains,

> Se acorderunt plus bel
> Ke ne fet la gemme en anel
> Kar de [tres]tut esteient un
> Sa seinte vie e son seint nun. (Fey, 25–28)
>
> [Went together more beautifully than does the gem in a ring, for both her holy life and her holy name were one.]

Fey is thus associated with an enclosure similar to that of the Christian believer, an enclosure that is expressed in the seamless fusion of her name and Life. The naming of Fey/faith becomes, through its connection with the saint, synonymous with a living of faith made accessible to the audience via the hagiographic text: *nun* [name] encloses *vie* [life] so that the two become indistinguishable from one another. Fey, as a symbol of the semantic and physical integrity of faith, therefore invokes belief by signifying and performing the enclosure it suggests. The immersion of the Christian subject in *ferme fei* is thus translated into the saint's own, complex embodiment of faith. The integrity of Fey's name and Life, like the correspondence between gem and ring, is an ideal representation of the integrity of the Christian subject invited to reinforce his enclosure in faith by listening to the *Vie*.

As far as the visualization of Fey's physical being is concerned, two features of this description should be underlined. First, what "Fey" connotes in a material sense is extremely difficult to pin down; conceptualizing the saint is far more reliant upon her name and the range of interconnected meanings that it invokes. Second, envisioning the saint implies contemplating a constellation of interrelated concepts that orbit around the notion of belief as a relationship of enclosure or spiritual fusion. This is in fact underlined later in the prologue, when the beauty of the correspondence of the saint's name and Life encapsulated in the notion of *fei* ostensibly supersedes the physical beauty of the holy virgin: Simon informs his audience that his text will narrate the life of the "seintissime pucele" [most holy virgin] who, although physically very attractive [*bele de vis*], is indisputably "de fei plus bele" [more beautiful of faith] (Fey, 19–20). The physical allure of the poem's heroine is thus supplemented and surpassed by its spiritual meaning; the beauty of the virgin is to be seen and interpreted through a lens of faith that obscures the saint's physicality in order to render it in spiritual terms.

I am not suggesting that the saint's femininity has no part to play in this initial description; on one level, Fey is quite clearly presented as a feminine object of desire for the *seignurs* to whom the poem is addressed. Nevertheless, it is worth underlining within this context that what this introductory presentation of the saint accomplishes is a dematerialization of the female martyr in which her very status as an object of vision is called into question. Fey is certainly an object of desire here; yet, this object does not directly correlate with an image of the female body, as some feminist critics have argued.[11] The implication of shifting attention from the beauty of the saint's face to the beauty of the *fei* she embodies is not simply a matter of exchanging one visual object for another: whereas the face potentially provides an image for contemplation, faith connotes a form of enclosure. Looking "at" the virgin's beauty in this sense does not allow for any relationship between viewer and object that would maintain their separation. What one "sees" is *Fey/fei*: that is, faith as an enclosure that extends outward to the Christian subject, enfolding him or her in a faith that must be intuited from within as well as from without.

I would suggest that the ramifications of this troubled vision carry over into the scenes of Fey's martyrdom witnessed by Capraise, where the complex status of the object of the gaze is linked to a more radical disruption of the visual encounter. Capraise's first, most significant encounter with the saint is clearly reliant upon ocular experience. As he is fleeing the town to escape persecution, Capraise finds himself on a rocky vantage point from where he can see [*veer*] everything occurring within the town he has just left. From this position,

Ses oilz vers la cité turna
E as granz turmenz esgarda
Ke seinte Fey la Deu amye

Suffri la pur le fiz Marie.
Kant il la vit pité en out
E des oilz tendrement plorout,
Ses meins devers le ciel tendi
E pria Deu k'il out merci
De seinte Fey ke pur sun nun
Suffri tant greve passiun,
E k'il li donast force e vertu
De veintre l'anguisse de fu
E ke victorie li donast
E par martire coronast. (Fey, 499–512)

[He turned his eyes toward the town and watched the great torments that Saint Fey, God's beloved, suffered there for the son of Mary. When he saw her, he took pity and tenderly wept from his eyes; he stretched his hands toward the heavens and prayed God to have mercy on Saint Fey, who suffered such a painful passion in his name.[12] And [he prayed] that [God] give her strength and fortitude/virtue to overcome the torment of the flames, and that he give [Fey] victory and crown her in martyrdom.]

As the repeated use of verbs such as *esgarder* [to watch, to look] and *voir* [to see] in this passage suggests, the role of vision here is central; yet what Capraise sees and the manner in which he responds to it are also significant. In the first four lines, the movement of the eyes introduces a telescoping effect whereby attention moves from the town to the saint's torments and from there to God, via the saint. What is presented as a simple visual encounter therefore already contains within it an interpretative element that blurs the distinction between seeing the sufferings of the saint and seeing her suffering for God (and thus, implicitly, bearing witness to the presence of God in her sufferings). Indeed, it is worth remarking upon the fact that what Capraise is looking at here is not the saint but rather her *turmenz* [torments]: the saint comes into view not so much as a female body but instead as one who suffers for God.[13] The subtlety of this distinction between visual objects should not blind us to the fact that the body is once again effectively eclipsed in this description, as attention alights upon the saint's sufferings and their significance in the context of her relationship to God. Seen in relation to the prologue, what seems to be implicit in these passages is that seeing Fey the saint and seeing her performance of faith through the sufferings she undertakes for God are, once more, one and the same thing.

Indeed, if there is a focus on any particular body part in this passage, it is upon Capraise's eyes, which not only draw him back toward the town to witness the saint's tortures but also initiate a physical and spiritual response to the events that he sees. This response, which takes the form of prayers and tears, at once reinforces the meaning of the saint's sacrifice and attempts to intervene in its outcome. This intervention is confirmed when Capraise's prayer that God aid the saint in her suffering and award her the crown of martyrdom has the effect of producing visually that which Capraise wishes for: the events for which he has prayed unfold before him, as a demonstration of divine grace. Although this experience is never described as a vision, the events that are shown to Capraise are part of an emphatically visual encounter with the divine, again repeatedly using verbs of seeing such as *esgarder* and *voir* to describe scenes in which God shows [*mustrer*] Capraise the glory of heaven by performing his requests.[14] Thus, once again turning his attention to the suffering saint, Capraise sees a pure white dove descend from heaven with a richly decorated crown of gold, which it places on Fey's head in recognition of her martyrdom (Fey, 526–50). The saint is then dressed in a brilliant white robe, whereupon Capraise sees and understands [*vit bien e entendi*] that Christ has given her victory, that her sufferings are over, and that her joys have begun (Fey, 551–60). Shortly after this, Capraise contemplates the unharmed saint in her divine accoutrements and, considering the glory and fortitude [*vertu*] that Christ has given her, decides to suffer martyrdom himself (Fey, 575–96).

What Capraise "sees" in this section of the poem is troubling in a number of ways. Perhaps most obvious in this respect is the fact that the events to which he is witness defy location within certain physical and temporal norms. The saint's coronation and robing take place in a space between heaven and earth in which she is at once roasted on a pagan pyre and crowned as a Christian martyr. This scene, although drawing on motifs commonly used to describe the posthumous accession to heaven of many saints, is therefore subtly different from such descriptions insofar as Fey's "posthumous" coronation and victory occur *alongside* her tortures. The outcome of the martyrdom she suffers for Christ is therefore enacted even as that martyrdom is played out, encouraging precisely the kind of retrospective reading that Capraise gives the scene, in which the saint's pain and suffering are infused with a meaning derived from the supposed outcome of her martyrdom. In so doing, this episode troubles the conventions of chronological time and linear narrative as a part of the experience of divine grace that it associates with Capraise's act of witness. The ultimate ideological function of such an experience, in which God ostensibly reveals [*mustrer*] the glory of heaven to the Christian subject, is to make meaning an immanent as opposed to a transcendent property of the event. In other words, the function of witness in this divinely inspired revelation is to ensure that seeing the suffering of the martyr is, to all intents and purposes, the same thing as seeing the meaning of that suffering within a Christian setting. This confusion of meaning and event is therefore achieved through a mode of perception that claims the self-evidence of visual experience while making that experience commensurate with the communication of the significance of what is seen: a form of what might be termed "hermeneutic vision."

Within this context, it is worth remarking that, in this intensely visual episode, the saint's body once again eludes the gaze of the spectator entirely. (The description of the beauty and whiteness of the heavenly dove in fact occupies more lines than does any description of Fey's physique.) The focus of Capraise's fascinated eye throughout this episode is on that which occurs *around* the saint, not on the saint herself. If there can be said to be an object of vision here (bearing in mind the particular mode of seeing that is implicit throughout this section) it is the peculiar conjunction of meaning and event expressed through Fey's martyrdom and coronation. This seems to be reinforced by Capraise's response to the scenes he witnesses, a response that, instead of dwelling on the female martyr, focuses on the implications of what he has seen happen to her and its possible ramifications for his own relationship to God:

Quant seint Capraisse out vëu
La gloirë e si la vertu
Ke Jhesu Crist aveit donée
A seinte Fey la bonurée
Ne se voleit plus long tapir,
Mes as peines voleit partir
Ke seinte Fey la Deu amie
Soffri la pur le fiz Marie;
Kar par tant sout ben k'il partireit
A cele gloire k'ele aveit;
De cele gloire esteit sëur
Pur ceo n'aveit de mort pöur,
Ne de nul autre gref torment. (Fey, 589–601)

[When saint Capraise had seen the glory and fortitude that Jesus Christ had given to the happy Saint Fey, he did not want to hide himself any longer, but instead wanted to go to [suffer] the pains that Saint Fey, God's lover, suffered there for the son of Mary; for, through this, he knew that he would have a share in her glory. Of this glory he was certain and for that [reason] he had fear neither of death nor of any other painful torment.]

As suggested by the first two lines of this passage, what Capraise has "seen" is the divine gift of glory and strength transmitted to the saint from Christ, just as Capraise previously requested. Furthermore, witnessing this gift leads Capraise—in a manner that possibly recalls the prologue to the poem—to a reinforcement of his Christian faith. Yet this confirmation of faith has its own, troubling effects. For, in reviewing what he has seen, Capraise imaginatively identifies himself with the position of the female martyr. Capraise wishes to suffer the pains that Fey suffered for Christ because he is certain to receive thereby the glory that he has seen her awarded on account of her torments. There is implicitly no question of performing a sacrifice that is *like* that of Fey here: Capraise will suffer the *same* pains in order to receive the *same* reward. It is worth underlining the visual dimension of this substitution. For, Capraise's first response to the scene he has witnessed is a desire to come out of hiding and to endure the same visual exposure as the saint, by being seen to suffer for God just as she has. What he sees is therefore rather more complex than might previously have been thought. Just as Capraise re-envisions Fey's martyrdom and heavenly reward as an event that occurs in both the recent past and in the future, so he sees himself performing the same scene as a series of events that similarly take place in the past and in the future. In the same way as the reward that the martyrs will later receive in heaven marks a moment in the future *and* refers to an event that has always already occurred, Capraise's martyrdom is both prefigured in this episode and has, in a sense, already taken place.

Thus, what Capraise sees in the prefiguration of the outcome of Fey's sacrifice is a model for his own death and salvation, and, by extension, for any martyr who gives their life to God. The visual encounter that underwrites this mimetic chain is not so much characterized by voyeurism as it is defined by narcissism. Narcissism in Freudian psychoanalysis is based upon a confusion between the love object and the self: it involves responding to the ego in its idealized form as an object of narcissistic satisfaction. Narcissism is thus both self-directed and object-directed; it relies upon a fundamental confusion of the object and the ego in its idealized incarnation.[15] As I have argued, Capraise's act of witness produces a similar confusion, enabling him to see Fey's martyrdom and his own performance of Christian sacrifice superimposed upon one another. It is in this sense significant that, just before Capraise witnesses the events for which he has prayed, he is described for the first time in the poem as a martyr, or, more to the point, as "li seint martir, / ke memes les peines suffrir / deveit pur le fiz Marie" [the holy martyr who would have to suffer the same pains for the son of Mary] (Fey, 523–25).[16] The visual experience of Fey's martyrdom therefore already implicitly connotes an alignment with the position of the martyr and, moreover, suggests a vicarious participation in the sufferings and glories to which she is subject. The two other martyrdoms that occur in the saint's life in fact seem to repeat this model: the brothers Primes and Felicien watch [*esgarder*] and marvel at Capraise's *vertu* under torture before being overcome by the holy spirit and deciding to suffer the same fate as the martyr (Fey, 752–802). They too observe the sacrificial spectacle and its meaning; they too "vit [*sic*] ke ceo fu lur confort / de suffrir pur Jhesu la mort" [saw that it was a solace to them to suffer death for Jesus] (Fey, 799–800); and they too decide on the basis of what they have seen to reenact that to which they have been witness.

There are of course many such instances in saints' lives, where, as a result of witnessing the miraculous events that occur around the martyr, those who are present convert to the Christian faith and, in certain cases, choose to sacrifice themselves as well. What is often less clear, however, is the process of identification that underwrites such events and the way this process relates to visual response. It may, therefore, be useful to compare an episode from another Anglo-Norman saint's life of more or less the same period in which the visual dynamics of witness and its implications for mimetic response are clearly in evidence. The saint's life in question is that of St. Alban: a poem extant in only one manuscript (Dublin, Trinity College MS 177), most probably written by Matthew Paris between 1230 and 1240.[17] In the second half of the poem, after Alban has been martyred and killed for his Christian faith, a group of male converts set out to find Amphibel, the Christian preacher who originally converted the saint. Having been successful in their quest and having submitted themselves to Amphibel as students, the converted party are approached by soldiers sent by the pagan ruler of Verulamium, who has given instructions that the Christians be killed unless they agree to revert to their pagan faith. The converts predictably refuse the offers made to them by the soldiers and a battle ensues in which massacre on an epic scale is depicted as Christian martyrdom. In a scene that is in some ways reminiscent of the episode in which Capraise watches Fey, Amphibel sees the slaughter as it unfolds:

> Tut ço veit Amphibal ki plure e gent de quoer;
> Ne puet sanz martire les martirs regarder—
> Cist sunt martir de cors, cist de quor, duluser—
> Mes a Deu les presente, ki les deigne apeler,
> E cist s'en vunt eu ciel sanz fin demurer. (Au, 1349–53)

> [Amphibel, who weeps and sighs in his heart, sees all this; he cannot look at the martyrs without himself suffering [*martire*]. They are martyrs of the body, and he of the heart; in pain, he commends them to God, who deigns to call them [to him] and they go to heaven to remain there for eternity.]

Amphibel's viewing of the martyrs as such seems to inscribe a form of mimesis that implicates him in that to which he is both witness and interpreter. The effect of considering the martyrs in this case is a vicarious martyrdom conferred upon the witness (Amphibel), who partakes of this suffering by contemplating their physical pain, and weeping and lamenting their plight. Amphibel is unable to see the martyrs without participating in their anguish; contemplation of their bodily pain [*martir de cors*] thus gives rise to an emotional pain located in the heart of the witness to their suffering [*martir de quor*]. Amphibel's visual contemplation of the slaughtered converts therefore performs its own version of the saints' suffering, a suffering located in the heart rather than the body and in the act of witness rather than in physical action or submission.[18]

As with Capraise, the outcome of such contemplation is Amphibel's own physical reenactment of the sacrifice performed by this martyred band of brothers, a reenactment that also recalls the sacrifice of Alban and the acts of witness and mimesis that this initial martyrdom inscribes. Witness in both of these texts therefore shares a number of common features. On a very basic level, seeing the saint involves considering physical pain in terms of the Christian interpretative framework that gives it meaning: the saint suffers for God and is therefore a martyr. What this rather obvious point implies, however, is that seeing the martyr as such always already implies a complex relation to the visual object. Vision and interpretation necessarily bleed into one another to produce what I have called hermeneutic vision. The visual encounter as it is described in saints' lives such as these consequently involves an engagement with the ideological dimension of sacrificial spectacle that goes beyond simply "seeing" something occur. The viewer is enclosed in the event in such a way as to suggest a form of vicarious participation in what is or has been seen, a participation that would suggest a narcissistic (rather than voyeuristic) involvement in sacrificial spectacle. In Capraise's case, this involvement occurs in the form of a retrospective (and predictive) narrative framing of sacrificial spectacle, as his own martyrdom and heavenly reward are read into the events he is shown by God. As mentioned earlier, on the one hand, Capraise is convinced to martyr himself as a result of the spectacle he witnesses; yet, on the other hand, he is presented as a martyr even as he witnesses these events. In relation to Amphibel, the vicarious participation in the scene of martyrdom is equally—if not more—pronounced. Seeing and experiencing martyrdom are here explicitly juxtaposed in a way that makes mimesis a part of the visual encounter. What is "seen" here again blurs the distinction between the viewing subject and the object of vision: seeing the *martir de cors* involves suffering with them and therefore, implicitly, seeing one's own suffering within the sufferings of others.[19]

Interpassive Vision

I would now like to explore how this investment in suffering—or, more specifically, how watching the suffering of another—might function both on a textual level and as a possible model for response to the saint's life.

I will do this by considering Slavoj Žižek's notion of interpassivity, as his elaboration of this concept enables a more detailed consideration of how identifications such as those described earlier might function and what might be at stake in such an investment. Where Žižek's work proves less useful is in considering how *vision* might operate within this framework; I will therefore go on to suggest how, in relation to my discussion, a notion of what I have termed "interpassive vision" might be possible.

The concept of interpassivity that Žižek advances in *The Plague of Fantasies* relies upon the Lacanian notion of the decentred subject.[20] Put simply, this is the idea that one's being-in-language involves a subjection to a symbolic order that is inevitably "outside" the self yet which nonetheless has a fundamental role in defining the very core of one's subjectivity. The subject of the enunciation in Lacanian theory is also subject to the symbolic order; that is to say, the subject only comes into being through its constitutive decentering within the symbolic. Because of this, the subject's agency is always in a sense indirect: the speech act itself is a gesture accomplished through the Other insofar as it is the symbolic order (the big Other) that speaks through me.

Žižek's argument is that, because this is the case, *both* active and passive responses (which are not, it must be emphasized, always easily distinguishable from one another) can be accomplished through another. In relation to active response, Žižek suggests that there are two types of the Other doing it for the subject: first, the Other does it for you but you do not recognize yourself in the gesture performed on your behalf. For instance, I think I do not believe in Santa Claus, but I believe through the Other (my children, my little brother or sister) and go to great lengths every year to convince them that Father Christmas exists. Thus, despite the fact that it is *you* who believe through the Other, you do not recognize yourself in a belief that is yours. The second kind of the Other doing it for the subject involves the opposite extreme: the subject believes that she acted but the Other did it for her. So, for example, this would be the point of including canned laughter in televised comedy programs: I think I laughed but it was in fact the Other who laughed for me. In this case, then, the subject misrecognizes the element of decentering in what she perceives to be her own response.

The obverse of this agency through the Other is, Žižek argues, interpassivity: instead of remaining passive while the Other acts for me, I am passive through the Other. In the case of interpassive response, then, it is passivity (rather than activity) that is given over to the Other so that I can remain actively engaged. Interpassivity is therefore a kind of degree zero of subjectivity insofar as it marks an alienation of passive experience that enables the subject to be active. Yet interpassivity also performs a more radical decentering of the subject than does interactivity, for, claims Žižek, it requires the displacement of the passive kernel of the subject's substantial identity. Whereas interactive response requires the substitution of the (active) signifier for the subject, interpassive engagement implicitly performs a more primordial substitution: that of the (passive) object for the subject. Although Žižek never explicitly considers the implications of this in relation to visual response, the language he uses implicitly associates passivity with visually induced inertia:

> The object which gives body to the surplus-enjoyment fascinates the subject, it reduces him to a passive gaze impotently gaping at the object; this relationship, of course, is experienced by the subject as something shameful, unworthy. Being directly transfixed by the object, passively submitting to its power of fascination, is ultimately unbearable: the open display of the passive attitude of "enjoying it" somehow deprives the subject of his dignity. Interpassivity is therefore to be conceived as the primordial form of the subject's *defence* against *jouissance*: I defer *jouissance* to the Other who passively endures it (laughs, suffers, enjoys. . .) on my behalf.[21]

In order to understand the relevance of this quotation for my discussion, some explanation is perhaps required. The position of the passive, fascinated observer here is a position characterized by its association with *jouissance*: that is, the excessive, unbearable, *painful* pleasure that lies beyond the limits placed upon enjoyment by the symbolic order (also known as the "pleasure principle"). What interpassivity does is therefore to prevent the subject from experiencing this transgressive pleasure directly, enabling her to displace it onto the Other who experiences it in her stead. Although not commented on by Žižek, what occurs in this displacement is a simultaneous transferal of the fascinated gaze of the observer: the Other not only endures/enjoys for me, it also, by extension, sees the unbearably fascinating object on my behalf.

Elsewhere in his work, Žižek explains the dynamics of interpassive identification in terms of a multiplication of the gaze.[22] This later exposition helps to clarify somewhat the interface between passivity and activity in Žižek's earlier description in that it posits a necessary relationship between these two forms of response. Interpassivity does not, he argues, simply symmetrically reverse interactivity, but instead represents a reflexive redoubling of the gaze. The subject can be active only insofar as passive fascination is transferred onto the Other, yet this transposition of passivity involves the concomitant assertion of a gaze that watches the "active" subject and thereby registers her acts in the symbolic. In other words, in delegating the role of passive observer to the Other, the subject imaginatively appears to this Other as an active subject. Seen in relation to his more detailed exposition of interpassivity in the *Plague of Fantasies*, Žižek's comments usefully emphasize the interrelationship of interactive and interpassive positions, both of which are imaginatively constructed around the subject's relationship to the gaze. Interpassive identification requires the subject to be in two places at once, to simultaneously occupy the role of the (passive) viewer and that of the (active) object of the gaze. Yet the subject does this indirectly, being both passive and active through the Other and thereby shielding herself from a direct involvement in *jouissance*.

Returning, then, to the visual dynamics of the scene of witness, a number of significant features should be underlined. I have demonstrated how the witness of martyrdom can function to trouble the separation between the viewing subject and the object of the gaze; viewed from the perspective of Žižek's notion of interpassivity, this vicarious participation in sacrificial spectacle comes more clearly into focus. In the case of both Capraise and Amphibel, the interpassive dimension of the visual encounter is clear: the martyr is passive on behalf of the viewing subject, who, in turn, suffers passively through the martyr. This model is already familiar from the archetypal sacrifice of Christ. However, for Capraise and Amphibel, this interpassive investment in suffering translates into a "real" reenactment of suffering, a reenactment that seemingly confirms the connection between the experience of sacrifice and the experience of it which occurs at one remove, through the act of witness. The question therefore arises as to what role the *narrative depiction* of such acts of witness has in the context of the saint's life and the ideological message it projects.

It is my contention that the proliferation of the gaze that Žižek claims to be inherent to interpassivity has a particular role to play in the identifications that the textual representation of such visual encounters is intended to encourage. Capraise and Amphibel are figures who, in an important sense, see on the reader/listener's behalf; in Žižek's terms, they stand for the unbearably transfixed and fascinated gaze that threatens to expose the subject to *jouissance*. Thus, in the *Vie de Sainte Fey* the narrative description of the miraculous scenes witnessed by Capraise has a dual function: on the one hand, this description is intended to offer a tantalizing glimpse of the agency of the divine from the perspective of the eyewitness. On the other hand, however, the text offers this experience in an inevitably mediated form: the auditor or reader "sees" the events described through a narrative representation of the experience of the eyewitness. What the reader or listener is ultimately confronted with, then, is a passive observer exposed to the almost unbearable pleasure of his glimpse of the glory of heaven: an observer who both sees and enjoys *instead of* the Christian subjects beyond the text and who also performs both of these tasks *on their behalf.* In other words, the text's consumers defer *jouissance* to the Other who passively enjoys/suffers the scene for them.

The ideological move here is therefore to create an impossible and inherently troubling object of vision (the divine) by depicting the transfixed gaze of the passive observer who "sees" and enjoys on the reading/listening subject's behalf. It should be emphasized that this representation of the Other's *jouissance* therefore has the effect of, on the one hand, depicting a painful excess of enjoyment that can be experienced vicariously by the subject and, on the other hand, deflecting the subject's own *jouissance* by preventing any direct or unmediated contact with it. Indeed, strictly speaking, *jouissance* is not displaced from the subject onto the Other: the saint's life presents the reader/listener with a glimpse of his own, *already displaced* encounter with *jouissance*. What the text therefore encourages is a misrecognition of the passive enjoyment of the viewer represented within the text (through figures such as Capraise and Amphibel) as a passive response to *jouissance* that the subject displaces onto the Other who enjoys for her. Doing so not only defers viewing and responding to the scene to the Other, it also crucially allows the Other to have faith in the ideological meaning of these events on the subject's behalf as well. Accepting that one's own, passive response is displaced (yet recognizable) in that of the Other represented in the text thus enables the kind of enclosure in faith described by Simon of Walsingham in the prologue to the *Vie de Sainte Fey*. The subject merges with the object of vision even as that object presents itself for contemplation: one both "sees" faith and inhabits it indirectly through the text. In this sense, it would seem that seeing (in a vicarious, textually mediated sense) really *is* believing.

In this respect, the notion of interpassivity might be used to contribute to recent debates concerning how the example set by saints' lives for readers or listeners was understood in medieval contexts. In what sense, for instance, did virgin martyrs set an example for real medieval women? How far was this identification taken? Thinking about reception in terms of interpassive vision can usefully redirect attention toward figures other than the saint with whom readers or listeners were encouraged to identify. For, as I have suggested, empathy with the saint can occur through a displaced participation in suffering that makes the primary object of identification for the reader/listener the witness rather than the martyr. Moreover, interpassivity provides a useful theoretical tool for thinking about issues of response insofar as it insists that identification occurs at the point where one's direct experience is deferred through its displacement onto another. This would mean that identification is the product of an experience of the text that is understood neither in terms of purely literal interpretation, nor as a failure to engage with the "real" content of what is presented. Seeing the reception of certain saints' lives in the context of an interpassive engagement such as that outlined here would insist upon considering the "authentic" experience communicated by the text as an alienation of direct subjective involvement in that which the narrative presents, an alienation that protects the subject from coming too close to the original even as it promises greater proximity to the divine.

Finally, to return to the question of gender with which I began, what thinking in terms of interpassive vision promotes is a consideration of the role of spectacle and specularity in saints' lives that complicates somewhat the notion of an appropriating male gaze. I have suggested that the voyeuristic model of looking at the saint for which certain feminist analyses have argued fails to account for the specific role that witness is accorded in accounts of martyrdom such as those examined here. Vision in these texts instead has a more narcissistic function, involving subject/object confusions that trouble the terms upon which visualization relies. My exploration of this relationship in connection with the notion of interpassive vision develops this model more specifically in the context of a visually negotiated response to the text. One of the implications of considering vision in accounts of martyrdom in these terms is to call into question the gendered positions claimed by interpretations that make these texts vehicles of the male gaze. For, if, as I have argued, interpassive vision troubles the boundaries between the subject and object of the gaze by allowing a vicarious occupation of both positions at once, the precise sense in which gender operates within this context needs to be readdressed. If, as in the case of Capraise and Fey, the viewing subject is identified with—or even *as*—the object of vision, it is surely not possible to separate masculine and feminine, or active and passive, in an unproblematic or meaningful way within this experience. This is not to say that the conditions for such an identification were never gendered or that sexual desire has no role to play in a critical exploration of response to saints' lives. However, we should be alive to the ways that the complex interpellations performed by the text might operate to bypass those features of subjectivity that might secure or normalize gender and sexuality in the context of narrative reception. By negotiating a complex investment in the gaze as a vehicle for experience of the divine, saints' lives such as the *Vie de Sainte Fey* encourage relationships between subjects and the objects of their supposed contemplation that can eclipse sex and gender through mechanisms of narrative visualization. In this respect, enclosure in the ideological space of the text depends in an important sense upon an interpassively troubled—and troubling—form of vision.

Notes

I would like to thank Simon Gaunt, Clare Lees, Bob Mills, and Jocelyn Wogan-Browne for their comments on earlier versions of this chapter.

1. The term "martyr" is etymologically based upon the notion of witness: from the Greek μαρτυς (*martus*, meaning witness).
2. Kathryn Gravdal, *Ravishing Maidens: Writing Rape in Medieval French Literature and Law* (Philadelphia: University of Pennsylvania Press, 1991), p. 24. Simon Gaunt usefully develops this point by incorporating the question of (male) voyeurism into a discussion of gendered response. See Gaunt, *Gender and Genre in Medieval French Literature* (Cambridge, UK: Cambridge University Press, 1995), esp. pp. 185–233.
3. Kathleen Coyne Kelly, "Useful Virgins in Medieval Hagiography," in *Constructions of Widowhood and Virginity in the Middle Ages*, ed. Cindy L. Carlson and Angela Jane Weisl (New York: Palgrave Macmillan, 1999), p. 156 [135–64].
4. Brigitte Cazelles, *The Lady as Saint: A Collection of French Hagiographic Romances of the Thirteenth Century* (Philadelphia: University of Pennsylvania Press, 1991), p. 53.
5. Arguments for the voyeurism of saints' lives have been critiqued from a variety of perspectives. However, these critiques often focus on questions of gender and historical context, rather than concerning themselves with the visual basis of the arguments they dissect. See for example Evelyn Birge Vitz, "Gender and Martyrdom," *Medievalia et Humanistica* n.s. 26 (1999): 79–99. Jocelyn Wogan-Browne makes the point that the visual is also the visionary in the Anglo-Norman Life under consideration here: Wogan-Browne, *Saints' Lives and Women's Literary Culture c.1150–1300: Virginity and Its Authorizations* (Oxford: Oxford University Press, 2001), pp. 57–90 (esp. pp. 70–72). On the problematics of vision in Old English hagiography, see (briefly) Clare A. Lees and Gillian Overing, "Before History, Before Difference: Bodies, Metaphor, and the Church in Anglo-Saxon England," *Yale Journal of Criticism* 2 (1998): 322–23 [315–34]; and, at greater length, Lees and Overing, *Double Agents: Women and Clerical Culture in Anglo-Saxon England* (Philadelphia: University of Pennsylvania Press, 2001), pp. 119–21 and 132–51. For a more general argument against feminist critical approaches in relation to Merovingian hagiography see John Kitchen, *Saints' Lives and the Rhetoric of Gender: Male and Female in Merovingian Hagiography* (Oxford: Oxford University Press, 1998), pp. 1–22. If taken seriously, Kitchen's objections to "the limited focus of contemporary research" on saints' lives would nonetheless invalidate most approaches interested in a theoretically informed exploration of gender in hagiography.
6. Gravdal, *Ravishing Maidens*, p. 24.
7. Arguments for seeing gender as obscured rather than manifested by saints' lives have been made by others; however, these arguments do not usually consider the representation of vision itself as one of the ways in which this is achieved. See for example Vitz, "Gender and Martyrdom," and Kitchen, *Saints' Lives and the Rhetoric of Gender*. For related comments on Old English material see Clare A. Lees, *Tradition and Belief: Religious Writing in Late Anglo-Saxon England* (Minneapolis: University of Minnesota Press, 1999), pp. 150–53.
8. Simon of Walsingham, "Vie Anglo-Normande de Sainte Foy, par Simon de Walsingham," ed. A.T. Baker, *Romania* 66 (1940–41): 49–84. Line numbers

from this edition are provided in parentheses; translations are my own. For context and dating see the introduction to Baker's edition (pp. 49–58) and M. Dominica Legge, *Anglo-Norman Literature and Its Background* (Oxford: Clarendon Press, 1963), pp. 257–58. Wogan-Browne provides an erudite description of the manuscript and its contexts, along with a table of contents, in *Saints' Lives and Women's Literary Culture*, pp. 6–11.

9. In the thirteenth-century section of the manuscript (which contains nine of the thirteen articles in the manuscript as a whole), the only other texts that lack such an initial are 5. *Le Romanz de sainte Marie Magdalene* by Guillaume le Clerc de Normandie (fols. 50v–55v) and 6. *Le Romanz de saint Edward rei* (Edward the Confessor) (fols. 55v–85v). The fourth article in the manuscript—the *Vie de saint Thomas de Cantorbéry* by Garnier de Pont-Sainte-Maxence (fols. 9r–50v)—is missing 138 lines at the beginning, making it impossible to know whether or not the text was originally accompanied by a picture of the saint. Fey's portrait initial may have been planned but inadvertently omitted, since the rubric appears on fol. 146v and the incipit on fol. 147r.
10. It should be noted that the use of *fermer* in the opening sections allows for slippage between different meanings. *Fermez* or *fermé* can often be translated as either "enclosed in" or "firm in" (the implication being that the one in some sense requires the other).
11. One might compare Cazelles's claim that, in the lives of female saints, "[beauty], rather than demonstrating [the saintly heroine's] ability to escape the temporal world, in fact hinders her spiritual progress. . . .These saintly maidens seek, in principle, to remain invisible; yet the logic of the narrative goes counter to this aspiration, and their ordeal can best be described as a process of forced visibility"; Cazelles, *The Lady as Saint*, p. 50.
12. *Pur sun nun* is ambiguous here. Although I have translated it as "in his [God's] name" it could also mean "on account of her name," implying that Fey is suffering for the faith after which she has been named.
13. Although concentrating on other features of this passage, Jocelyn Wogan-Browne similarly points out that the body of the saint is not the primary focus of Capraise's gaze. See Wogan-Browne, *Saints' Lives and Women's Literary Culture*, pp. 71–72.
14. The number of occurrences is as follows: *Esgarder*: 526, 538, 577; *Voir*: 529, 530, 532, 535, 551, 555, 576, 578, 589.
15. Sigmund Freud, "On Narcissism: An Introduction," in *Freud's "On Narcissism: An Introduction,"* ed. Joseph Sandler, Ethel Spector Person, and Peter Fonagy (New Haven: Yale University Press, 1991), pp. 3–32. On the fundamentally relational dimension of Freud's concept of narcissism see the article by Heinz Hensler in the same volume: "Narcissism as a Form of Relationship," pp. 195–215.

16. Before this, other terms are used: "hom de grant religiun" (459), "bacheler" (460), "seint" (493).
17. Matthew Paris, *La Vie de seint Auban: An Anglo-Norman Poem of the Thirteenth Century*, ed. Arthur R. Harden, Anglo-Norman Texts Society 19 (Oxford: Blackwell, 1968). (Line numbers from this edition are provided in parentheses.) A date for this text before 1230 is possible, however (see Harden's introduction, pp. xv–xvii). The poem has been associated with women readers of the court of Eleanor of Provence; Wogan-Browne suggests that the text was probably known to Isabella of Arundel, who is named by Matthew Paris in the flyleaf to the manuscript. Wogan-Browne, *Saints' Lives and Women's Literary Culture*, pp. 151–76.
18. One might compare the notion of the *martir de quor* here with passages from a thirteenth-century Life of Andrew the Apostle in Oxford Bodleian Library MS Canonici Miscellaneous 74. In the introductory section to this text, we are told that "doble maniere / poomes nos soffrir martire / u enz el cors u el corage" [we can suffer martyrdom in two ways: either in body or in spirit] (69–71). These different—yet comparable—forms of martyrdom are then examined at some length in the poem, which claims that spiritual martyrdom precedes physical martyrdom even in the case of those holy men who lived a long time ago. See "The Passion of Saint Andrew," ed. A.T. Baker, *Modern Language Review* 11 (1916): 420–49.
19. As others have pointed out, this is a mode of perception common to a great deal of later medieval devotional literature and art. For a consideration of this investment in suffering and its relationship to vision see Robert Mills, "A Man Is Being Beaten," *New Medieval Literatures* 5 (2002): 115–53; and Mills, "Ecce Homo," in *Gender and Holiness: Men, Women and Saints in Late Medieval Europe*, ed. Samantha J.E. Riches and Sarah Salih (London: Routledge, 2002), pp. 152–73. See also Sarah Stanbury, "The Virgin's Gaze: Spectacle and Transgression in Middle English Lyrics of the Passion," *PMLA* 106 (1991): 1083–93.
20. Slavoj Žižek, *The Plague of Fantasies* (London: Verso, 1997), pp. 86–126 (esp. pp. 111–22).
21. Žižek, *The Plague of Fantasies*, p. 115. Compare his discussion of the gaze as an object of fascination for the viewing subject in film: Žižek, *Looking Awry: An Introduction to Jacques Lacan Through Popular Culture* (Cambridge, MA: MIT Press, [1992] 2002), pp. 114–116.
22. Žižek, "Class Struggle or Postmodernism? Yes, please!," in Judith Butler, Ernesto Laclau, and Slavoj Žižek, *Contingency, Hegemony, Universality: Contemporary Dialogues on the Left* (London: Verso, 2000), pp. 90–135 (esp. pp. 116–117).

CHAPTER 6

SEEING FACE TO FACE: TROUBLED LOOKS IN THE KATHERINE GROUP

Robert Mills

This chapter explores the connections between vision and identity in early Middle English anchoritic writings, taking as its starting point an engagement with Foucauldian and psychoanalytic models of the gaze.

The point of gaze always participates in the ambiguity of the jewel.

—Jacques Lacan, *The Four Fundamental Concepts of Psycho-analysis*

A visual hermeneutic can be perceived throughout the cluster of thirteenth-century religious prose works known collectively as the Katherine Group; indeed, it could be argued that vision is one of the Group's unifying features. Acts of looking and metaphors of sight are central features in the three saints' lives that appear in the collection, those of Katherine (after whom the Group is named), Margaret, and Juliana.[1] What these texts have in common, however, is not a focus on vision per se but a desire to organize or to structure vision as it is manifested in various textual identities or "positions." Sight, the legends imply, is something that can be manipulated, appropriated, or exchanged by the various protagonists within an economy that associates it with power and subjectivity. At the same time, by mobilizing vision within a framework that is itself discursive and rhetorical—a framework that becomes especially apparent when viewed against the backdrop of the virgin martyr's verbal eloquence—these texts also have the capacity to generate zones of ambivalence and contradiction. *Seinte Margarete*, for instance, is structured around a conflict between several different fields of vision: the look of the martyr, who prays to God that she may lay her "ehnen o þe luðre unwiht þe weorreð aȝein me" [eyes on the wicked devil who is waging war against me] (*SM*, 56); the look of the devil himself, who appears in the form of a dragon with eyes that "steareden steappre þen þe steoren ant ten ȝimstanes, brade asce bascins" [gleamed brighter than stars or jewels, broad as basins]; the look of the pagan tormentor, Olibrius, who announces that, when Margaret has been torn limb from limb, he will count all her sinews "in euchanes sihðe þe sit nu ant sið þe" [in the sight of everyone sitting here now] (*SM*, 56); the look of those same spectators, who express sorrow when they "seoð" [see] the saint's soft, lovely body cruelly ripped to pieces (*SM*, 52), and gasp with horror at the sight of the dragon "glistinde as þah he al ouerguld were" [glittering all over as if he had been gilded] (*SM*, 58); and, of course, the imagined looks of the author and audiences of the narrative, who are afforded the option of identifying with any or all of these positions of viewing.

Looking likewise features heavily in the didactic texts included alongside the saints' lives in the Katherine Group. *Hali Meiðhad*, a letter addressed to a "seli meiden" [innocent maiden] (*HM*, 34) who has, or is about to, commit herself to virginity, implies that the whole purpose of adopting the virtue is to enable the soul to both "opene to understonde me þe ehnen of þin heorte" [open the eyes of your heart to understand me] (*HM*, 2) and "schine ase sunne" [shine like a sun] (*HM*, 40) in the sight of the Lord; the text begins by comparing virginity to the tall tower in Jerusalem called Zion, a name that corresponds in English, the author asserts, to the notion of "heh sihðe" [high vision] (*HM*, 2). Similarly *Sawles Warde* mediates between a vision of hellfire that "ne ȝeueð na liht, ah blent ham þe ehnen þe þer beoð wið a smorðrinde smoke" [gives no light, but blinds the eyes of those who are there with a choking smoke] (*SW*, 90) and a vision of angels and archangels in heaven who give so much "murhðe" [pleasure] that Love of Life, one of the allegorical messengers of the text, cannot "longe hwile elleshwider lokin" [look elsewhere for a long time] (*SW*, 100). Finally *Ancrene Wisse*, closely related in style, audience, date, and dialect to the texts of the Katherine Group, contains, in the part discussing ways of guarding the heart through the five senses, a much-discussed section devoted to the topic of sight and the evils that arise from looking. Making a variety of claims for the troubled and troubling effects of vision, all the woes of the world, the text claims, ultimately "com of sihðe" [came from sight].[2]

The question I wish to raise in this chapter is not whether the *Ancrene Wisse*'s claim that "al com of sihðe" can be substantiated, so much as whether the connections that early Middle English anchoritic writings posit between sight and identity are communicated to the reader in any stable or coherent manner. Modern critics of these texts have sometimes assumed that sight is a position and point of origin: that there is a connection between vision and identity in anchoritic writings; that the looks that appear can be categorized in terms of gender and sexuality; even that such texts betray an appreciation of modern or medieval "gaze theory." Elizabeth Robertson, debating the question of whether the anchorhold offered women a medieval version of Virginia Woolf's "room of one's own," suggests that the *Ancrene Wisse*'s discussion of the dangers of sight shifts the focus of its Latin sources, which deploy references to vision in support of a theological argument about curiosity, by stressing instead the immediate practical consequences for the anchorite of looking at men or allowing men to look at her; this is an example, for Robertson, of the ways in which the text reminds women of "their inferior status, in their present bodies and historically as well."[3] Susannah Mary Chewning argues that acts of looking in *Wohunge* Group—a collection of thirteenth-century devotional texts probably also intended for anchorites—allow the female speaker to be "masculinized" through her visual ability: while admitting a variety of possible identifications for readers of the *Wohunge* meditations, Chewning states that the speaker's "act of looking at Christ is another way that she appropriates masculinity or, here, the masculine gaze."[4] Sarah Salih reads the Katherine Group life of St. Margaret and finds that to be the audience of the spectacle of martyrdom is to occupy "a dangerous and uncertain position" since "to be a spectacle can be a position of power."[5]

I do not wish to claim that vision has nothing to do with gender and empowerment in medieval writings, or that acts of looking do not contribute to the construction of identity; the examples presented in this chapter suggest that vision is implicated in both. What I would like to argue is that writings like those collected in the Katherine Group foreground discourses of sight and visibility that, in their unresolved and fraught interrelationships, also betray a degree of non-convergence between identity and vision—a mismatch that is potentially "troubling." Those critics who comment on the scopic dimensions of the Katherine Group generally do so as they inform the saints' lives of the collection.[6] Here I shall concentrate instead on the two didactic texts in the Group—*Hali Meiðhad* and *Sawles Warde*—since, while these texts, like the saints' lives, are frequently investigated in the context of research on medieval virginities, their ocular dimension has been less well studied or understood. Because recent analyses of vision in anchoritic literature have often been informed, implicitly or explicitly, by the perspectives of contemporary feminist film theory, my analysis will be framed with a consideration of the critique of that body of theory put forward by the psychoanalytic critic Joan Copjec.

Panoptical Vision

In the opening chapter of her book *Read My Desire*, an analysis of the relationship between psychoanalysis and historicism in modern cultural discourses, Copjec suggests that at the basis of much recent film theory is a misconception about its psychoanalytic heritage. Feminists on film, for instance, are generally more amenable to the assumptions of Foucault than to the ideas of Freud or Lacan; they are in fact more likely to sympathize with the disciplinary power of Foucault's *Discipline and Punish*, in particular the notion of panoptical vision, than with a rigorously psychoanalytical conception of the gaze.[7] Foucault deploys the architectural figure of Jeremy Bentham's *Panopticon*, a model prison composed of a central, all-seeing tower enveloped by a ringlike arrangement of cells, to describe the features that, for him, characterize modern disciplinary arrangements. The major effect of the Panopticon, Foucault writes, is

> to induce in the inmate a state of conscious and permanent visibility that assures the automatic functioning of power. So to arrange things that the surveillance is permanent in its effects, even if it is discontinuous in its action; that the perfection of power should tend to render its actual exercise unnecessary; that this architectural apparatus should be a machine for creating and sustaining a power relation independent of the person who exercises it; in short, that the inmates should be caught up in a power situation of which they are themselves the bearers.[8]

Copjec points out that the seeing/being seen dyad by which the panoptic gaze is structured is, in turn, installed by film theory as defining the total visibility of women under patriarchy. Citing the pronouncement in the introduction to *Re-vision*, a collection of essays by feminists on film, that, in terms of her visibility, woman "carries her own Panopticon with her wherever she goes, her self-image a function of her being for another," Copjec asks whether this view is reconcilable with a Lacanian argument on vision.[9]

We might, in this context, cite two formulations that have been influential in medieval studies and that share some of the principles the *Re-vision* editors impart. The first in fact precedes the publication of Foucault's *Discipline and Punish* by several years and also, indeed, most film theoretical discussions of the topic themselves. John Berger's *Ways of Seeing*, discussing the presentation of female nudes in European oil painting, has the following comment to make:

> *men act* and *women appear*. Men look at women. Women watch themselves being looked at. This determines not only most relations between men and women but also the relation of women to themselves. The surveyor of

> woman in herself is male: the surveyed female. Thus she turns herself into an object—and most particularly an object of vision: a sight.[10]

This concept of a dichotomously gendered look, internalized by women so that they become both the object and the internal bearer of an emphatically male gaze, anticipates the sentiments of a more explicitly film theoretical analysis: Laura Mulvey's much cited and much debated article "Visual Pleasure and Narrative Cinema," which alleges a close alliance between the look of the cinematic camera and a voyeuristic, fetishistic gaze that transforms the bodies of women into erotic spectacles for men. Mulvey writes:

> In a world ordered by sexual imbalance, pleasure in looking has been split between active/male and passive/female. The determining male gaze projects its phantasy on to the female figure which is styled accordingly. In their traditional exhibitionist role women are simultaneously looked at and displayed, with their appearance coded for strong visual and erotic impact so that they can be said to connote *to-be-looked-at-ness*.[11]

Both formulations have, in their own ways, been subject to heavy scrutiny and critique and the point of repeating them here is not simply to replicate the now well-worn debates about the relative merits and drawbacks of "male gaze" theory. What I should like to suggest is that the assumptions to which they have given rise, particularly in the context of their alignment with Foucauldian analyses of power, have had a knock-on effect in other areas of academic writing, not least in medieval literary and art historical studies.

One of the effects that a "Foucauldization" of gaze theory has had is that feminist medieval studies are often now animated by a desire to locate possible pockets of resistance to the spaces of power–knowledge that a panoptical gaze puts in place. Just as some commentators have attempted to create an opening for feminist cinema, or to clear a space for feminist art history,[12] certain critics of medieval anchoritic literature have made efforts to appropriate these texts as, to some degree, "liberating," whether for the women who read them or for the virginal identities that they effect. One recent example of this approach—and I cite it not because I think there is anything especially mistaken in the reading but because it is a particularly clear and well-managed articulation—is Salih's analysis of spectacle in the Katherine Group *Seinte Margarete*. Salih distinguishes the pagan gaze of the narrative from the notion of a dichotomously gendered "masculine gaze," since, as she notes, the audience of the martyr's torments, both externally and internally, was not entirely male. She then makes a case for the view that "the virgins take control of the sights of their naked bodies, subverting the meanings intended by their persecutors" and that martyrs are "spectacles on their own terms."[13]

I wish to enter into a dialogue with Copjec's analysis of the Foucauldization of Lacan in feminist film theory by asking to what extent panoptical vision is a defining feature of other texts in the Katherine Group. Can the model of power and resistance that critics like Salih envisage in the context of the saints' lives fully explicate the workings of vision in the didactic texts too? *Hali Meiðhad* is literally dominated by the image of a watchtower, the tower of Zion that, as already noted, is interpreted by the text's author as conveying a sense of "high vision" (based on the idea of an etymological connection between the words "Syon" and "sihðe"). This tower, we are told, signifies

> þe hehnesse of meiðhad, þe bihald as of heh alle widewen under hire ant weddede baðe. For þeos, ase flesches þrealles, beoð i worldes þeowdom, ant wunieð lahe on eorðe; ant meiden ston þurh heh lif i þe tur of Ierusalem. Nawt of lah on eorðe, ah of þe hehe in heouene þe is bitacnet þurh þis, of þet Syon ha bihalt al þe worlt under hire. (*HM*, 2–4)
>
> [the high state of virginity, which as if from a height sees all widows below it, and married women too. For these, as slaves of the flesh, are in the servitude of the world, and live low on earth; and the virgin stands through her exalted life in the tower of Jerusalem. Not from low on earth, but from the height in heaven which is signified by this, from that Zion she sees all the world below her.]

The image of the tower certainly has elements in common with a panoptical structure of looking. Virginity is an identity positioned at a locus of visibility: the virgin sees "al þe worlt," and women in other states, widows and wives for example, are presented as being comparatively underprivileged in their access to vision. Moreover the subject's claim to know is bound up with her ability to see, a conflation that arguably finds its counterpart in the scientific, and ultimately Aristotelian, insistence on the primacy of sight as a medium of knowledge.[14] Given that *Hali Meiðhad* is a text that was presumably written for the encouragement of prospective virgins as well as for those who have already committed themselves to the virtue, the implication is that readers should aspire to a spiritual height in which they will be able to participate in the virgin's all-seeing, all-knowing gaze. Indeed they are asked to consider virginity, as it is presented in the text, as a nexus of what Foucault might term "vision–knowledge" relations. To paraphrase Berger's formulation, virgins look at women; women watch themselves being looked at.

This modification points to the existence of what could be termed the "virginal gaze," a phenomenon that critics reproducing the conventional film theory paradigm might be tempted to interpret as an appropriation of a masculine interpretive stance.[15] Yet it is important to note that the panoptical tower of *Hali Meiðhad* is itself an object of vision, besieged by Lechery and attacked by the people of Babylon, the army of the Devil of hell. The virgin's privileged position of looking is an object of desire that the Devil himself attempts to appropriate:

> Nu bihalt te alde feond, ant sið þe i þis mihte stonde se hehe, ilich hire ant hire sune, as engel in heouene, i meiðhdes menske, ant toswelleð of grome; and scheoteð niht ant dei his earewen, idrencte of an attri healewi, towart tin heorte to wundi þe wið wac wiul, ant makien to fallen, as Crist te forbeode! (*HM*, 12)
>
> [Now the ancient enemy looks on, and sees you stand so high in this virtue, like her and her son, like an angel in heaven, in the glory of virginity, and swells with fury; and night and day he shoots his arrows, dipped in a venomous potion, towards your heart, to wound you with weakness of will and cause you to fall, which Christ forbid!]

The Devil's arrow is lecherous desire, and Lechery's first help is sight: "ȝef þu bihaldest ofte ant stikelunge on ei mon, Leccherie ananriht greiðeð hire wið þet to weorrin o þi meiðhad, ant secheð earst upon hire nebbe to nebbe" [if you look often and intently at any man, Lechery at once prepares herself with that to make war on your virginity, and first advances on her face to face] (*HM*, 14). In these passages, a position of looking—the virginal gaze being emitted from the tower—is besieged by two other fields of vision: the envious look of the Devil and the lustful look of Lechery. Moreover the latter, though characterized as attacking virginity, is implicitly and paradoxically on the side of the virgin, in that the troubling look is her own. This complicates the idea that the virginal gaze is a purely panoptical—and what might be read as gendered—gaze, since the virginal gaze is also simultaneously an object of vision, subject to the looks of Lechery (gendered grammatically female in the text) and the Devil (gendered grammatically male). The logic of the previous sentence is deliberately paradoxical: the virgin, I am claiming, is both object and subject, since her status as a sight endows her with the capacity to see. Like the virgin martyrs elsewhere in the Katherine Group, the virgin is positioned here as a spectacle that enables her to confront "nebbe to nebbe" [face to face] the problematic looks that she has been regarding thus far from on high. The specular standoff between Lechery and virgin in *Hali Meiðhad* produces a scene in which the position of the virgin is aligned visually with the position of the saint: just as in *Seinte Margarete* the martyr is constituted as a figure besieged by the lustful looks of Olibrius and subsequently transformed by him into a dismembered, torn-apart body, the consequence of allowing Lechery to make its assault in *Hali Meiðhad* is that virgins are "tolimet, lið ba ant lire" [torn to pieces, limb from limb] (*HM*, 18). The paradox of vision-besieged is also, indeed, a feature endemic in certain feminist accounts of the structure of patriarchal looking, which imply that, by rendering *visible* the male gaze's structure—its parallels with, say, the watch-tower of Bentham's prison—a subversive reappropriation of the gaze that is nonetheless a defining condition of female subjectivity might be set in motion.

Hali Meiðhad concludes by evoking a different field of vision altogether: the sight of, and looks produced by, the virgin's heavenly husband. After the well-known section on the tribulations of marriage, which constructs an image of earthly husbands abusing and beating their wives like slaves, the text turns to a preferred object of desire: "ȝef þet tu wlinest were þe muche wlite habbe, nim him of hwas wlite beoð awundret of þe sunne ant te mone, upo hwas nebschreft þe engles ne beoð neauer fulle to bihalden" [If you want a husband who is very handsome, take him whose beauty the sun and moon admire, whose face the angels are never weary of gazing at] (*HM*, 34–36). In this way, the heavenly lord is himself portrayed as a lure for vision, beneath which is only the sight of heavenly virgins themselves. Virgins in heaven, the text tells us, have robes that shine above all others, since they walk next to God wherever he goes: "Ant alle ha beoð icrunet þe blissið in heouene wið kempene crune; ah þe meidnes habbeð upo þeo þe is to alle iliche imeane a gerlondesche schininde schenre þen þe sunne" [And all who rejoice in heaven are crowned with a victor's crown; but the virgins have, over and above what is common to all alike, a circlet shining brighter than the sun] (*HM*, 20). Moreover, the shining light of the virgin's virtue provokes what is the final mention of sight in the text, the look of the husband: "Eadi Godes spuse, haue þeos ilke mihte, þet tu ne þunche þeostri ah schine ase sunne i þi weres sihðe" [Blessed spouse of God, have this virtue, that you may not seem dark but shine like a sun in your husband's sight] (*HM*, 40). The virgin is thus positioned as a vision, a gleaming state to which she should continually aspire. God looks at virgins; virgins watch themselves being looked at.

These extracts demonstrate that vision, or what might be termed in film theoretical vocabulary "the gaze," is distributed in the text in a variety of ways. Acts of looking can be visible sites of knowledge—architecturally structured, panoptical ones at that. But the subjects who inhabit those sites of knowledge can themselves become the point of origin for a different kind of look, the look that plummets to the ground and invites physical lust; they can also constitute the battleground for a struggle between the looks of the Devil and the heavenly king; they can indeed provide a model for subjects external to the text to open the "ehnen" of their hearts in order to see more clearly. So, remaining within a Foucauldian frame, we can say that vision is a hermeneutic that permits both power and resistance, registering a conflict of positions and discourses that simultaneously threatens panoptical power and inscribes it. Identifications of various kinds are produced in the course of this process, since the multiplication of looking corresponds to a multiplication of subject positions. But this multiplication does not in itself undermine, or step outside of, the pact between knowledge and power, since each position is precisely that, a *position*—a determinate point of view.

The Gaze as a Locus of Meaning

The seemingly determinate status of vision–knowledge relations in a text like *Hali Meiðhad*, where a variety of subject positions are imagined that, in their own ways, attempt to effect mastery over all they survey, corresponds to another element in the Foucauldization of film theory that Copjec perceives: the notion of the gaze as a locus of meaning, which determines the subject in the visual field. The description of vision offered by film theory, says Copjec, founds itself on a reading of psychoanalytic theory that foregrounds the gaze's subjectivizing properties.[16] This reading draws its inspiration especially from Lacan's early essay "The Mirror Stage as Formative of the Function of the I" (which plays, for instance, an important role in Mulvey's analysis of mainstream cinema).[17] The ego, Lacan submits in this essay, is formed by a process of identification with its self-image, a narcissistic relation with a mirrored reflection that leads to an imaginary sense of mastery. Thus an act of seeing (the beholding of the mirror image) constitutes a fundamental element in the structure of subjectivity. But a superficial glance at the series of seminars Lacan gave in 1964 (Seminar XI) that were subsequently gathered together under the heading *The Four Fundamental Concepts of Psycho-analysis*, suggests that the alignment of subjectivity and vision is also at issue here, in the context of the psychoanalyst's extended discussion of what he terms *le regard* or, in English translations, "the gaze." Lacan's discussion here presents a notion of the gaze that, while being fundamentally dissociated from "the eye" of the subject, implicates that subject in a process of to-be-looked-at-ness. As he puts it: "In the scopic field, the gaze is outside, I am looked at, that is to say, I am a picture . . . . What determines me, at the most profound level, in the visible, is the gaze that is outside."[18]

This idea has been interpreted by film theory as referring to the fact that *le regard*, in Lacanian theory, is literally that which gives meaning. By mapping the subject onto a grid of intelligibility, an imaginary order that establishes the I in the visible, the gaze effectively coincides with the subject, since the subject is thought to identify with the gaze as the ultimate source of knowledge. To put it differently, the gaze is imagined as a subject, an all-seeing, all-knowing subject, with whom the object of the gaze learns to identify and thus to gain a modicum of subjectivity.[19] On the surface it appears that we have not really traveled so far—both in the Lacan of the mirror stage and the Lacan of "the gaze"—from the notion of panoptical vision, which, as we saw in the context of *Hali Meiðhad*, may be represented both as an external, visible structure (the panoptical tower) and as an internalized, identified-with field (virginal virtue) that is in both cases a locus of subjectivity.[20]

In thinking through this conception of the subjectivizing gaze—which I will characterize in conclusion, like Copjec, as in some senses "pseudo-psychoanalytic," not least in its appropriation by film criticism—I now wish to consider the status of vision in the other didactic text in the Katherine Group, *Sawles Warde*. This work is an allegorical treatise describing how two messengers, one from heaven (Love of Life) and the other from hell (Fear), visit members of an imaginary household governed by a housewife (Will) and mastered by a husband (Reason); the messengers warn of the dangers that may beset the inner servants, who, in all kinds of ways, plot to "please" the housewife and consequently set her against the will of God. A visual framework is central to the text and indeed is somewhat enhanced in comparison with its Latin source—*Sawles Warde* is based on a treatise called *De custodia interioris hominis* ("On the Custody of the Soul") that was commonly ascribed in the Middle Ages to St. Anselm.[21] One moment where the Middle English author seems to augment the visual dimensions of the text is in the section introducing the two messengers in the narrative. In *Sawles Warde*, Death's messenger Fear comes from a place whose darkness is so thick that it cannot be grasped, whereas Love of Life enters the household and lights the place up—we are informed that the householders "beoð alle ilihtet ant igleadet, ham þuncheð, of his onsihðe, for al þet hus schineð ant schimmeð of his leome" [are all cheered, and the very sight of him makes them feel happy, for all the house shines and shimmers with his radiance] (*SW*, 98). No such descriptions of light and dark are forthcoming in the Latin treatise at these points in the dialogue.[22] Moreover, in *Sawles Warde*, Love of Life brings word of a more entrancing vision still, that of Christ sitting on his Father's right side, "se unimete feier þet te engles ne beoð neauer ful on him to bihalden" [so immeasurably beautiful that the angels are never weary of gazing at him] (*SW*, 100). He adds that he has seen, in turn, the places of Christ's wounds; Mary shining brightly on her throne, "hire wlite se weoleful, þet euch eorðlich liht is þeoster þeraȝeines" [her face so radiant, that every earthly light is darkness compared with it]; and the angels and archangels, in whose "onsihðe" [appearance] he took so much "murhðe" [pleasure] that he could not "longe hwile elleshwider lokin" [look elsewhere for a long time]. While the source text certainly acknowledges these visions in the speech attributed to Love of Life (in Latin, "Desiderium Vitae Aeternae"), the author of *Sawles Warde* makes one important shift with respect to the visualization of virgins: whereas in Latin virgins are described as coming "postremo" [last, in the rear],[23] a somewhat anticlimactic mode of introduction that does little to convey the ocular splendors of chaste existence, Love of Life's evocation of the visual pleasures of heaven in *Sawles Warde* ends with an uplifting and lengthy portrait of "þet schene and þet brihte" [that radiant and shining] company of virgins, of whose "feierlec. . .ne mei na tunge tellen" [beauty. . .no tongue can tell] (*SW*, 102). At the same time, the Latin and Middle English texts correspond in one important respect: the bliss common to all those described is that their lives make possible a vision, and knowledge, of God. In *De custodia interioris hominis*, the messenger states: "Vita eorum est visio et cognitio beatae Trinitatis" [Their life is a vision and knowledge of the blessed Trinity].[24] In *Sawles Warde*, Love of Life asserts:

> Ant hare lif is Godes sihðe ant Godes cnawlechunge, as ure Lauerd seide: þet is, quoð he, eche lif, to seon ant cnawen soð Godd ant him þet he sende, Iesu Crist ure Lauerd, to ure alesnesse. Ant beoð forþi ilich him, i þe ilke wlite þet he is, for ha seoð him as he is, nebbe to nebbe. (*SW*, 102)
>
> [And their life is the vision of God and the knowledge of God, as our Lord said: that is eternal life, he said, to see and know the true God and him whom he sent for our salvation, Jesus Christ our Lord. And therefore they are like him, in the same glory as he is himself, because they see him as he is, face to face.]

Statements to this effect in both *Sawles Warde* and its source assume that visual pleasure is a determining, subjectivizing phenomenon, coextensive, more often than not, with being a subject. The members of the household are literally en*light*ened by the presence of Love of Life—his light is what prevents the household's shaken resolve, after hearing Fear's terrifying words, from degenerating into despair. God, we are told, "iseh ow offruhte ant sumdel drupnin of þet Fearlac talde of Deað ant of helle, ant sende me to gleadien ow" [saw you afraid and rather downcast because of what Fear said about Death and hell, and sent me to cheer you] (*SW*, 98). The household is thus made conscious that they are always in the sight of God, the beatific vision that is, from the point of view of Christian orthodoxy, the ultimate point of origin, source of meaning, and longed-for object. Moreover, they are enlightened by the messenger's words—his descriptions of the glorious visions of heaven. The gaze in these evocations is dual, both directed toward and emerging from the visions portrayed. In a sense, its structure is partly reminiscent of the medieval scientific matrix by which the eye is a source of radiance that impresses its objects (extramission) and also a receptor that is impressed by light radiating from its objects (intromission).[25] The subjectivizing gaze can be aligned both with the messenger's vision of the shimmering wonders of heaven, which brings the household hope, and the light that beams back from the wonders themselves, which presents a forceful contrast to earthly sources of illumination. Finally, the brilliance that emanates from the virgins is what heralds the culminating image of a marvelous convergence between light, vision, and knowledge: virgins, like other members of the company of heaven, are able to fulfill Christ's request on behalf of the apostles in John 17.3 that "they might know thee the only true God." It is significant that, at this moment, the author of *Sawles Warde* adapts the biblical citation to include concepts of seeing, as well as knowing. (The word "seon" does not have an equivalent in the original verse from John, a modification which supports the view that vision in *Sawles Warde* functions especially as a source and medium of knowledge; the Latin source text likewise includes no verb of seeing at this juncture.)[26] One of the implications of the text's climactic moment is that it is possible for the gaze of the Other (God) and that of the subject (virgin) to be crucially mirrored, "nebbe to nebbe," face to face.

The Gaze as Contentless

The focus on mirroring in *Sawles Warde* and *Hali Meiðhad*—especially the appearance in both texts of the phrase "nebbe to nebbe"—suggests an obvious parallel with Lacan's conception of the mirror stage as that which precipitates "the assumption of the armour of an alienating identity."[27] Staring God in the face in *Sawles Warde*, like identification with one's own specular image, betrays a promise of future wholeness that is nonetheless, within a Christian framework, continually deferred. Just as Lacan's mirror stage may be interpreted as a permanent structure of subjectivity, in the sense that it sustains the ego in a state of constant anticipation that it will achieve completeness (which it can never actually attain), *Sawles Warde* ends with Fortitude's observation that they continue to be separated ("tweamen") from God and the narrator's account of how the words of the messengers inspire each member of the household to accordingly "inȝong his warde" [maintain his watch] (*SW*, 106). The face-to-face motif in *Hali Meiðhad* figures forth an encounter between the look of the virgin and the look of Lechery that is itself confused in its lines of sight and precarious as a consequence. (While the conceit of the text is that Lechery advances on the virgin "nebbe to nebbe," the look of the virgin is also potentially and implicitly *coextensive* with that of Lechery.) Thus, in both texts, motifs of mirroring evoke a field of vision that is conceived as both attainable (in the future) and a domain of ceaseless and unremitting potentiality.

In this final section, I wish to draw out the significance of face-to-face encounters further, in order to reveal spaces where, despite numerous attempts to organize vision as a function of identity in these texts, the connections between motifs of sight and textual positions cannot finally be sustained. I propose that engagements with the mirror in anchoritic writings occasionally trouble the alignment of identity with vision. First, though, I wish to return to the issue of the psychoanalytic gaze. I suggested in the fore-going section that certain Lacanian concepts might, on the surface, be perceived as reinforcing links between vision and subjectivity; I argued that film theory's appropriation of these readings has produced a "pseudo-psychoanalytic" conception of the gaze. But, as Copjec explains, in Lacan's Seminar XI *le regard*, far from creating the possibility of a centered and transcendent subject, far from being aligned with a subject, is in fact *unoccupiable*; the subject is unable to be situated or situate itself in the field of the gaze, since this field denotes the subject's eradication.

This is a complex point and requires further elucidation. Let me backtrack with reference to the previously quoted passage from Seminar XI: "In the scopic field, the gaze is outside, I am looked at, that is to say, I am a picture. . . . What determines me, at the most profound level, in the visible, is the gaze that is outside."[28] Lacan is not suggesting here that there actually *is* a determining outside gaze in the sense of a gaze that is synonymous with a subject—he is not saying that the subject and the Other can ever be as one (in the way that, say, the virgins of *Sawles Warde* meet God face to face). The Lacanian maneuver is actually more radical than that. What is at stake is a concept of the gaze in which the subject, far from corresponding with or identifying with the gaze, is in fact *completely split off* from it. The gaze, Lacan states, is "not a seen gaze, but a gaze imagined by me in the field of the Other"—it is an imaginary phenomenon, established in the context of desire.[29] Copjec puts it thus:

> Lacan does not ask you to think of the gaze as belonging to an Other who cares about what or where you are, who pries, keeps tabs on your whereabouts, and takes note of all your steps and missteps, as the panoptic gaze is said to do. When you encounter the gaze of the Other, you meet not a seeing eye but a blind one. The gaze is not clear or penetrating, not filled with knowledge or recognition; it is clouded over and turned back on itself, absorbed in its own enjoyment. The horrible truth. . .is that *the gaze does not see you*. So if you are looking for confirmation of the truth of your being or

> the clarity of your vision, you are on your own; the gaze of the Other is not confirming; it will not validate you.[30]

In this way, Lacan constructs a very different hypothesis from that erected by so-called psychoanalytic film theory. In what might be taken as a radical, atheistic stance, Lacan's gaze is a contentless impossibility.

This is not to say that the gaze does not have any significance in a psychic fantasy—Lacan's point is that the subject is a desiring being who hankers after an impossible real (impossible because, beyond the field of imagery and signification, there is actually nothing); the fact that representation seems to gesture to something beyond itself—a gaze, a signified—is what causes a subject's desire, what, in short, founds the subject. The plentiful associations between vision, knowledge, and identity in anchoritic literature demonstrate the importance of a subjectivizing, signifying gaze in the lives of religious writers and devotees. As a modern nonbeliever I find the institutional framework of this fantasy less compelling, but still it sustains me to the extent that my integrity is grounded in the illusion that the Other *does* exist, that it *is* complete (if I am to put my faith instead, that is, in a psychoanalytic conception of subjectivity as a site of misrecognition). What I do take to be the implication of a reading process that refuses the religious—or fantasmatic—dimensions of a medieval text is that it pinpoints elements in that text where the process appears to fail.

One moment when this failure may potentially be seen to surface in *Sawles Warde* is the passage describing the messenger Love of Life's vision of the heavenly king. When asked by Prudence, one of the daughters of God who have come to assist the head of the household, whether he ever "sehe" God Almighty, Love of Life answers in the affirmative: "ȝe, i soð. . .Ich habbe isehen him often" [Yes, certainly. . .I have seen him often].[31] But the messenger qualifies this with another statement, that he has seen him

> nawt tah alswa as he is—for aȝein þe brihtnesse ant te liht of his leor þe sunne-gleam is dosc ant þuncheð a schadewe, ant forði ne mahte Ich nawt aȝein þe leome of his wlite lokin ne bihalden, bute þurh a schene schawere bituhhe me ant him schilde mine ehnen. (*SW*, 100)
>
> [not as he really is—for compared with the brightness and light of his countenance the sunlight is dark and seems like a shadow, and therefore I could not look towards the brilliance of his face or hold my gaze, except through a shining mirror between me and him which shielded my eyes.]

The Latin source text's evocation of this vision is briefer but similarly communicates, in the language of 1 Cor. 13.12, the notion of God's unrepresentability: "Vidi deum, sed per speculum et in enigmate" [I have seen God, but through a glass, darkly]. By the messenger's own admission, he requires a mirror envisaged as a screen—a *schawere* in Middle English or a *speculum* in Latin—in order to stomach the significance of the point of light that he claims is beyond. This confirms Lacan's supposition that apprehensions of the gaze would be traumatic, in that to encounter the Other in its radical nothingness is to experience dissolution—even a messenger from heaven is forced to look through a mirror *in enigmate*. Everything that the messenger *can* grasp is at the level of the signifier: Christ's suffering body, and the locations of his wounds. (Indeed, it is at Christ that the angels themselves never tire of looking.) The beyond of Christ's body, which is of course a figment of the imagination in Lacan's nontheological stance, is an impossible, if continually sought-after, space in the context of medieval religion. Just as Lacan, in Seminar XI, places considerable emphasis on the function of the screen in the structure of the visual domain—it is that which, as a field of mediation between the eye and the gaze, is "opaque" and, like the surface of a jewel, untraversable—the virgin-in-making who aspires to the position of a heavenly virgin in anchoritic texts can only do so by way of a mirror image (the heavenly virgin with whom she identifies) that is conceived as a screen (the space of identification that produces a point of contact with the gaze of God that is nonetheless impossible to bear).[32]

What I am suggesting, then, is that there is a degree of confluence between Lacanian gaze theory and early Middle English anchoritic writings, with the important difference that the latter make a considerable effort to resist the traumatic effects of approaching a gaze that is not all-seeing and all-knowing, that is impossibly and inaccessibly Other. In anchoritic discourse the Other is, of course, represented as inherently possible. But what if, in the midst of a continuing reiteration of this position, a reader refused to believe? What if they momentarily lapsed in their acceptance of the perceived links between vision and knowledge, or subjectivity and the gaze? These questions have implications for our understanding of the connections between vision and gender, and the relationship between medieval literary criticism and film theory. In a Lacanian argument *no* position produces a stable identity so that it is not possible to clear a space for the category of "woman" that is inhabitable as such. Anchoritic literature likewise allows no earthly space for the category of "virgin," which is, in fact, possible, since the virginal gaze that meets with God "face to face," the inhabitation of the panoptical tower of "heh sihðe," must always be postponed—at least, until one dies and goes to heaven. One is not born a virgin, nor can one simply become it; one has to desire the state, and desire is produced by generating the suspicion that something, beyond representation, is being hidden. These texts create that suspicion, and plenty of it. But they do not necessarily do so within a framework of dichotomous gender. The looks with which readers may identify shift variously between masculine and feminine positions: the reader of *Hali Meiðhad* is asked to periodically identify with the panoptical virginal gaze and to look down on other states of women; to imagine being beset by the looks of Lechery and the Devil; to reject the position of an abused, enslaved and objectified wife; and to shine like a sun in the sight of God. The author of *Sawles Warde* produces a mapping of vision in which the face of the Other is blinding and can only be apprehended "through a glass, darkly," while at the same time stressing the extent to which inhabitants of heaven are sights that are a pleasure to behold. In deflecting my analysis of these medieval writings through a reading of Foucauldian and Lacanian theories of vision, the point I am making is essentially straightforward in its implications: film theoretical discussions of "the gaze" arguably parallel the shifts and dissonances of vision that I have also attempted to uncover in anchoritic writings, between what might be perceived as a scientific tradition associating vision with knowledge and power, an "ocularphobic" tradition emphasizing the unrepresentability and invisibility of God, an extra-religious stance that asserts the impossibility of the Other's gaze, and a medieval doctrine of incarnation that asserts the ultimate visibility of, for example, Christ's body. These tensions create, in the Katherine Group, identities that maneuver between stability and potentiality, while at the same time being synonymous with neither. In both *Hali Meiðhad* and *Sawles Warde* the reader is asked to imagine positions simultaneously without and within identity: virgin-in-waiting and virgin-confirmed, Other-in-discourse and Other-in-fact. But these are not always positions that can be easily or stably organized into positions of empowerment and victimhood, or masculine and feminine. Virginity potentially disrupts views of selfhood as a fixed and immobile state, just as a visual hermeneutic sometimes complicates conceptions of an omnipotent, all-embracing space of knowledge—and the looks that inhabit anchoritic narratives do not necessarily allow this disruption to be contained.

Notes

1. I refer throughout to the following edition of the Middle English texts and translations: Bella Millett and Jocelyn Wogan-Browne (eds.), *Medieval English Prose for Women from the Katherine Group and* Ancrene Wisse (Oxford: Clarendon Press, 1990). Page numbers are provided in parentheses in the text and the following abbreviations have been used: *Seinte Margerete* (*SM*), *Hali Meiðhad* (*HM*), *Sawles Warde* (*SW*).

2. *The English Text of the Ancrene Riwle: Ancrene Wisse, from MS Corpus Christi College, Cambridge 402*, ed. J.R.R. Tolkien, Early English Text Society, original series 249 (Oxford: Oxford University Press, 1962), p. 31. For readings of *Ancrene Wisse* that foreground, like me, the unfixed and unstable elements of virginal identity, see Sarah Beckwith, "Passionate Regulation: Enclosure, Ascesis, and the Feminist Imaginary," *South Atlantic Quarterly* 93 (1994): 803–24; Anke Bernau, "Virginal Effects: Text and Identity in *Ancrene Wisse*," in *Gender and Holiness: Men, Women and Saints in Late Medieval Europe*, ed. Samantha J.E. Riches and Sarah Salih (London: Routledge, 2002), pp. 36–48; and Sarah Salih, "Queering *Sponsalia Christi*: Virginity, Gender, and Desire in the Early Middle English Anchoritic Texts," *New Medieval Literatures* 5 (2002): 155–75.
3. Elizabeth Robertson, *Early English Devotional Prose and the Female Audience* (Knoxville: University of Tennessee Press, 1990), p. 57.
4. Susannah Mary Chewning, "The Paradox of Virginity within the Anchoritic Tradition: The Masculine Gaze and the Feminine Body in the *Wohunge* Group," in *Constructions of Widowhood and Virginity in the Middle Ages*, ed. Cindy L. Carlson and Angela Jane Weisl (New York: Palgrave Macmillan, 1999), p. 127 [113–34].
5. Sarah Salih, *Versions of Virginity in Late Medieval England* (Cambridge, UK: D.S. Brewer, 2001), pp. 80–81.
6. For instance, in addition to Salih's discussion of spectacle in the legends of the three saints in *Versions of Virginity*, pp. 74–98, Jocelyn Price [Wogan-Browne], "The Virgin and the Dragon: The Demonology of *Seinte Margarete*," *Leeds Studies in English* n.s. 16 (1985): 337–57, presents a reading of *Seinte Margarete* that takes its visual hermeneutic as symptomatic of a broader thematic interest in the text in the distinction between the *unsehen* (un-seen) and the *unsehelich* (un-see-able); Gayle Margherita places the obsession with acts of looking in *Seinte Iuliene* in a psychoanalytic context in "Desiring Narrative: Ideology and the Semiotics of the Gaze in the Middle English Juliana," *Exemplaria* 2 (1990): 355–74, and *The Romance of Origins: Language and Sexual Difference in Middle English Literature* (Philadelphia: University of Pennsylvania Press, 1994), pp. 43–61; and Jocelyn Wogan-Browne considers, briefly, the trajectories of the tyrants' and saints' gazes in the Katherine Group in "The Virgin's Tale," in *Feminist Readings in Middle English Literature: The Wife of Bath and All Her Sect*, ed. Ruth Evans and Lesley Johnson (London: Routledge, 1994), pp. 178–81 [165–94].
7. Joan Copjec, "The Orthopsychic Subject: Film Theory and the Reception of Lacan," in *Read My Desire: Lacan against the Historicists* (Cambridge, MA: MIT Press, 1994), pp. 15–38. Copjec interrupts her analysis of film theory's relationship to Lacan with a review of what she describes as "orthopsychicism," a concept produced in response to the work of Gaston Bachelard and a topic that, for the sake of clarity, remains beyond the scope of my discussion here.
8. Michel Foucault, *Discipline and Punish: The Birth of the Prison*, trans. Alan Sheridan (London: Penguin, 1977), p. 201.

9. Copjec, "Orthopsychic Subject," pp. 16–19, citing Mary Ann Doane, Patricia Mellencamp, and Linda Williams (eds.), *Re-vision: Essays in Feminist Film Criticism,* The American Film Institute Monograph Series 3 (Los Angeles: University Publications of America, 1984), p. 14.
10. John Berger, *Ways of Seeing* (London: BBC and Penguin, 1972), p. 47. A.C. Spearing, *The Medieval Poet as Voyeur: Looking and Listening in Medieval Love-Narratives* (Cambridge, UK: Cambridge University Press, 1993), pp. 22–24, cites Berger's formulation as an influence.
11. Laura Mulvey, "Visual Pleasure and Narrative Cinema," *Screen* 16.3 (1975), 13 [6–18], reprinted in Mulvey, *Visual and Other Pleasures* (London: Macmillan, 1989), pp. 14–26. See the comments again of Spearing, *Medieval Poet as Voyeur*, pp. 23–24; and Madeline H. Caviness, *Visualizing Women in the Middle Ages: Sight, Spectacle, and Scopic Economy* (Philadelphia: University of Pennsylvania Press, 2001), pp. 25–27.
12. See for example Lorraine Gamman and Margaret Marshement (eds.), *The Female Gaze: Women as Viewers of Popular Culture* (London: Women's Press, 1988), and Griselda Pollock, *Vision and Difference: Femininity, Feminism, and Histories of Art* (London: Routledge, 1988).
13. Salih, *Versions of Virginity*, p. 85. See also Wogan-Browne, "The Virgin's Tale," pp. 178–81, for a comparable argument about the "rescripting" of the gaze in the Katherine Group saints' lives.
14. For a summary of medieval scientific discourses on vision, see Suzannah Biernoff, *Sight and Embodiment in the Middle Ages* (New York: Palgrave Macmillan, 2002), esp. pp. 63–84.
15. Discussions of the "virginal gaze"—the line of sight associated with virginal identity—have to date centered largely on the figure of the Virgin Mary: see, especially, Sarah Stanbury, "The Virgin's Gaze: Spectacle and Transgression in Middle English Lyrics of the Passion," *PMLA* 106 (1991): 1083–93. Stanbury, locating herself within a film theoretical frame, argues that the Virgin's gaze in fifteenth-century passion lyrics frequently stands in for the gaze of an (implicitly or explicitly) male spectator/reader, but suggests that the representation of such a mode of looking also constructs an important space for female potency since it "jockeys with and even at times resists textual strategies for controlling her [the Virgin's] lines of sight" (p. 1091).
16. Copjec, "Orthopsychic Subject," p. 22.
17. Jacques Lacan, "The Mirror Stage as Formative of the Function of the I as Revealed in Psychoanalytic Experience," in *Écrits: A Selection*, trans. Alan Sheridan (London: Routledge, 1977), pp. 1–7. For a helpful discussion of the role of vision in Lacanian theory, see Martin Jay, *Downcast Eyes: The Denigration of Vision in Twentieth-Century French Thought* (Berkeley: University of California Press, 1993), pp. 339–70; for a concise, but lucid, account of the mirror stage in Lacan's thought, see Dylan Evans, *An Introductory Dictionary of Lacanian Psychoanalysis* (London: Routledge, 1996), pp. 114–116. Mulvey's exploitation of the mirror stage argument occurs in "Visual Pleasure and Narrative Cinema," pp. 9–10.

18. Jacques Lacan, *The Four Fundamental Concepts of Psycho-Analysis (Seminar XI)*, ed. Jacques-Alain Miller, trans. Alan Sheridan (London: Vintage, 1998), p. 106.
19. This version of the gaze parallels Jean-Paul Sartre's analysis of *le regard* as that which allows the subject to recognize the subjectivity of the Other: "my fundamental connection with the Other-as-subject must be able to be referred back to my permanent possibility of *being seen* by the Other. It is in and through the revelation of my being-as-object for the Other that I must be able to apprehend the presence of his being-as-subject"; Sartre, *Being and Nothingness: An Essay on Phenomenological Ontology*, trans. Hazel E. Barnes (London: Routledge, 1958), p. 256. As Evans points out, although Lacan initially embraced Sartre's conception of the gaze, he went on to develop a theory of the gaze quite distinct from Sartre's in that for Lacan the gaze is always on the side of the Other; Evans, *Introductory Dictionary of Lacanian Psychoanalysis*, p. 72.
20. Thus it might be argued that the panoptic gaze that Copjec critiques in *Read My Desire* is a construct that is not as unamenable to a psychoanalytic viewpoint as Copjec makes out: after all, Jacques-Alain Miller, the editor of Lacan's seminars and a practicing psychoanalyst, published an essay on the subject in 1975 that interprets Bentham's machine in terms that recall Foucault's political analysis in *Discipline and Punish* (published in French in the same year) while at the same time resonating with the Lacanian theory of the split between eye and gaze that is the basis for Copjec's conclusions about representation. See Jacques-Alain Miller, "La Despotisme de l'utile: la machine panoptique de Jeremy Bentham," *Ornicar?* 3 (1975): 3–36, translated as Jacques-Alain Miller, "Jeremy Bentham's Panoptic Device," *October* 41 (1987): 3–29. Nonetheless, as I argue in the final section of this chapter, there are aspects of the Lacanian gaze that are irreconcilable with the panoptical apparatus to the extent that, for Lacan, *le regard* is not an eye that sees or is filled with knowledge.
21. The Latin text of *De custodia interioris hominis* on which I draw here is reproduced in *Memorials of St. Anselm*, ed. R.W. Southern and F.S. Schmitt, Auctores Britannici Medii Aevi 1 (Oxford: Oxford University Press, 1969), pp. 354–60; an almost word-for-word Middle English translation of the treatise is contained in Dan Michel's fourteenth-century *Ayenbite of Inwyt*, ed. Richard Morris, Early English Text Society, original series 23 (London: Trübner, 1866), pp. 263–71. For discussion, see Millett and Wogan-Browne, *Medieval English Prose for Women*, pp. xxv–xxvii. Anne Eggebroten mistakenly identifies the original context for the Latin source as Hugh of St. Victor's *De Anima*, when *De custodia interioris hominis* is in fact an independent work associated in the Middle Ages, as I have already suggested, with Anselm. Nonetheless, the comparisons Eggebroten draws between *Sawles Warde* and the Latin text in the context of gender are insightful: see Eggebroten, "*Sawles Warde*: A Retelling of *De Anima* for a Female Audience," *Mediaevalia* 10 (1984): 27–47.
22. *De custodia interioris hominis*, pp. 356, 358.

23. *De custodia interioris hominis*, p. 359.
24. *De custodia interioris hominis*, p. 359.
25. Biernoff, *Sight and Embodiment*, pp. 71–73.
26. *De custodia interioris hominis*, p. 359: "Haec est vita aeterna, ut cognoscant te deum verum, et quem misisti Iesum Christum" [This is eternal life, that they might know you the true God and Jesus Christ whom you have sent].
27. Lacan, "Mirror Stage," p. 4.
28. Lacan, *Four Fundamental Concepts*, p. 106.
29. Lacan, *Four Fundamental Concepts*, p. 84.
30. Copjec, "Orthopsychic Subject," p. 36. Margherita, characterizing the legend of Juliana as "excessive in its fetishistic relation to the act of looking," makes a case for the construction of a "putatively extrasemiotic gaze" on the side of the saint, metaphorically linked to the omnipresent "eh-sihðe" of Christ, that evokes a Lacanian-style split between eye and gaze, where the gaze is nonetheless "finally unapprehensible"; Margherita, *Romance of Origins*, pp. 52–53.
31. *De custodia interioris hominis*, p. 358.
32. Lacan, *Four Fundamental Concepts*, p. 96.

PART THREE

TROUBLED REPRESENTATIONS

CHAPTER 7

VISION BEYOND MEASURE: THE THRESHOLD OF IACOPONE'S BEDROOM

Cary Howie

This chapter articulates and extends the relationship among eros, space, and visuality in the lyrics of the thirteenth-century devotional poet and polemicist Iacopone da Todi. Hyperbolic vision, vision beyond measure, exemplifies that intensification of the senses that Iacopone's participatory poetics at once spatially confines and sets loose.

There is a sense in which medieval visionary literature offers its readers a lesson in visual hyperbole: in these texts one does not just see; one pushes vision to its breaking point. In Julian of Norwich's writings, for example, it is a question of a dialectic of the seen and the hidden, intensified by meditation: "At one time," she writes, early in her *Revelation*, "I saw how halfe the face, begyning at the ere, overrede [overrode, overspread] with drie blode til it beclosid to the mid face, and after that, the tuther halfe beclosyd on the same wise."[1] This chapter argues that—for a tradition of medieval piety that extends from Julian's lexicon of enclosure perhaps as far back as Augustine, whose epiphany with Monica takes place, after all, precisely at the window of a villa—a mode of spatial intensification might accompany this kind of sensory intensification. More specifically, the following pages attempt to delineate the contribution of the Italian poet Iacopone da Todi (d. 1306) to a spatial optics that would also be a kind of poetics. That vision is, for certain modes of medieval devotion, not necessarily discrete from the other senses, especially touch, has been eloquently argued in a recent book by John Milbank and Catherine Pickstock. Their claims, made vis-à-vis Aquinas, will haunt this chapter as it addresses to what extent sensation, in the lyrics of this radical Franciscan, might participate (never immanently but analogically) in transcendence, and to what extent this participation might be figured in terms of space.[2]

Despite his lack of fame in the anglophone world, Iacopone da Todi remains the most significant of Italy's medieval devotional poets: a convert from the bourgeois dynamism that characterized so much of thirteenth-century Umbria, he spent several years as a wandering penitent before officially entering the Franciscan Order relatively late in life. His poems, composed in the dance-like meter of the *lauda*, vary widely in tone and content, having in common at most a commitment to extravagance (or immoderation, *esmesuranza*) in the exposition of the penitential and contemplative lives. Even within the corpus that modern scholarship has deemed more or less certainly of his hand, Paolo Canettieri observes, "it is not in fact possible to make Iacopone's literary production fit into a unifying frame, either thematically or metrically."[3] Iacopone thus gives a unifying name to a heterogeneous group of texts, in a paradox of authorship and authority that would no doubt have suited his taste for contradiction. He remains, for Lino Leonardi and Francesco Santi, "second only to Dante in the *duecento*, for both the dimensions of his body of work and its manuscript diffusion."[4]

Still, if *esmesuranza* is the fulcrum of Iacopone's poetics, and if one concedes (with Contini and all more recent scholarly appraisals) that this immoderation is steeped in a profound Latin and theological culture,[5] it is worth asking just how Iacopone inflects this crucial term. A typical utterance lies at the heart of laud 92, "Sopr'onne lengua amore," when Iacopone asks, "Amor esmesurato, perché me fai empascire?" [Measureless Love, why are you driving me crazy?] (92, l. 145).[6] Yet, even as the crucial phrasing of the divine "beyond" remains the "ultra esmesurato" (39, l. 90), Iacopone can argue that a brief moment of earthly delight may have as its reward measureless punishment, or measurelessness *as* punishment [*penar 'n esmesuranza*] (19, l. 48). Indeed, laud 44, "O anema mia, creata gintile," uses *esmesuranza* more synthetically, to describe both the heart's callous self-surrender to the senses (44, ll. 32–35) and the transcendence that it forfeits in doing so (44, ll. 57–58). *Esmesuranza* can thus be mapped, I would argue, onto the semantic field of outrage, comprising both offense and excess.

It is worth recalling that Dante uses the term only once, to indicate not divine transcendence but the most outrageous pride, and to indicate it within—or actually beyond—the field of vision. At the entrance to the pit, which will lead the pilgrim and Virgil to hell's final frozen circle, Dante asks: "S'esser puote, io vorrei / che de lo smisurato Brïareo / esperïenza avesser li occhi miei" [If it is possible, / I'd like my eyes to have experience / of the enormous one, Briareus]. Virgil informs the pilgrim that he will have to content himself with another giant, Antaeus: "Quel che tu vuo' veder / più là è molto / ed è legato e fatto come questo, / salvo che più feroce par nel volto" [The one you wish to see lies far beyond / and is bound up and just as huge as this one, / and even more ferocious is his gaze].[7] Dante thus presents Briareus's "smisuranza" as a (denied) object of vision, located "più là," in a beyond that mirrors, and reverses, the divine "ultra esmesurato" of which Iacopone speaks. The measureless thus marks the place at which virtue and vice are *visibly* difficult to tell apart, where conversion and perversion meet at the barest point of turning. It is, likewise, a situation not of spatial mediocrity but of spatial extremity: the seat of the *Deus absconditus* in the very belly of hell.[8] Francesco Santi observes that, for Iacopone, "il crocefisso è posto per così dire al confine estremo del cosmo: al di qua è il niente; al di là è il tutto" [the Crucified is placed so to speak at the extreme boundary of the cosmos: on this side, nothingness; on that side, the all].[9] Even the most abject forms of nothingness—here figured as the "lost" sinner or the "measureless" hell-bound giant—participate in this "tutto," which should not be understood metaphysically but, instead, as the very name of participative recuperation.

Measure is a crucial category of sensation for no less a thinker than Bonaventure, to whose treatise on *The Soul's Journey to God* [*Itinerarium mentis in Deum*] Iacopone's angelology, but also much of his neoplatonic repertoire in general, is heavily indebted (for example, lauds 77, 84). It will come as no surprise, in the light of this neoplatonism, that measure is *visible* for Bonaventure. According to the first chapter of the *Itinerarium*, the sensory perception of the world takes account of things in themselves, "see[ing] in them their weight, number and measure" [videt in eis pondus, numerum et mensuram]. Furthermore, measure is defined as that "by which things are determined" [quam limitantur], and is associated, through the ensuing parallelisms, with "order" [ordinem] and "activity" [operationem]. But Bonaventurean measure is, above all else, one means of rising from creation to Creator: "From all these considerations the observer can rise, as from a vestige, to the knowledge of the immense power, wisdom, and goodness of the Creator" [Ex quibus consurgere potese sicut ex vestigio ad intelligendum potentiam, sapientiam, et bonitatem Creatoris immensam].[10] It is clear that Iacopone shares Bonaventure's association of measure with order: in a famous moment of mystical backtalk, Iacopone responds to God's demand to "ordena questo amore" [set this love in order] (89, l. 147) by asserting, "Quanno sì esmesurato me tte davi, tollivin' da me tutta mesuranza" [When you gave yourself to me so immoderately, you took all moderation from me] (89, ll. 189–90). Yet if measure, precisely in its limiting quality [quam limitantur], allows the observer visually to rise up to God, why does Iacopone need to emphasize the measureless? That is to say, is not Bonaventure's notion of measure already, and sensorially, ecstatic?

This is, in fact, the lesser-known antecedent to Iacopone's poetics of the measureless. For, as Elena Landoni has most recently observed, Iacopone is responding here to the rhetoric of Occitan lyric as well: in his famous exposition of the virtuous "mean" or "middle way" (laud 43, "O mezzo virtüoso, retenut'a bataglia"), Iacopone "clarifies unequivocally that to reach that 'mean' one must laboriously pass through a stage of being caught up, without reservation or remainder, in the two opposite extremes of love and hatred. . .and so on: a radical reversal of reasonable, aristocratic *mezura*."[11] Landoni makes fleeting reference to the late troubadour Guilhem de Montanhagol when describing the reluctance of even late Occitan verse to relinquish a courtly commitment to *mezura*; what remains to be made explicit in her argument is the extent to which moderation (and its rejection in Iacopone) can be construed spatially and sensibly. If Montanhagol's sincere lover "non es desmezuratz" [is not immoderate], and this moderation is situated *between* two terms, "entre .l trop e .l pauc mezura jatz" [too much and too little], Iacopone's "mezzo virtuoso" [virtuous mean] is still more dynamically spatialized.[12] In laud 43, the mean is a "travaglia," an ordeal, and Iacopone's sequence of opposites results less in synthesis than in a sense of fundamentally unstable, dynamic aporia. While Montanhagol's restful *mezura* lies down, "jatz," as if suspended in a hammock, Iacopone's *mezzo* consists of, among other things, "sperare e desperare stare enn una masone" [hope and despair staying in one house] (43, l. 13), and "escecurtà e temore demorar 'nn una corte" [security and fear abiding in one court] (43, l. 17): a series of cohabitations culminating not in a happy marriage but, instead, sharp contrast. Iacopone warns, "Altro è lo patere che l'odirlo parlare" [Hearing about this and enduring it are two different things] (43, l. 38); similarly, "A chi non l'à provato non lo pò emagenare" [he who has felt it can't conjure its image for someone who hasn't] (43, l. 50). Sight and sound signally part ways here: sight is, like "provare," vicariously inaccessible, whereas sound marks the very place of this vicarious (and useless) sensation. Whereas sound is on *this* side of feeling, sight is over there, just a bit beyond and within.

Iacopone, furthermore, ends this exposition of the *mezzo* by placing himself, as it were, close to the knives: "demoro entro le forfece, ciascun coltel m'affétta, / abrevio mea ditta, en questo loco finare" [I abide between the scissors, each blade cuts me, / I'll shorten my speech, to end in this place] (43, ll. 61–62). This paradoxical place is not unlike that of a magician's assistant closed inside a box stuck through with swords. It is bound up with a crucial speech act (the abbreviated "ditta" like an abracadabra) and rests upon a simultaneity of places—inside and outside, between the blades and pierced through by them—sustained by an optical illusion. For evidence of this mystical optics, we must look to the sixty-fifth laud in Mancini's edition, bound up as it is with the very technique of abbreviation, which both marks the "loco" of contradiction and brings it to an end here. First, however, let me merely emphasize that Iacopone's emphasis upon such an unbearable *mezzo* is precisely the Bonaventurean, and thus philosophical, inflection of what will elsewhere appear as specifically anti-courtly *esmesuranza.* Stated positively (as aporetic *mezzo*) or negatively (as excessive *esmesuranza*), the place of spiritual ordeal remains, paradoxically, the contradictory house whose roof gets broken open by anagogic "consurgere," whose walls are torn by scissors.

Evelyn Underhill, one of the first and most prolific modern scholars of mysticism, notes, in her 1911 "spiritual biography" of Iacopone, that "Omo chi vòl parlare," laud 65 in Mancini's edition, "can hardly be offered to the modern reader," inasmuch as it contains "a peculiarly daring and detailed description of the Spiritual Marriage."[13] Her move is not unlike that of many medieval exegetes of the Song of Songs, a text that puts the S/M in Spiritual Marriage: one must be careful that these precariously theological erotic texts don't fall into the wrong hands.[14] Underhill says to her readers: look at what I'm *not* showing you; hear the thud of bedroom noises behind my "daring and detailed description." Underhill thus very primly lets her tongue slip through the alliterative gap in her denial, as the cataphatic presence at the heart of her negation.[15]

Iacopone's poem begins by asserting its own status as discourse, and specifically "brief" discourse. Brevity has a range of meanings for Iacopone, only some of them stylistic: "abrivïare" indicates sensory mortification in laud 19, for example,[16] while it serves a mnemonic purpose in laud 40,[17] and designates the humility of the Incarnation in laud 44.[18] Here, however, Iacopone admits, "el longo abrivïare / sòle l'om delettare" [abbreviating what is long / generally gives men pleasure] (65, ll. 7–8). It is just such "delettare" that abbreviation is supposed to *remedy* in laud 19's account of the senses. Abbreviation thus becomes the stylistic sign of apophasis: it at once produces and denies delight, foregrounding the sensory component of poetry (the mnemonic value, but also the humility, of rhythm and rhyme) while inscribing a negation at the heart of the sensible. In this way, the dialectic of length and brevity, delight and mortification, which abbreviation makes sensible, renders in more erotic form the structure of speech and closure in the poem on the virtuous mean. Abbreviation is thus a companion to irony, while more explicitly concerned than the latter with an aporetic *recuperation* of what it denies: delight, length, and sense.

Having thus situated his poetic practice in an apophatic theology, Iacopone announces that he will give an account "De l'omo ch'è ordenato / La 've Deo se reposa, / Ell'alma ch'è sua sposa" [of the ordered man, / that place where God rests / in the soul which is his bride] (65, ll. 14–16). Keeping in mind that order and measure are intimately connected both for Bonaventure and for Iacopone, and that the place of the rapt soul is precisely associated in laud 92 with what is *beyond* order and measure, it is curious to see Iacopone's description of the *ordered* man as this amalgam of bride and bridal bed, place and spouse, wherein God rests. It is as though Iacopone were spelling out here, in abbreviated form, the way in which metonymy draws participation (of body in place, place in God) from contiguity. But something more is at work here, even at the level of tropes. Iacopone proceeds to elaborate the characteristics of this body/bed as though it were a traditional schematic *allegory*, thus radicalizing the allegorical through the participative contamination established through the poem's initial metonymies. The ordered mind, according to this metonymic allegory, is a bed with four feet [*la mente sì è 'l letto*] (65, l. 17). Its frame is bound with rope; a blanket lies on top of its mattress, which itself lies on top of a coarser mattress [*saccone*] laid directly upon the rope supports. The lower parts of the bed correspond to parts of the soul: the feet, for example, are the four cardinal virtues (prudence, justice, temperance, fortitude). Yet, as the description ascends, the soul's place in the allegorical tenor gives way to Christ: the mattress is "Cristo pro me pazzo" [Christ crazy for me] (65, l. 46) and the headboard "Cristo ch'en croce sale" [Christ ascending the cross] (65, l. 50). The bedsheets, however, are "lo contemplar che vola" [contemplation in flight] (65, l. 54), a surface enclosure that comprehends both Christ's humanity and the virtuous soul. The allegory of the bed thus depends upon the cohesion of its contiguous components: they touch, and thus merge, into the contemplative flight where distinguishing subject from object is no easy task.

But this segue from contiguity to participation does not merely occur as something *transferred* from the allegorical vehicle (the sheet-swathed bed) to its tenor (the contemplatively enclosed God-and-soul). The allegorical tenor, in fact, *touches* its vehicle; Iacopone thus fills in the gap that separates them, inscribing metonymy at the heart of allegory:

Coperto è de speranza
A ddarme ferma certanza
de farme cittadino
en quell'abbergo devino.
La caritate 'l iogne
e con Deo me coniogne;

iogne la vilitate
cun la divina bontate.
Ecco nasce un amore,
c'à emprenato el core,
pleno de disiderio,
d'enfocato misterio.
Preno enliquedisce,
languenno parturesce;
e parturesce un ratto,
nel terzo cel è tratto. (ll. 57–72)

[[The bed] is covered with Hope,
to give me a firm certainty
of becoming a citizen
of that divine lodging.
Charity reaches [joins] it,
and joins me with God;
it joins my lowliness
with God's goodness.
Behold, a love is born,
which has [for charity has] impregnated the heart,
full of desire,
of inflamed mystery.
Thus filled it liquefies,
languishing it gives birth;
it gives birth to rapture
and is drawn up into the third heaven.]

Iacopone effectively *inflates* the space of the allegorical vehicle, allowing Charity, ostensibly part of the tenor, to touch it, and thus to be comprehended within it. The bed thereby exceeds the sterile and vaguely two-dimensional world of correspondence, entering into an active relation with a term that it would ordinarily be expected to *represent*. To spell this out: Charity reaches the bed, slips under the covers, but also *joins* it (this is the double meaning of "iogne") as a kind of acting-out, in the literally virtuous terms of the earlier correspondence-allegory, of that joining which is then made explicit as that which happens between "God" and "me." To be more precise, it is only through Charity's humping the bed that God and I can come together. In fact, Charity and the bed are joined just as God and I are joined, but this "just as" indicates not the gap of a comparison but the common border whereby one term, or pair of terms, *participates* in the other. One could almost say that allegory passes, through metonymy, into something like a new literalism, a spaced-out (and thus no longer immanent) immediacy.

Iacopone's poem thus offers, among other things, a critique *avant* or *dans la lettre*, of Paul de Man's reading of symbol and allegory. According to de Man, the symbol's structure, in Romantic poetics, "is that of the synecdoche, for the symbol is always a part of the totality that it represents." In allegory, as in irony, "the sign points to something that differs from its literal meaning and has for its function the thematization of this difference," a difference articulated *temporally*.[19] Inasmuch as, for de Man, parts that ostensibly represent wholes more often than not reduce to the very totalities they claim to represent, they cannot accommodate temporality as the mark of internal difference. Allegory, according to this reading, not only accommodates such difference but knows it does so. In response to de Man, I would argue that metonymy offers a relationship of contiguity (indeed, contiguity as enclosure) that does not swallow part into whole but, rather, preserves each of its terms in the *surface* upon which they touch. Metonymy is thus the trope of borders, tact, and the very *spaciousness* of these.

To be sure, there are precedents for the bed's pivotal role in binding discrete terms, rhetorical and otherwise, into a basic sameness. Indeed, one wonders whether the medieval ear would have been able to hear the participative proximity of *legare* [to bind] to *leggere* [to read], and from *letto* [read] to *letto* [bed]. Bernard of Clairvaux allows spatial contiguity, spatial enclosure, and sameness to overlap in his classic exposition of nuptial union with God: "They [Bride and Bridegroom] share the same inheritance, the same table, the same home, the same marriage-bed, they are flesh of each other's flesh."[20] With the turn to Christ's passion in thirteenth-century devotion, it is inevitable that this bed should become conflated with the cross. Angela of Foligno, Iacopone's contemporary, uses precisely this conflation to inscribe the crucifixion, and its material exhaustion, at the heart of the soul's ineffable union with God. This latter "darkness" enables Angela to see neither more nor less than Christ's humanity: "In short, what proceeds from those eyes and that face [of Christ] is what I said that I saw in that previous darkness which comes from within, and which delights me so that I can say nothing about it."[21] Indeed, Angela's reiteration of the "joy of the humanity of Christ" causes her to break into song:

> At this moment, my desire is to sing and praise:
>
> I praise you God my beloved;
> I have made your cross my bed.
> For a pillow or cushion,
> I have found poverty,
> and for other parts of the bed,
> suffering and contempt to rest on.

> When I, brother scribe, asked her for a better explanation of what she had said, Christ's faithful one added: This bed is my bed to rest on because on it Christ was born, lived and died. . .On this bed I believe I die and through this bed I believe I am saved. I cannot describe the joy which I expect from those hands and feet and the marks from the nails which pierced them on that bed.[22]

This is, fascinatingly, the only poem—strictly speaking, a *lauda*—in the entire text of the *Memorial.* Its structural symmetry to Iacopone's poem is striking: the bed's "parts" correspond to the various components of abjection, just as Iacopone's bed begins by corresponding to the various virtues. Yet the bed remains a *surface* here, a plane on which Angela can identify with Christ, suffer with Him; Angela does not meld with the bed, and Christ does not join it as he joins her. In this way, it stops short (though just barely, and perhaps with a sense of the participative abbreviation we have seen in Iacopone) of Iacopone's impregnating junction of space and time, divine and mortal bodies, tenor and vehicle, allegory and metonymy.

For Iacopone's bed of contiguous union is also a childbearing bed. While theologically similar to Meister Eckhart's "birth of God in the soul," it nonetheless suggests, where Eckhart describes the "detachment" of the soul from materiality, the metonymic participation of the material in the strictly spiritual.[23] In a construction sandwiched between giving birth to love and giving birth to rapture (and it is unclear, and for Iacopone beside the point, whether this is really one birth or two), the heart becomes pregnant and liquefies, swells up and dissolves. Birth precedes and follows a dissolute pregnancy. And when rapture is born, it drags the heart, as though by its umbilical cord, into the third, seraphic, heaven. If this is so, Iacopone is suggesting that mystical ascent is not a matter of levitating gracefully upward, toes flexed toward the earth; rather, if rapture is the child pulling its mother to heaven, it is pulling her by the womb, and she (or he) is ascending upside-down, her (or his) legs in the air.

This inverted ascent, with its echoes of metonymy's "dragging" [*trahit*] in the *Ad Herennium*,[24] thus appears to participate quite literally in what Sarah Beckwith has called the "violently inverting tactics" of Franciscanism.[25] These "tactics," namely "replacing health with sickness, embracing the leprous and the maimed, the high with the low, its embrace of filth and flesh, its emphatic fetishizing of Christ's torn and bleeding body as the object, indeed subject, of compassion and passion," are, in Iacopone, also *tactile.* There is no doubt that Iacopone is playing here with gender as a kind of *coincidentia oppositorum.* True, Evelyn Underhill once swooned at the thought of Iacopone's masculine prowess: in the course of her study, she speaks of his "rough male brutality" and his "virile spirituality."[26] And every account of Iacopone's life is careful to give him a wife, usually named Vanna, who dies tragically when the balcony she is dancing on collapses, thus securing our hero's heterosexuality and observance of gender oppositions just in time to cut them short. Yet if Iacopone's "omo" is a manly man, he is pregnant in the way that too much testosterone can cause a weightlifter's breasts to swell: masculinity spills over, swells out, into the feminine. This would not necessarily be surprising, if we consider a Franciscan faithfulness to the letter of scripture in light of Stephen Moore's reading, in *God's Gym*, of the ways in which the masculine excesses of the Old Testament God have distinctly (or actually indistinctly) feminizing consequences.[27] This would give new, or perhaps merely radical, meaning to Francesco Santi's observation of the "hermaphroditism" that underlies Iacopone's poems.[28]

Yet this is perhaps the least radical aspect of what is happening in Iacopone's bed. To sum up: love is born of the bed, and all of a sudden we are bounced right up to the third heaven, but something has come out of us in the meantime, pulling us by the womb (but let's say also—against an abiding prudishness about saints' bodies not shared by saints themselves, and with a commitment to contiguous zones—by the twat, by the asshole, by the balls) into that realm of *esmesuranza* that Iacopone elsewhere describes, and undescribes, in great detail. In fact, inasmuch as these paradoxes draw upon sensory language, we might ask how we know what we're seeing in this scene of rapture, birth, and generative dry humping. The only time Iacopone calls attention to visual mechanics in the poem is when he announces that the bed has four feet to rest on, "como en figura el vidi" [just as I saw it in a figure] (65, l. 20). Sight is linked to representation. The bed is based on another bed. Plato, curiously, gives a reading of the bed as object of representation (or the bed of representation) in *Republic*, to emphasize the aporia between Ideas and material imitations.[29] I nonetheless prefer to see Iacopone's bed as *conforming* to its model, its "as" [*como*] participating in God's "como esmesurato" [82.3]: *leaning* imitatively, reaching out to touch its "figura" just as charity reaches it, joins it, engenders with a touch. A metonymic connection is inscribed at the heart of representation: in Plato's terms, the bed here binds Idea, painter, and carpenter together.

Furthermore, in laud 92, "Sopr'onne lengua amore," Iacopone radically deconstructs the notion of the figural or the representative. He asks God, "Enfigurabel luce, / chi te pò figurare?" [Light beyond all figures, / who can figure you?] (92, ll. 17–18). At greater length, later on, he adds:

Se te vai figurando
imagen' de vedere
e per sapor sapere
que è lo esmesurato,

cridi poter, cercando,
enfinito potere,
sì com'è, possedere,
multo parm'engannato. (92, ll. 137–44)

[If you go figuring for yourself
an image to look at,
and strive to know by sensory knowledge
what the measureless is,
you believe that by seeking
infinite power
you can possess it,
and that seems to me very deceived.]

The poem is saturated with this kind of disfigured figuration, and develops a notion of visuality to support it: taken up and "trasformato" in God, the soul "sente que non sentio, / que non conubbe vede" [feels what it had not felt, and sees what it had not known or sensed] (ll. 73–74). *It even sees its own rapture*: the poem speaks of "là," there, that place, "v'el se vede ratto" [where he sees himself rapt] (l. 96). The mystical bedroom has mirrors on the ceiling, outdoing even the self-consciousness of de Man's allegory. And yet this vision is not immanent or exhaustible or, in the strongest sense, comprehensible. As if he has not been clear enough about this, Iacopone suggests that "Onne fede se cessa, / ché lli è dato vedere / . . . Vedere ciò che pensava, tutt'era cechetate" [All faith ceases, for now he is given sight. . .And seeing what he had previously thought, it was all blindness] (ll. 281–82, 289–90). I would like to suggest that Iacopone is not, perhaps even in spite of himself, denying sensation but rather opening up new sensory and, as it were, transsensory possibilities. This surplus of sight, and of the figuration that sight perceives and transmits to the refiguring powers of "volere" and "parlare," creates space: the "there," "là," where the soul's rapture is visible to itself. When the soul, in "Omo chi vòl parlare," gives birth to a rapture that pulls it (by the surplus) into the seraphic heaven, it gives birth to the bedroom, to the interstices between where it is and where it is going.

Thus the Song of Songs' entreaty, "come into my bedroom" [intra in cubiculum meum], is reworked in the following way: the heart's body, the "cor" that shapes the "corpo," gives birth to, expels, even as it is drawn inside, the place of its rapture. It is this heart-shaped bedroom that Iacopone invites us to see, with eyes that no longer constitute points from which a glance is thrown but which themselves dilate and contract, contain and, dissolving, give birth to what they see and where they see it. *And yet they do this because they have been touched.* The "inside" into which Iacopone's bed draws us, its contiguously generated enclosure, resonates thus with a stunning passage on space in Jean-Luc Nancy's *The Sense of the World*:

> In order to be understood as a world of sense—of "absent sense" or exscribed sense—the world must also be understood in accordance with the *cosmic* opening of space that is coming towards us. . .[with] the almost immobile speed of movements that do not so much *traverse* space as *open* it and *space it out* with their motives and motions, a universe in expansion and/or implosion. . .of which the unity is nothing but unicity [*unicité*] open, distended, distanced, diffracted, slowed down, differed, and deferred within itself.[30]

What Nancy maps out cosmologically could be said to resemble Iacopone's heart-shaped bedroom, and Nancy's non-immanently unitive "unicité" likewise echoes the "unione" in "trasformazione" that the bed of the heart engenders. Moreover, the notion of "spaces that are fleeing, curved back, invaginated, or exogastrulated" not only resonates with Iacopone's upside-down ascent to God, but dovetails nicely with his elliptical way of locating God in space. The first quatrain of "Sopr'onne lengua amore" hurls its oblique prepositions like boomerangs at their elusive object:

> Sopr'onne lengua amore,
> Bontà senza figura,
> Lume for de mesura,
> Resplende en lo mio core. (ll. 1–4)
>
> [Love above every tongue,
> Goodness without representation,
> Light outside all measure,
> Shines in my heart.]

Iacopone shows us the way back to the heart, but the *itinerarium* is one of going too far and coming up short, "sopra" and "senza," outside and inside, "for" and "en." The impression is of a heart convulsing: this is the pulse, the throb, the engendering spasm of a bed that beats.

Iacopone's bed thus acquires, through the rhythm of this oscillation of paradoxes, exactly the sort of *temporality* that rescues it from de Man's critique of the symbol. What is more, it conforms to a Franciscan poetics "whereby," according to Beckwith, "through the medium of Christ's body, identities are restored, transformed, revived, absorbed and submerged."[31] Iacopone's radicalization of Franciscan thought consists precisely in his *collocation* of crossing, all the transformations of "trans," at the heart of the heart, the body, the eyes, and the bed. When the soul's desire is "collocato / en quello esmesurato / d'onne ben Donatore" [placed / within the measureless / Giver of every good] (92, ll. 194–96), its enclosure is transitive, dynamic.

Gender, too, metonymically touches upon and participates in space: it is a masculine subject who sees himself rapt, just as it is a masculine subject who is urged, in the laud praising St. Francis, to "largatece morire / ['n] la font'ennamorato" [let yourself die / of love in that fountain] (40, ll. 187–88). If this masculine look, as subject, is in danger of a solipsistic vision in which it sees only itself, it is nonetheless, as object, always already touched, given, situated, spaced out. Looking at itself through God's specular place, the soul undergoes what might be called an "excorporative identification," right at the site, the mirror, which Lacan calls the "threshold of the visible world."[32] The soul does not assimilate what it sees; it is acted upon, it touches the seen, and is thereby drawn out of itself, across itself, into the edge of something new. The threshold stretches.

Notes

1. Julian of Norwich, *A Revelation of Divine Love*, ed. Marion Glasscoe, rev. edn. (Exeter: University of Exeter Press, 1993), p. 14.
2. See John Milbank and Catherine Pickstock, *Truth in Aquinas* (London: Routledge, 2001), p. 77. Space in this essay is never to be taken as *absolute* space, along the lines of the utter spatialization Pickstock describes and denounces in *After Writing: On the Liturgical Consummation of Philosophy* (Oxford: Blackwell, 1998), but rather as space *within* the absolute.
3. "non è infatti possibile far rientrare la produzione di Iacopone in un quadro unitario, relativamente ai temi come alle forme metriche utilizzate"; Paolo Canettieri, "*Laude* di Iacopone da Todi," in *Letteratura italiana: le opere*, ed. Alberto Asor Rosa, 8 vols. (Turin: Einaudi, 1992), 1:126 [121–52].
4. "secondo solo a Dante, nel Duecento, sia per l'ampiezza dell'opera, sia per la diffusione manocritta"; Lino Leonardi and Francesco Santi, "La letteratura religiosa," in *Storia della letteratura italiana*, ed. Enrico Malato, 10 vols. (Rome: Salerno, 1995), vol. 1, *Dalle origini a Dante*: 369 [339–404].
5. See for example Gianfranco Contini, *Poeti del duecento*, 2 vols. (Milan: Ricciardi, 1960), 2:62.
6. All references to Iacopone's poems cite laud and verse according to Mancini's edition: Jacopone da Todi, *Laude*, ed. Franco Mancini (Rome: G. Laterza, 1974). The translations are mine. An English version of the *Laude* nonetheless exists, which captures Iacopone's spirit while remaining too free for close textual scrutiny: Jacopone da Todi, *The Lauds*, trans. Serge and Elizabeth Hughes (London: SPCK, 1982).
7. *The Divine Comedy of Dante Alighieri*, trans. Allen Mandelbaum (Berkeley: University of California Press, 1980), p. 273 (*Inferno* 31.97–99, 103–105).
8. This is also an anti-dualistic gesture, and thus fully in the Augustinian tradition from which Bonaventure also draws heavily.
9. Francesco Santi, "La mistica di Iacopone da Todi," in *Iacopone da Todi: Atti del XXXVII Convegno storico internazionale, Todi, 8–11 ottobre 2000* (Spoleto: Centro italiano di studi sull'alto medioevo, 2001), p. 66 [47–70].

10. Saint Bonaventure, *Itinerarium Mentis in Deum*, trans. Philotheus Boehner, (Saint Bonaventure, NY: Franciscan Institute/Saint Bonaventure University, 1956), p. 45 (I.11). It is worth noting that the Platonic ascent is classically driven by vision: see Plato, *Phaedrus*, trans. C.J. Rowe (Warminster: Aris and Phillips, 1986).
11. "La stupenda descrizione del 'mezzo virtuoso,' in 43, chiarisce in modo inequivocabile che il faticoso raggiungimento di tale 'mezzo' passa attraverso un coinvolgimento senza riserve negli opposti estremi dell'amore e dell'odio. . .eccetera: rovesciamento radicale dell'aristocratica e ragionevole *mezura*"; Elena Landoni, *Il "libro" e la "sentenzia". Scrittura e significato nella poesia medievale: Iacopone da Todi, Dante, Cecco Angiolieri* (Milan: Vita e Pensiero, 1990), p. 40.
12. Peter T. Ricketts, *Les poésies de Guilhem de Montanhagol* (Toronto: Pontifical Institute of Medieval Studies, 1964), p. 111 (11, ll. 28, 30).
13. Evelyn Underhill, *Jacopone da Todi: A Spiritual Biography* (London: Dent, 1911), p. 84.
14. For a detailed philosophical account of Eros and monastic anxiety vis-à-vis the Song, see Denys Turner, *Eros and Allegory: Medieval Exegesis of the Song of Songs* (Kalamazoo: Cistercian Publications, 1995). Also useful is E. Ann Matter, *The Voice of My Beloved: The Song of Songs in Western Medieval Christianity* (Philadelphia: University of Pennsylvania Press, 1990).
15. "Cataphatic" names the affirmative, predicative strain of mystical (or, really, any) discourse. Turner explains: "there is a very great difference between the strategy of *negative propositions* and the strategy of *negating the propositional*; between that of the *negative image* and that of the *negation of imagery*. The first of each of these pairs belongs to the cataphatic in theology, and only the second is the strategy of the apophatic"; Turner, *The Darkness of God: Negativity in Christian Mysticism* (Cambridge, UK: Cambridge University Press, 1995), p. 35.
16. The five senses here compete to see which of them can most thoroughly renounce itself: "la loro delettanza leve / ciascheun brig' abriviare" [their frivolous delight / each one must abbreviate] (19, ll. 3–4).
17. Iacopone declares that he has "abbreviated" the seven "figures" of the cross shown to St. Francis "in order to count them" [.iole abbreviate / per poterle contare] (40, ll. 9–10).
18. "O esmesuranza en breve redutta, / cel, terra tutta veder 'nn un vasello" [O Measureless one, reduced to such brevity; / to see all of heaven and earth in one little vessel!] (44, ll. 57–58).
19. Paul de Man, "The Rhetoric of Temporality," in *Blindness and Insight: Essays in the Rhetoric of Contemporary Criticism* (Minneapolis: University of Minnesota Press, 1983), pp. 187–228 (esp. 191, 209).
20. Bernard of Clairvaux, *On the Song of Songs*, trans. Killian Walsh and Irene Edmonds (Kalamazoo: Cistercian, 1971), 7.2. Stephen D. Moore's provocative reading of this passage, and the Song of Songs commentaries in general, shares my sense of the queerness of mystical erotics, while

concentrating on earlier material and diverging significantly from my rhetorical concerns. See Moore, *God's Beauty Parlor, and Other Queer Spaces in and around the Bible* (Stanford: Stanford University Press, 2001), pp. 21–89.

21. Angela of Foligno, "Memorial," in Angela of Foligno, *Complete Works*, trans. Paul LaChance (New York: Paulist, 1993), p. 205.
22. Angela, "Memorial," pp. 205–206.
23. See Oliver Davies' account of Eckhart in "Later Medieval Mystics," in *The Medieval Theologians: An Introduction to Theology in the Medieval Period*, ed. G.R. Evans (Oxford: Blackwell, 2001), pp. 226–27 [221–32]. Iacopone may not be unique among male mystics in using the language of childbirth to speak of mystical union, but his emphasis on generation does break with what Caroline Bynum has described as the Cistercian preference for the nurturing aspect of motherhood. See Caroline Walker Bynum, *Jesus as Mother: Studies in the Spirituality of the High Middle Ages* (Berkeley: University of California Press, 1981), p. 150 [110–69]. Bynum's reading remains useful in mapping the differences between the Cistercian tradition and the later affective literature, especially Franciscan, inspired by it. On the Franciscan debt to the white monks, specifically in their "devotion to the person of Jesus," see R.W. Southern, *Western Society and the Church in the Middle Ages* (London: Penguin, 1970), p. 273 [240–99].
24. For the dragging or drawing forth of semantic continuity from contiguity, see *Rhetorica ad Herennium*, trans. Harry Caplan (Cambridge, MA: Harvard University Press, 1989), p. 335 (4.32.43).
25. Sarah Beckwith, *Christ's Body: Identity, Culture and Society in Late Medieval Writings* (London: Routledge, 1993), p. 52.
26. Underhill, *Jacopone da Todi*, pp. 89, 113.
27. Moore offers a disturbing complement to Bynum's account of Jesus as mother in his study of Yahweh as bodybuilder: "So hypermasculine did he become that his body ceased to be merely male, and began to sprout female parts. Far from being assuaged, his insecurities about this masculinity now had something new to feed on—a pair of female breasts"; Stephen D. Moore, *God's Gym: Divine Male Bodies of the Bible* (London: Routledge, 1996), p. 100.
28. He does so, however, with a more conservative notion of gender complementarity in mind. See Santi, "La mistica di Iacopone da Todi," pp. 58–59.
29. See Plato, *Republic*, trans. Desmond Lee (London: Penguin, 1974), pp. 422–26 (596b–598d).
30. Jean-Luc Nancy, *The Sense of the World*, trans. Jeffrey S. Librett (Minneapolis: University of Minnesota Press, 1997), p. 37.
31. Beckwith, *Christ's Body*, p. 52.
32. See Kaja Silverman, *The Threshold of the Visible World* (London: Routledge, 1996), pp. 10–37.

CHAPTER 8

SEX AND THE MEDIEVAL CITY: VIEWING THE BODY POLITIC FROM EXILE IN EARLY ITALIAN VERSE

Catherine M. Keen

This chapter considers representations of gender in the work of four Italian poets. Keen argues, in each case, that the use of courtly discourse to describe the realities of political domination troubles the lyric's visual imaginary, figuring the feminine "body politic" as the site of desire but also of shame and violence.

It may seem incongruous to borrow the title of a contemporary television series to open an investigation of medieval lyric poetry and, indeed, I will not attempt to draw any overextended connections between the two in the main body of this essay. My title however has a more than merely facetious intent, for one of the key points in my investigation of a selection of fourteenth-century Italian political lyrics is the importance of the city as the locus of contention over power and autonomy, expressed in terms of viewing and desiring the female body. In the Sex and the City programs, alluring images of the female body, and contention over the dynamics of power and desire, are explored in a specifically metropolitan context, which, the series' title suggests, qualifies these issues in a particular way. In my fourteenth-century texts, such qualification extends so far that the female body *is* the city: for I am concerned with a strand of political verse that addresses not a woman, but the feminine personification of a town.[1] Civic and social desires or aspirations are enunciated in these lyrics in terms of desire for the alluring city-lady [*città-donna*], object of the poetic subject's gaze.

This gaze does not imply mastery, for the spectator–speaker in the poems is positioned outside the city boundaries, in exile from the feminized body politic.[2] The problematic political and social relationship of the exile to his homeland—and the speakers here invariably assume a male voice—is explored through a range of visualizations of the *città-donna*. The corporeality imagined onto the city through the terms of the allegory often proves troubling, as indeed do the gender roles assigned to both city and poet. Although the poets normally speak from a male position, both they and the cities are represented sometimes as dominant and "masculine," sometimes as weak and "feminine," in the political/sexual roles that the allegories assign them. The *città-donna*, too, takes ambiguous shape under the gaze of the lover, who varies between desire and repulsion, action and passivity, in his relationship to the feminized corporeality imagined for her.

Personification of the city is a common device in the Old Testament, where the political vicissitudes of the chosen people are often expressed through the allegory of Jerusalem as widow, adulteress, or whore.[3] The lyrics that concern me undoubtedly draw on such biblical traditions, but their predominant idiom is courtly or pseudo-courtly. They borrow from the vernacular love tradition in order to represent the lyric "I" as the supplicant lover, lamenting his rejection by his beloved, the personified town. This courtly convention provides the frame of reference for verse by both serious courtly and/or moralistic writers and for those normally classified as non-courtly or *giocosi* [jocose]. Intriguingly, the personification device adds a categorically sexual element to these compositions almost regardless of conventional classifications of register, thanks to their inevitable concern with penetration.[4] The speakers' pleas for the favors of the *città-donna* have the ultimate, concrete objective of breaching the walls and gates that exclude them from the urban space, which the allegory visualizes as a female body. While verse that appears to address real women can remain ambiguous about what kind of union with the beloved is sought—hence the contention that has been generated around the notion of "courtly love"—the nature of the personification allegory makes an exile's desire for entry into the city into an unavoidably corporeal and sexual matter.[5]

In the lyrics, fulfillment of such desire is always problematic: the position of exile that the poets articulate effectively precludes successful union between lover and beloved, or at best postpones it to an indeterminate future. The relationship between the excluded lover and his excluding *città-donna* is represented in the courtly terms of *amor de lonh* [distant love].[6] To substitute, but also to exacerbate, frustrated desire, the exile is sometimes able to fix his gaze on the forbidding exterior of the city; at other times even vision is denied, or can be deputed only to the poet's imagination or to his works, playing on an Ovidian contrast between the physical constraints on the exile and his texts' free circulation.[7] As already noted, the lyrics predominantly mark the distance between the looker (the male exile) and his object (the female city) as signifying the former's absence of power. Even when the gaze seems to imply masculine objectivity or mastery in the allegorical love relationship, it is almost always in the negative framing context of a continuation of political disempowerment through exile. The lyric "I" thus occupies a position of emotional and sexual frustration that entails not only isolation but also disgrace, once the metaphors of distance are re-literalized back into the environment of city politics. The allegorized political subject matter of my selected lyrics makes it very evident that beneath their erotic metaphors lies an explicitly social and political agenda. Their writers are ultimately concerned with success in a primarily male, civic environment—and this again renders ambiguous the allegories' gender systems, that feminize the political community of the city (by representing it as a woman), and often cast the lyrics' male speakers in positions of emasculating disempowerment.[8]

Traditional courtly discourse uses the feudal imagery of powerful, semi-masculinized *donne* [ladies] and dependent male *serventi* [servants] to assign gender roles.[9] It may seem surprising that writers from the republican milieu of the Trecento Italian city-states should adopt this discourse to describe their political experiences. However, feudal metaphors had perhaps greater consequence for the cities' sociopolitical reality than initially appears. In the world of the city-states, the body politic was frequently under threat from internal factional violence, from the colonial rapacity of neighboring towns, or from claims to feudal dominion by superior powers such as papacy or Empire. By visualizing the city itself as a powerful *donna* imbued with seigneurial power, a figure that employs the imagery of the more hierarchical and more constitutionally normative world of feudalism, the poets can attempt to turn the tables so as to assert the strength, viability, and worth of their civic society.[10] At the same time, however, the fact that the writers assume the subservient position of the traditional courtly lover in their exiled relationships to the personified cities may reveal doubts about the ordering of this society. Indeed, not only are the lyric protagonists excluded from the *città-donna*'s aura of nobility and supremacy, but the allure of their desired but distant beloveds often proves deceptive.

The political circumstances framing these erotic allegories lead the lyricists almost invariably to cast their *donne* in ambiguous situations that undermine the discourse of courtliness. Some lyrics use misogynist stereotype to accuse the city herself of abandoning her idealized courtly attributes and of behaving with capricious female fickleness in favoring the rival political faction responsible for the speaker's banishment.[11] In other cases, the city is instead portrayed as a victim reduced by political vicissitude to an abject position of poverty, servitude, or dishonor; sometimes, too, the writers linger disturbingly over corporeal images of possession, which take on overtones of sexual violence or rape committed by the warring factions.[12] As the powerful *donna* puts off her elevated attributes, whether voluntarily or by force, the lover's constancy in turn becomes less a badge of merit and more a sign of madness [*follia*], one of the cardinal sins against the courtly code. Strains in the urban poets' use of courtly discourse become evident, as the female body politic, which we first envisaged as a locus of desire, is exposed as vulnerable or even repulsive, in suffering the consequences either of inconstant concupiscence or of violence and debasement. Thus the kind of cultural or political values that are represented by the gendered personifications of this political poetry emerge as increasingly insecure.

★ ★ ★

The political theme of exile first appears in Italian vernacular poetry in the mid-thirteenth century, in compositions emanating primarily from the city-states of Tuscany. The *caposcuola* [leader] of the early Tuscan writers, Guittone d'Arezzo, wrote several *canzoni* on politics and exile, relating both to his native Arezzo and to other Tuscan centers such as Pisa and Florence.[13] Only one of these sustains the device of city personification at any length: "Magni baroni certo e regi quasi" [Great barons indeed and almost kings], addressed to the joint heads of the Pisan *Comune*, Ugolino della Gherardesca and Nino Visconti.[14] Given Guittone's stern religious convictions, it is unsurprising that he represents Pisa's political decline in language that draws extensively on the biblical traditions mentioned earlier. He echoes both Lamentations and Ezekiel in describing the downfall of "la migliore / donna de la provincia e regin' anco" [the best mistress of the provinces and their queen too] (ll. 70–71), who has become "d'onor dinudata, / di valor dimembrata" [naked of honor, dismembered of worth] (ll. 75–76).[15] The lyric depicts Pisa not as the ruler's wife or lover but as "la cità madre vostra" [the city your mother] (l. 48), her body generating the bonds of civic brotherhood (ll. 55–57, 64–65).[16] Such Pisan brotherhood, however, naturally does not include the Aretine poet; although the *canzone* employs personification to powerful effect, providing a significant point of reference for later practitioners, it differs from my central selection of lyrics in addressing a city not the poet's own and in preferring biblical to courtly discourse.

In the cases of exile poetry to which I now turn, the poets are writing about their own cities, and the ambiguity of an exile's relationship to his homeland is emphasized by depicting the city not as a nurturing mother but as a capricious, courtly beloved. My first example comes from medieval Italy's most famous political outcast, Dante Alighieri; next, I will consider a lyric by his close friend and poetic associate, Cino da Pistoia. These first two texts, both *canzoni* and dated to the first decade of the fourteenth century, provide examples of verse written in an explicitly courtly vein about the relationship between the exile and his beloved *città-donna*. I will then turn to the so-called *comico-realistica* [comic-realistic] tradition, looking at examples by two poets of the following generation, the Lucchese Pietro dei Faitinelli, and the Trevisan Niccolò del Rosso. While one of Faitinelli's two selected sonnets has a burlesque quality, the other texts display a serious, moralistic attitude to political matters that raises questions about the writers' conventional classification as *giocosi*.

Dante Alighieri, famously, was exiled from his native city of Florence following a faction coup in January 1302. He soon came to build his condition as an exile into his public persona, and to endow it with an ethical and religious significance that went far beyond questions of *realpolitik*, drawing on the Christian traditions about *peregrinatio* that he had already begun to exploit well before his banishment, in the composition of his confessional *Vita nuova*.[17] For current purposes, I am interested in a *canzone* composed apparently in the early years of his exile; its *congedo* treats his estrangement from Florence from a historical and secular, rather than a meta-historical and religious, viewpoint, using traditional courtly language to explore his desire for the personified city. The so-called "montanina" *canzone*, "Amor, da che convien pur ch'io mi doglia" [Love, since I am anyway compelled to suffer], does not however present this desire straightforwardly; rather, it is one of several conflicting passions dominating the despairing "I" who speaks in the poem.[18]

The main body of the lyric deals with the speaker's suffering over his cruel treatment by a woman, apparently real, described as "bella e ria" [fair and harsh] (l. 20), and presents a conventional plea for death to release him from the pain of unrequited love.[19] In fact, so little explicitly political material appears in the first five stanzas that Guglielmo Gorni has recently suggested that they may have been composed in the 1290s, with the exilic *congedo* added only later.[20] The first, indirect hints of the theme of exile, or at least of distance, appear in the fifth stanza, which describes the geographical environment of the love experience and matches the harshness of the woman with the harshness of an inhospitable landscape outside Florence, "in mezzo l'alpi" [in the heart of the mountains] (l. 61). Here no courtly companions may be found to comfort the speaker: "non donne qui, non genti accorte / veggio, a cui mi lamenti del mio male" [I see no ladies here, no discerning people, to whom I may lament my woe] (ll. 67–68).

The beloved herself is so unresponsive to the courtly codes that she is described as exiled [*sbandeggiata*] (l. 71) from the court of the personified Love to whom the *canzone* is addressed, a shield of pride protecting her from the arrows of his masculine amorous aggression (l. 73).

In the *congedo*, Dante turns to his own situation as a political exile, and to his personified city:

> O montanina mia canzon, tu vai:
> forse vedrai Fiorenza, la mia terra,
> che fuor di sé mi serra,
> vota d'amore e nuda di pietate;
> se dentro v'entri, va' dicendo: "Omai
> non vi può far lo mio fattor più guerra:
> là ond'io vegno una catena il serra
> tal che, se piega vostra crudeltate,
> non ha di ritornar qui libertate." (ll. 76–84)

> [Oh my mountain song, go now: perhaps you will see Florence, my city, who locks me out from herself, empty of love and naked of pity. If you enter inside there, go and say: "Now my maker can no longer make war on you: back there where I have come from he is so bound by a chain that, even if your cruelty relents, he has no freedom to come back here."]

Dante deputes to his *canzone* the attempt to approach [*vai*] and to gaze at [*vedrai*] the city. Like the woman of the previous stanzas she rejects these advances, repelling penetration by anything more substantial than—perhaps—the poet's words.[21] Like the beloved in the mountains, Florence is characterized only by an absence of courtly feminine attributes. The visual imagery chosen to describe this, with the imagined stripping [*nuda*] and disemboweling [*vota*] of the Fiorenza who repels her male lover's approach, disturbingly emphasizes the corporeality of the personified *città-donna*. The lyric protagonist uses an aggressive internal fantasy to turn the tables on the city; the imagined words spoken by his *canzone* are calculated to disempower personified Florence by preemptively asserting their creator's invulnerability to her rejection.

It is true that the latter part of the *congedo* reveals that this defiance is only possible at the price of a painful and emasculating submission to another woman, the alpine beloved who has imprisoned the speaker with a locked chain. The repetition of the rhyme-word *serra* in lines 78 and 82 stresses the protagonist's vulnerability: both of the cruel women who dominate his imagination threaten him with humiliation and enslavement. But if political and amorous exclusion from the objects of his desires weaken the figure of the exile-poet, other devices in the *canzone* tend to strengthen his position. The close similarities between the two women that emerge from the *congedo* allow the possibility that Dante will eventually offer the same rejection to his *donna* as to his *città*; a possibility strengthened by the reminder, repeated in the first and the fifth stanzas, that the speaker's true *signore* [lord] is Love (ll. 12, 72), rather than either of the women. The desires and the power of the male speaker fluctuate as he toys with visions both of feminine strength and of feminine vulnerability: the beloved in the mountains wields shield and chain, and Florence is secure behind her locked gates; but the city is also *vota* and *nuda*, the woman *sbandeggiata* from courtly company. Yet, since both women are entirely estranged from love [*sbandeggiata, vota*], the feudal bond linking the speaker and the personified male figure of Love suggests that masculine force and solidarity may eventually overcome female rejection, and either penetrate for real beyond the defenses that surround the desired body or else reject both the recalcitrant objects of desire, whose rebellion against Love's authority diminishes their worth.

Cino da Pistoia was a close friend of Dante's, strongly influenced by the latter in his own poetic work, and like Dante he suffered a period of political exile from his hometown (probably 1303–06).[22] In his *canzone*, "Sì m'ha conquiso la selvaggia gente" [So far has the wild people conquered me], Cino outlines a situation in which the lover, speaking from an exiled position of weakness and dejection, confronts a personified city stripped of courtly attributes, as did Dante in the *montanina* lyric.[23] Cino, however, asserts that the city herself is directly responsible for the absence of admirable qualities. The *canzone* in fact addresses the city's population, rather than explicitly personifying the city herself, but the feminine, singular grammatical gender of this *gente*, and its tendency to act collectively (even, paradoxically, when dividing itself into faction groupings, l. 18), makes it permissible, I think, to include the *canzone* in the present study.[24]

The first epithet applied to the people of Pistoia is "selvaggia" [wild] (l. 1). This label not only stresses the uncontrolled nature of the citizens' behavior, but also alerts the reader to the possibility of reading the lyric in an amorous key, since "Selvaggia" is also the *senhal* [poetic name] of the ever-unattainable Pistoian lady Cino often addresses in his love poetry. Other poems suggest that Selvaggia's family belonged to a rival political faction;[25] the opening assertion that Cino is the conquered victim of the *selvaggia gente* may therefore imply that his erotic suffering has a real as well as a metaphorical female correlative inside the city from which he is estranged.

Cino's treatment by and relationship to the woman and the city show differences, however. He normally represents the woman Selvaggia as deliberately calculating when she causes him to suffer,[26] but he is less clear about the intentions motivating the perverse conduct of the city's *selvaggia gente*. Although the *gente* is powerful, "fatta sì per farmi penar forte" [made so as to make me suffer greatly] (l. 6), her conduct is irrational and uncontrolled, manifested in "atti nuovi" [strange/unfamiliar actions] (1.2). Her actions do not let him see her "gaia ed allegra /. . .d'un cor piano" [gay and happy with a peaceful heart] (ll. 16–17), as the courtly lover would hope: instead, in the *canzone*'s most explicit political statement, we learn that she has become "bianca e negra" (1.18), that is, divided by the factionalism of the Black and White parties that dominated Pistoian urban politics. The internal unease evoked by the bizarre visual image of the parti-colored *gente* has not only failed to give the city satisfaction, it has also broken the courtly codes of decorous concealment to make her situation a byword, so that "ogni strano / che del suo stato intende, n'ha pesanza" [all strangers who hear of her state, are saddened by it] (ll. 19–20). Unsurprisingly, therefore, those who love her suffer more and the speaker, who claims amorous preeminence, more again: "dunque io, che son quel solo / che l'amo più, languisco maggiormente" [therefore I, who am he alone who loves her most, suffer the most] (ll. 23–24).

Strangely, it is after this climactic moment when the speaker declares himself the most severely afflicted of the witnesses to Pistoia's destruction that he actually starts to reassert his own relative self-control. As we have seen, the poem opens by depicting the speaker as the captive of a conquering people; he is crushed, suffering, and on the point of death. The first full stanza provides a brief moment of self-mastery, as the poet enunciates his rational conclusion that "ogni partenza di quel loco è saggia, / che è pien di tormento" [all departures from a place that is full of torment are wise] (ll. 11–12). But this magisterial pronouncement is prompted by a reflection about the departure of the lifeforce from his heart, in the context of a hyperbolic exclamation about the imminence of death. In the third stanza, however, the speaker regains sufficient autonomy to cast himself as an ambassador for Pistoia to his *signore* (l. 32); this overlord must from the context be the personification of Love. The active role the poet now assumes hints not only at his poetic prowess—his pleas take the form of "piatosi lai" [pitiful lays] (l. 31)—but also at the historical Cino's high standing in the real world outside the poem, as an academic lawyer and as a member of Pistoia's political class; a class he metaphorically reenters, despite exile, in his embassies to Love. True, he stresses that his advocacy is doleful, reflecting the excess of sorrow inside his heart (ll. 33–34), but he appears less weak than before, by comparison with Pistoia's now extreme abjection.

The lack of control that was initially implied in describing the people as *selvaggia* is extravagantly realized toward the end of the poem. The

Pistoian community is so masochistically self-destructive that she presents a disturbing spectacle to the onlooking poet, and through him to the lyric's audience:

> Cotal gente già mai
> non fu veduta, lasso, qual è questa,
> ch'è crudel di se stessa e dispietata,
> che in nulla guisa resta
> gravar sua vita come disperata,
> ché non si cura d'altra cosa omai. (ll. 25–30)
>
> [No people like this have ever been seen, alas, for she is cruel and pitiless to herself, and never abstains from burdening her life as if desperate, for she pays no attention now to anything else.]

The hypothetical vision of happy Pistoia—"se gaia. . .vedesse" [if I were to see her happy] (ll. 16–17)—is replaced with the visible reality [*veduta*] of insanity. Pistoia has become inescapably a victim, turning the corrosively disdainful qualities of a courtly lady onto herself rather than onto her lover. However unhappy the speaker claims to be, he endows himself by comparison with a degree of objectivity. By the end of the *canzone*, the abject male figure of the opening stanzas has achieved greater autonomy than the inward-turning personification, whose conduct is fixed in a vicious circle of self-abasement. The *congedo* to the poem confirms the paradoxical liberty that the initially *conquiso* speaker has attained. It presents a conventional courtly appeal to Death, again in the guise of a female personification, as the lady who represents his last hope of pleasure: "vieni a me, che mi se' sì piacente" [come to me, for you please me so much] (l. 38). While conventionally macabre and pessimistic, Cino's desire for the unequivocal finality of the courtly lady Death's embrace appears almost rational, when compared to the masochistic self-degradation promised by any further pursuit of his polity's *selvaggia gente*.

With my next lyrics, we move on a decade or so from these early Trecento productions by two of the leading courtly *stilnovisti*. While Dante and Cino are undisputedly influential contributors to the Italian vernacular tradition, my remaining two poets are very much minor figures, usually classified as *poeti giocosi*. It is interesting, however, to note that much of their political rhetoric is closely comparable to that of the "serious" writers we have just reviewed—and whose courtly discourse has proved to display such ambiguities in negotiating political and/or erotic desires.[27]

The Lucchese Pietro dei Faitinelli offers interesting developments of the personification trope in a pair of sonnets on the theme of his exile. In the first, "Onde mi dée venir giuochi e sollazzi?" [From where may entertainment and pleasures come to me?], the poet only hints at his outsider condition, devoting as much attention to the vicissitudes suffered by his city as to those endured by himself.[28] The first six lines explore the speaker's unhappy condition and announce his entire deprivation of all sources of courtly pleasure. The opening quatrain represents his frustrated desire for entertainment, while instead he receives only torments that are driving him to insanity [*eo impazzi*] (l. 4). In the next quatrain, he reveals the reasons for the despondency that has settled in his heart: Lucca has been made subject to Pisa, and the Lucchesi have become servants [*servi*] (l. 8) to the ignoble Pisans.

Up to this point, the poet has not made explicit use of the personification trope, beyond a hint of amorous involvement indicated by a reference to the speaker's heart (l. 6), implying desire, and the possessive appellation "Lucca mia" [my Lucca] (l. 7). It is doubly shocking therefore when the courtliness of the opening sections dissolves into a sequence of vivid and violent corporeal images in the tercets. The first description of Lucca as a woman is brutalizing: "ontata, nuda ed abitata / non da lo suo antico abitatore, / ma da color che l'hanno sì guidata" [shamed, naked, and inhabited not by her old inhabitants but by those who have driven her to this] (ll. 9–11). As in Dante's *canzone*, the imagery makes Lucca the object of disturbing physical violence. Her body is stripped bare and becomes the object of rival claims to possession and domination by the former and the present inhabitants. Habitation, in this context, implies possession or penetration of the *città-donna*'s body, and together with the stress on shame and nudity, carries aggressive sexual overtones. Even more disturbing is the choice of the speaker to present himself as a spectator to these events, maintaining a deliberate distance from the events his gaze records. The verb *vedere* is used emphatically in lines 7, 9, and 12, and suggests a voyeuristic attitude to the spectacle of Lucca's sexual/political violation. Faitinelli tells us that the vision of Lucca disgraced threatens to attack both his heart and his reason, but he remains a passive presence within the sonnet, *looking* at the *città-donna*, but apparently unable or unwilling to pursue any active line of conduct in her regard.

In what seems to be a companion poem, the sonnet "S'eo veggio en Lucca bella mio ritorno" [If I see my return into beautiful Lucca], the poet by contrast becomes an enthusiastic actor, though admittedly only in the context of a dream-like fantasy.[29] The speaker imagines his future return to the *città-donna*, now praised for her physical beauty, and describes the incomparable happiness that will then fill his heart. Selective citations might suggest that the sonnet is written in a courtly tone; but in fact, the vivid physicality of Pietro's vision of return into the city develops in the second quatrain into bizarre, burlesque images of his enthusiastic licking of the city's walls and inhabitants: "le mura andrò leccando d'ogn' intorno / e gli uomini" [I shall go round licking the walls in every direction, and the men] (ll. 5–6). If the city's walls are imagined as her skin, the image becomes blatantly erotic, strengthening the less-explicit sexual suggestion of the opening image of entry to the city. The imagined pleasure of the exile's return, indeed, creates an exuberance that breaks down binaries of gender, as of politics. Faitinelli extravagantly combines heterosexual and homosexual desire, in the erotic vision of affirming his civic reinstatement through pleasurable congress with the bodies of both the female city and the male citizens. This enthusiastic erotic physicality is accompanied by an interest in other sensual pleasures, such as eating and sleeping. The return is imagined to take place "quando la pera fie ben mézza" [when the pear will be rather overripe] (l. 2), an ambiguous expression that not only reveals an interest in food, but may also bear a sexual implication (pears are frequently associated with sex and sexuality in medieval literature).[30] In the first tercet, sensual imagery recurs as the speaker protests his preference for coarse bread and a straw mattress in Lucca, to fine bread and feather pillows elsewhere (ll. 9–11); but with the extravagant sexuality of the lover's moist kisses in mind, his acceptance of imaginary austerities can be only partial.

In this lyric, the position of the passive spectator that Faitinelli's "I" adopted in the previous sonnet is abandoned and he gives himself up to sensual experience of all kinds. He takes an active role in the pursuit of different pleasures and abandons all restraint in his enthusiastic embraces of the *città-donna* and of her inhabitants. This action, though, all occurs in the context of an internal fantasy, introduced with the hypothetical "s'eo veggio"; the final tercet returns to contemplation of reality. The closing lines, with ironic hyperbole, welcome even faction enemies (White Guelfs and Ghibellines) into the exuberant passion of post-exile satisfactions. This political promiscuity is undercut, however, by a pessimistic prediction of the indefinite extension of the pains of exile, which stresses the impotence and suffering of the reality outside the fantasy:

> Ch' i' ho provato sì amaro morsello,
> e provo e proverò, stando esiticcio,
> che 'l bianco e 'l ghibellin vo' per fratello. (ll. 12–14)
>
> [For such bitter pain have I endured, do endure and will endure, remaining outside, that I want the White and the Ghibelline for a brother.]

My final exile lyric is a sonnet produced by the Trevisan Niccolò del Rosso, "Oi terra, ch'eri de delicie arca" [Oh city, you who were an ark of delights].[31] In Niccolò's long sequence of sonnets on the Trevisan politics of the 1320s,[32] this is the only one to employ the city personification device—although it is used in slightly confusing alternation with comparisons of the city to the inanimate space of a court, port, or coffer, as in the first line. The figure of the exile plays an important part in the sonnet, although there is no hint that Del Rosso himself has been banished from the city. His opening quatrain echoes Cino and Faitinelli, employing the *Ubi sunt?* topos to contrast the past grandeur and present misery of personified Treviso. Courtliness is specifically invoked, with the city described as formerly "d'onni gran deletto dolze corte" [sweet court of every great delight] (l. 2), while modern Treviso is exposed as the antithesis of courtly. Aggressive images of female enslavement and evisceration appear in the description of the *città-donna*: "di tutto bene vòita, forte / porto di planto, d'angossa se' carca" [empty of all good, distressed port of grief, you are burdened with anguish] (ll. 3–4). The feminine adjectives *vòita* and *carca*, and the second person singular address, make it plain that Treviso is here visualized as a woman, although the masculine *porto* deploys topographic imagery alongside the prosopopeia.

In this first quatrain, Del Rosso ascribes no particular blame to any party in the city's disgrace. The second quatrain focuses on the relationships between the city and her population and opens a still more ambiguous development of the corporeal imagery. Reviewing the attitude to political events of the city's inhabitants, Del Rosso switches back in part to topographical representation of Treviso. He focuses on the groups least well-placed to complain or criticize.

> per ti l'essul e 'l pover se rimarca,
> quando vengono dentro a le tue porte:
> vezendo le zentil cortesie morte,
> lassano ti planzendo ed oltra varca. (ll. 5–8)
>
> [the exile and the poor man express disappointment over you when they come inside your gates: seeing the noble courtly values dead, they leave you, weeping, and travel onward.]

Approaching the city from outside, the poor and the exiled may imagine emotional and corporeal fulfillment to lie behind its closed gates, but when they penetrate into the urban space they find life and sex replaced by death. The personification allegory begins to disintegrate, and the single, feminized body of the city as viewed from outside disappears from view. Instead, the travelers witness a massacre of civic values; whether they originally desired female Treviso herself, or the grammatically feminine *cortesie*, the body or bodies exposed to their gaze once the gates have been penetrated offer no hope for satisfactory union. Even the most disenfranchised of citizens proves unable to tolerate this state of affairs; after physically seeing what Treviso has become in his absence, the exile chooses continued, voluntary separation from his degraded city.

As the poem moves on to its climax, the tercets develop the sexual implications of the second quatrain's evocation of union and separation, and further transform the already disturbing visualizations of city and civic values, as the tone shifts from lament to sarcasm. The first tercet contemptuously mocks the disgraced city's submission to her new rulers, using transparent sexual innuendo to label them "quigli che ti gode" [they who enjoy you] (l. 11). The last line of the sonnet, its impact heightened by a pause of mock-hesitation, makes unavoidably explicit what the creeping corporeal imagery has already implied, that Treviso has prostituted herself beyond redemption: "tu se' de vici un enorme bordello" [you are an enormous brothel of vices] (l. 14). The poet's disgust and his harsh, vituperative language culminate in this image of the disgraced female figure of a city that has changed from court to brothel, from courtly lady to prostitute. The reification of the female body in prostitution is underlined by Del Rosso's shift to the inanimate image of the brothel, while still continuing to employ second person verbs.

The troubling aspects of the allegory, which have already portrayed the feminized city's vulnerability to rape and enslavement, shift again, as the poet proceeds toward misogynistic condemnation of Treviso's complicity with her seducers. The speaker himself is clearly morally, if not actually, claiming membership of the group of former devotees represented by the poor and the exiles. His moral distance from his city's changed values has cancelled all possible desire and created an absolute caesura between the sensual and spiritual pleasures of the past and the repellent verities of the present. Despite its protests of reluctance—"el parlare non mi pare bello" [to speak of it does not seem pleasant to me] (l. 13)—Del Rosso's sonnet is designed to publicize the degradation of Treviso, exposing the violence perpetrated against the body politic in disturbing images of attacks against the female body. The lyric's visual rhetoric has progressively undermined the certainties implied by its courtly opening, as the female city's body is imagined successively as a site of sweetness and delight (ll. 1–2), of sorrow and anguish (ll. 3–8), and finally of degradation and vice (ll. 9–14), as the prosopopeia unfolds.

⋆ ⋆ ⋆

Niccolò del Rosso achieves probably the most extreme development of the sexual imagery associated with this kind of personification metaphor, but he is only carrying it to its logical conclusion. All the lyrics reviewed here employ disturbing sexual imagery to convey their political comment; they represent only a small selection from a fairly large corpus of contemporary Italian verse on this theme. The lyrics reveal ambiguities in their adoption of courtly convention that I believe may be seen as symptomatic of broader anxieties about the social and political legitimacy of the Italian *Comuni* as constitutional entities.[33]

In all the examples that we have seen, attempts to apply the language of courtly desire to the city as love object have broken down. The cities, whether they are agents or patients in the process, have been thoroughly stripped of refinement and autonomy—even Faitinelli's fantasy of sexual satisfaction, while avoiding the violence imagined in other lyrics, involves a burlesque physicality that undermines pretensions to refinement and stability. The allegory of the *città-donna* exposes a polity's physical and also moral vulnerability, suggesting underlying anxiety about the social and political organization of the city-states. The male protagonists of these lyrics remain largely powerless, passive spectators to aggression against the female cities. In matters of politics, represented through their gendered allegories, they seem unable to achieve firm action, or to articulate stable identities. If Del Rosso retains sufficient autonomy to choose departure from the city (itself a negative outcome), the other lyrics represent the dissolution of political and sexual energy in acceptance of disgrace and death—as we saw, even Faitinelli's exuberance in fantasy is undermined at the end of the sonnet. The writers thus seem trapped by their own rhetoric. Their lyrics reveal an uneasy awareness that the social realities of urban Italy cannot be comfortably accommodated into the metaphorical discourse of courtliness; yet they persist in their attempts. The sexual and physical violence of so much of the visual rhetoric associated with the *città-donna* and with her hapless exile-lover, offers an exploration of the tensions and fragilities of societies whose dynamics of development involved painful and frequently violent ruptures with the conventions traditionally governing both politics and culture, and reveals uncertainty about where to turn in the quest for a new stability.

Notes

I would like to express my thanks to the reviewers of this volume for their constructive comments on earlier drafts of this essay, and to Emma Campbell and Robert Mills for their exemplary patience and courtesy as editors. My attendance at the "Seeing Gender" conference was funded by the University of Leeds.

1. The feminine grammatical gender in Italian of the noun *città* and of city names readily invites female-gendered personification allegory.
2. Although there is only space here to consider a few examples, numerous exile lyrics employ this type of personification allegory. Useful recent studies of Italian exile that include considerations of exile verse include: Randolph Starn, *Contrary Commonwealth: The Theme of Exile in Medieval and Renaissance*

Italy (Berkeley: University of California Press, 1982); Jacques Heers and Christian Bec (eds.), *Exil et civilisation en Italie, XIIe–XVIe siècles* (Nancy: Presses Universitaires de Nancy, 1990); Georges Ulysse (ed.), *L'Exil et l'exclusion dans la culture italienne: Actes du colloque franco-italien* (Aix: Publications de l'Université de Provence, 1991).

3. See Julie Galambush, *Jerusalem in the Book of Ezekiel: The City as Yahweh's Wife* (Atlanta: Scholars Press, 1992); Peggy L. Day, "Adulterous Jerusalem's Imagined Demise: Death of a Metaphor in Ezekiel XVI," *Vetus Testamentum* 50 (2000): 285–309.
4. The problematic nature of the label *giocoso*, often applied to eminently serious poets or works on grounds especially of their sexual "immorality," is ably discussed by Steven Botterill, "Autobiography and Artifice in the Medieval Lyric: The Case of Cecco Nuccoli," *Italian Studies* 46 (1991): 37–57; similar problems are raised over the notion of register in troubadour lyric by Simon Gaunt, "Poetry of Exclusion: A Feminist Reading of Some Troubadour Lyrics," *Modern Language Review* 85 (1990): 311–312 [310–29].
5. The bibliography on the vexed issue of "courtly love" is vast: see Roger Boase, *The Origin and Meaning of Courtly Love: A Critical Study of European Scholarship* (Manchester: Manchester University Press, 1977); also Gaunt, "Poetry of Exclusion," pp. 310–11, 329.
6. A survey of this theme is provided by Michelangelo Picone in "Adii e assenza: storia di un motivo lirico dai trovatori a Petrarca," *Vox Romanica* 53 (1994): 34–48.
7. On visual disempowerment, see Simon Gaunt, "Poetry of Exclusion," pp. 323–24; and his essay in this volume, Chapter Four, which also touches on *amor de lonh*. On the themes of memory and imagination in exile poetry, see my essay, "Images of Exile: Distance and Memory in the Poetry of Cino da Pistoia," *Italian Studies* 55 (2000): 21–36. The Ovidian trope of the mobile *libellus* derives from the *Tristia* (see for example I.1) and his letters *Ex Ponto*; see Michelangelo Picone, "Dante, Ovidio e la poesia dell'esilio," *Rassegna europea della letteratura italiana* 14 (1999): 12 [7–23].
8. See Margaret Brose, "Petrarch's Beloved Body: 'Italia mia,'" in *Feminist Approaches to the Body in Medieval Literature*, ed. Linda Lomperis and Sarah Stanbury (Philadelphia: University of Pennsylvania Press, 1993), pp. 3–10 [1–20]; and more generally, Michelangelo Picone "Le città toscane," in *Lo spazio letterario del medioevo*, vol. 2, *Il medioevo volgare*, part 1.2, *La produzione del testo*, ed. Pietro Boitani, Mario Mancini, and Alberto Vàrvaro (Rome: Salerno, 2001), pp. 695–734.
9. See Sarah Kay, *Subjectivity in Troubadour Poetry* (Cambridge, UK: Cambridge University Press, 1990), pp. 85–86, 91–95, 115–117, 129–31; Gaunt, "Poetry of Exclusion," pp. 311, 314, 317–318, 320–21.
10. On the anomalous constitutional status of the *Comuni*, see J.K. Hyde, *Society and Politics in Medieval Italy: The Evolution of the Civil Life, 1000–1350* (Basingstoke: Macmillan, 1973), pp. 63–64, 84–87; Philip Jones, *The Italian City-State: From Commune to Signoria* (Oxford: Clarendon, 1997), pp. 335–43.

11. See Kay, *Subjectivity*, pp. 87–91, 95; Gaunt, "Poetry of Exclusion," pp. 310–11, 329.
12. See Brose, "Petrarch's Beloved Body."
13. See Picone, "Le città," in *Lo spazio letterario*, pp. 695–97, 707–709.
14. Guittone d'Arezzo XII [xlvii], in *Poeti del Duecento*, ed. Gianfranco Contini, 2nd edn., 2 vols. (Milan: Mondadori-Ricciardi, 1995), vol. 1. Contini dates this lyric to 1285. For this poem, as for all the poems discussed in this chapter, line numbers are provided in parentheses in the text. The modern notoriety of Guittone's dedicatees derives from their appearances in Dante's *Commedia*, respectively in *Inferno* 32–33 and *Purgatorio* 8.
15. Lam. 1.1: "How is she become as a widow. . .that was great among the nations, and princess among the provinces"; Ezek. 16.39–40: "They shall strip thee also of thy clothes. . .and leave thee naked and bare. . ..They shall stone thee with stones, and thrust thee through with their swords." See Day, "Adulterous Jerusalem," pp. 299–300, 304–305.
16. On maternal personification, see Brose, "Petrarch's Beloved Body," pp. 10–11.
17. See, briefly, Keen, "Images of Exile," pp. 23–26.
18. Poem 53 [CXVI], in Dante Alighieri, *Rime*, ed. Gianfranco Contini (Turin: Einaudi, 1946). Line numbers are provided in parentheses in the text.
19. The woman has been ascribed many different historical or allegorical identities: see Guglielmo Gorni, "La canzone 'montanina' *Amor, da che convien pur ch'io mi doglia* (CXVI)," *Letture classensi* 24 (1995): 132–33, 144–45 [129–50].
20. The *canzone* is conventionally dated to ca. 1307/08, the probable date of *Epistle* IV, which provides a partial commentary on the text; Gorni, "La canzone," discusses its dating in detail.
21. Given the feminine grammatical gender of the personified *canzone*, its gaze and its imagined penetration of the city open the possibility of a queer reading of the lyric; the feminine *canzone*, however, remains the male poet's deputy, rather than autonomously expressing female desire.
22. See Keen, "Images of Exile," p. 23.
23. Cino da Pistoia CIII, in *Poeti del dolce stil nuovo*, ed. Mario Marti (Florence: Le Monnier, 1969). Line numbers are provided in parentheses in the text. See Keen, "Images of Exile," pp. 27–29.
24. Cino's concern with Pistoia's *gente* represents a clear example of the feminization of the citizenry, and of the consequent ambiguity of the allegory's expression of political/sexual desire, since the political class represented as a feminine *gente* is presumably composed of biologically male citizens.
25. Poems CXVIII, CXIX, CXXIII, CXXIV, *Poeti del dolce stil nuovo*.
26. See poems LII, LIII, LV, LXII, CXVIII, *Poeti del dolce stil nuovo*.
27. In the following remarks, I am unfortunately unable to accommodate reaction to the very recent article by Fabian Alfie on the exile theme in the *giocosa* tradition, which appeared only as this volume went to press: "Cast Out: The Topos of Exile in Cecco Angiolieri, Pietro de' Faitinelli, and Pieraccio Tedaldi," *Annali d'italianistica* 20 (2002): 113–26.

28. Pietro Faitinelli 15, in *Poeti giocosi del tempo di Dante*, ed. Mario Marti (Milan: Rizzoli, 1956); Marti dates this poem and the following to ca. 1314. Line numbers are provided in parentheses in the text.
29. Faitinelli 16, in *Poeti giocosi*. The poem displays echoes of Cecco Angiolieri's exilic sonnet on Siena, "Se Die m'aiuti, a le sante guagnèle" [If God helps me, by the holy Gospels], poem 32, *Poeti giocosi*. Both poems are ably discussed in Alfie, "Cast Out."
30. See for instance, Day 7 story 9 of Boccaccio's *Decameron*, or Chaucer's *Merchant's Tale*.
31. Niccolò del Rosso 62, in *Poeti giocosi*, dated by Marti to ca. 1324. The image of Treviso as *arca* and *corte* echo Guittone's exile poem, "O dolce terra aretina" [Oh sweet Aretine city], poem VIII [xxxiii] in *Poeti del Duecento*, 1.
32. The sequence covers his poems 55–79, in *Poeti giocosi*.
33. See Margaret Brose, discussing the personification of Italy rather than of a city alone: "Petrarch's Beloved Body," pp. 7–17.

PART FOUR

TROUBLED READINGS

CHAPTER 9

READING READING WOMEN: DOUBLE-MIRRORING THE *DAME* IN *DER RITTER VOM TURN*

Anne Simon

This chapter examines textual and visual strategies employed in the German Book of the Knight of the Tower *for directing women's reading and the space for maneuver allowed by reading against these strategies.*

Es sprechent aber viel lütt / das sy nit wolten das jre wyber der geschrifft gelert werden / weder mitt schriben noch mitt lesen / Es ist aber eyn vnwyßheit / Dann es ist sonders gůt das frowen leßen kŏnden / dann sy dar durch den glouben vnnd das heyl jrer selen dest baß erkennen / vnnd acht nemen mŏgen / Vnnd vnder hunderten ist nitt eyne die dest arger oder bŏßer sy.

[However, many people say that they do not want their wives taught about the Scriptures and other written works, neither how to read them nor how to write themselves. That, however, is folly, since it is particularly good for women to know how to read as this enables them all the better to recognize their faith and [what is good for] the salvation of their soul and to pay heed to it. And out of a hundred you will not find one who is any the wickeder or more evil for it.][1]

This view on the desirability of women's reading is found in *Der Ritter vom Turn* (1493), the German version of the *Livre du chevalier de la Tour Landry*. It is prompted by the story of Deborah, whose wisdom, culled from Holy Scripture, enabled her, according to the Knight, to convert her hard-hearted, evil husband from his wicked ways into a just and peace-loving man. While the biblical Deborah was a judge, prophetess, and military leader who led a coalition of Israelite tribes to a victory on the plain of Esdraelon over the superior Canaanite forces commanded by Sisera (Judges 4–5), the

Knight turns her into a model of feminine piety and domestic virtue whose book learning furnishes her with weapons for the taming not of her people's enemy but of her tyrannical spouse.

Given that the *Livre du chevalier* was written for a female readership, this recasting of the results of a woman's learning is hardly surprising and is typical of the work as a whole. Reading as a path to active female virtue is the stated purpose of this particular text. The purpose of this chapter is threefold: first, to explore the ways in which both translator—in the German version—and narrator—in French and German versions—attempt to determine women's reading of the text through a rigid framework of commentary and exegesis; second, to examine textual and visual models of women readers in the work; and, third, to ascertain whether women readers have any scope to establish a reading of their own.

The German version of the *Livre* was first published in Basel in 1493 by Michael Furter for Johann Bergmann von Olpe, probably best known as the publisher of Sebastian Brant's *Narrenschiff* [*Ship of Fools*], which appeared in Basel in 1494. The translation and adaptation of the *Livre* was undertaken by the Swabian aristocrat Marquard vom Stein primarily for his two daughters, Elsa and Jakobea, but also for others unable to read French (87).[2] The first German edition is distinguished by its forty-six woodcuts, all cut specifically for the work rather than re-used from other sources. Scholars differ as to the attribution of the woodcuts: suggestions include Matthias Grünewald, Hans Baldung Grien, Hans Süss von Kulmbach, the anonymous master of the Bergmann workshop, Johann Wechtin, and the young Albrecht Dürer.[3] Currently, opinion seems to favor Dürer,[4] who was in Basel between early 1492 and May 1494 and is thought to have contributed at least some of the woodcuts to Brant's *Narrenschiff.*

The *Livre du chevalier de la Tour Landry* is a courtesy text intended to instruct young ladies of the aristocracy and upper bourgeoisie in virtue and seemly behavior, both before and during marriage. Instruction is provided through *exempla* of virtuous and evil women taken from the Bible, Classical literature, saints' lives, chronicles, *fabliaux*, legends, a collection of didactic tales for use in sermons,[5] and even the Knight's personal experience. In the German version these *exempla* are located within a double textual frame: the German translator's preface and the Knight's own. The former explains Marquard's decision to translate the work, the latter the Knight's motives for compiling the *Livre* in the first place. Together the prefaces set up a clear framework for women's reading and understanding of the text. In its turn the text constructs a model of behavior for women's lives that itself encourages female readers to internalize male expectations, not least through its demonstration—visual as well as textual—of the rewards for compliance and penalties for disobedience.

The preface to the German translation initially appears unrelated to the text since Marquard maintains that fallen man's natural state is activity:

> Dann so fer der mensch anschowet den spiegel der heiligen geschrifft Erlernet er im für alle tugenden vfgesetzt / sin ůbung vnnd arbeit gůter dingen / vnd můssyg gon vermyden. Do er anfangs von der geschöpft der hochsten wysheit vßgeschlossen / Vnd in das irdysch paradiß gesatzt / ist im für alle tugenden vfgelegt sich ze ůben / das paradiß alda zů gebuwen / zů arbeiten / vnd nit můssig zů gönde. (85)
>
> [Then in so far as man looks into the mirror of the Holy Scriptures he learns one virtue above all others, namely to cultivate and toil at good works and to avoid leisure. When he was, in the beginning, shut out of the Creation of the highest wisdom and set into this earthly Paradise, he was charged with one virtue above all: to be industrious in cultivating this Paradise, to toil, and not to go idle.]

Deviation from this natural state in the form of sloth has devastating consequences since it renders mankind open to seduction by Satan:

> Bedüt vnnß der heilig sant Augustin / der da sprichet / Das trackheit gůter ůbungen / vnnd můssig gon / der gröst jnfal sye zů kranckheit der selen vnnd des libs / Wann der lystig tüfel jn allen anfechtungen vnnd widerwertikeiten / so er menschlichem geschlecht ye bewysen hat / clůger vrsach nie gehabt / den menschen an zů fechten / dann in syner still růw vnd můssigung. (86)
>
> [Saint Augustine makes it clear to us when he says that sluggishness in the performance of good works and idleness are the greatest sign of sickness of the body and soul. For of all the temptations and tribulations which the Devil has ever visited on mankind, he, in his cunning, has never possessed a cleverer means of leading man into temptation than that to be found in his stillness, inactivity, and leisure.]

This openness results in "liblicher vergeilung" [lasciviousness] and "vngehüren sünnden" [monstrous sins] (86), fatal not just for the individual but for all mankind. To support his argument Marquard names Classical and Christian authorities (Aristotle, Roman history, the Bible, and Augustine), attributing the Flood, Solomon's apostasy, and the decline of the Roman Empire to sloth and self-indulgence (86–87). Hence Marquard's own reading and translating of the *Livre* have been occasioned by his wish both to avoid idleness himself and to keep his daughters occupied and thereby virtuous: young ladies may be prevented from sinning through the very activity of reading since it helps them to avoid idleness and teaches them appropriate behavior. In short, women's reading of *Der Ritter vom Turn* is determined by a rigid framework of industry and propriety, one reinforced by implied guilt for and resultant fear of the moral and social decline resulting from individual—especially female—deviation from the activity that constitutes man's natural state.

The Knight's preface apparently subverts Marquard's stance as the classic *locus amoenus* with which it starts transports the reader into the realm of courtly love poetry and romance:

> Als ich mit namen / der Ritter vom thurn / Eyns tags zů vßgőndem Aprillen / mit etwas schwermůtikeit beladen / Vnd für vffenthalt kurtzwyle / vnnd ergőtzung jn eynen gartenn / vnder eyns boums schattenn gangen / Da selbst sytzend was / hort ich da von dem gefügel der galander trostlen vnd nachtgallenn / Die sich gegen der zyt des sommers frőwen warent / sőllichen lieplichen vnnd sůssen gesang / Das mir die selben jre frőlichen stymen / vnnd loblich sůß getőnen / all myn vnmůt vnnd beschwerd hin namen. (88)
>
> [Then I, who am called the Knight of the Tower, went, laden with melancholy, into a garden one day in late April and sat in the shade of a tree, hoping to stay there to pass the time in pleasure and delight. Sitting there I heard such a charming and sweet song from the larks, thrushes, and nightingales, who were rejoicing in the advent of summer, that with their cheerful voices and praiseworthy sweet tones they took away all my displeasure and troubles.][6]

The courtly vein is reinforced by the Knight's memories of his youthful enslavement to Venus and to one fair, virtuous lady for whom he himself composed love songs. However, the Knight is then prompted by the advent of his naïve young daughters to recall the amorous zeal of the men he knew in his own youth and their carelessness in damaging women's reputations (88–89). Thus personal experience rather than biblical or Classical sources shapes the Knight's view of human morality; individual *exempla* illustrate his misgivings and provide positive and negative role models for his daughters:

> Daruß [from the book] vor byld vnd lere zů nemen das gůt zů gebruchen / vnd sich vor dem argen zů verhůten / dann vil mannen gewonheit ist / eyn frow oder junckfrowen vnder ougen an lachen / vnnd hynderwertz enteren vnnd verspotten. (89)
>
> [Take from this [book] example and precept so that you practice what is good and guard against what is evil, for it is the custom of many men to smile to a woman's face and impeach her reputation and mock her behind her back.]

The aim of the *exempla* is to teach the Knight's daughters the ways of the world, to aid them in avoiding the pitfalls of love, and in guarding their good name. Rather than lack of industry the Knight considers flirtatiousness and the attraction of erotic love to be the main threats to women's virtue.

Since the Knight's frame for women's reading of the text differs from that of Marquard, it might alter our interpretation of the latter. Marquard's observations on idleness and industry apply to men and women, highlighting models of behavior desirable in both. His examples from the Bible and Roman history infuse individuals' actions with an importance beyond the merely social and contemporary. By contrast the Knight's concerns, rooted in the aristocratic courtly tradition, are confined to the personal and social. Nonetheless, both fathers share a didactic intent and the wish for their daughters to internalize patterns of appropriate public and private conduct that will prevent them from bringing opprobrium on their fathers and later their husbands. Marquard sums up their thinking thus:

> Dann wo sy die selben minen doͤchtern / jn steter gůter uͤbung vnd zymlichen wesen hyeltenn / Wer mir vß vatterlicher liebe besonder froͤd. (87)
>
> [For if they [the two books compiled by the Knight] ensured that my very own daughters maintained constant good habits and seemly behavior it would be to me, in my paternal love, a particular delight.]

Women's reading of the German version is, then, paternally, even patriarchally determined, set in a tradition derived from Aristotle, the Bible, and the Church Fathers, and directed toward the maintenance of male reputation. Not only is the text framed by two male-authored prefaces, but its sources are also chosen by the male clerics charged by the Knight with this task and are themselves in all probability male-authored. A further constraining factor is the constant intrusion by the narrator in the form of the father, who addresses his daughters directly to drive home the moral of each story, a strategy that limits female readers' space to negotiate the text to suit their own ends. Let one example stand for many. The first tale is about the Emperor of Constantinople's daughter, who is saved from illicit sex, pregnancy, disgrace, and death by the souls of the dead she has prayed for. Their ghosts frighten away her lover as he is about to enter her bed (91–92), whereas her sister, less assiduous in prayer and therefore less protected, becomes pregnant by her nocturnal visitor. Their father orders her secretly drowned and her lover flayed alive.[7] When the Emperor's surviving daughter is questioned by her chastened lover, she realizes she was saved from her own death by the already dead. The Knight concludes:

> FVrbaß lieben doͤchtern / Das erst werck / das ir am morgen / so ir vff gestanden / tůn / So soͤllen ir den dienst gotz volbringen / vnd üwer zyt vnd gebet mit andacht sprechen / vnd das tůn mit gůtem hertzen / on wyter oder andre gedencken. (92)
>
> [Indeed, dear daughters, the first task you should perform on getting up in the morning is to worship God and say your hours and prayers with deep

devotion and do so with a pious heart without letting your thoughts wander to other things.][8]

This "indeed, dear daughters" echoes in variations throughout the work. The conversational tone adopted by the father-narrator brings him closer to the reader. In the silence of his daughters, who have no voice at all in the text, the female reader assumes the daughters' place as direct recipient of paternal advice.[9]

Thus the Knight's comments constitute what could be called—using twentieth-century terminology—a "voice-over" to the individual *exempla.* Kaja Silverman, in her article "Dis-Embodying the Female Voice," analyzes the female subject's access to discourse within a film soundtrack.[10] Her observations provide a useful summary of narrative strategies in *Der Ritter vom Turn*. She characterizes the sort of male voice-over heard in documentaries and "B" movie police thrillers as "a pure distillate of the law" that "speaks with an unqualified authority" and remarks: "The capacity of the male subject to be cinematically represented in this disembodied form aligns him with transcendence, authoritative knowledge, potency and the law—in short, with the symbolic father."[11] This alignment between the father's voice, "authoritative knowledge" and "potency" permeates the text. The Knight-narrator figure becomes a "symbolic father" to all female readers of the work, fictional and actual; his exegesis becomes the "law."[12]

Having discussed the translator's and narrator's strategies for determining women's reading, let us look at the women established as model readers within the text itself: Deborah and St. Katherine of Alexandria. Deborah is extolled by the Knight as the woman reader whose study of Holy Scripture led to wisdom, prophecy, holiness, and the taming of a husband, Lappidoth, barely mentioned in the Bible.[13] Since the reform of violent, lascivious, and evil husbands is a worryingly recurrent topic in the *Ritter vom Turn*, her story figures one function of the work as a whole: women's reading as a source of men's virtue. Katherine of Alexandria was a fourth-century virgin saint and mystic bride of Christ, martyred by the Roman Emperor Maxentius, who desired her and sought to undermine her Christian faith. He dispatched fifty philosophers to this end; Katherine's faith and her erudition—before her conversion she had been particularly fond of Aristotle and Plato—enabled her to convert them to Christianity. The philosophers' conversion resulted in their instant death. Maxentius had Katherine tortured on a specially devised spiked wheel and eventually beheaded. Her reconstituted body was translated by angels to Mount Sinai, where it rests to this day.[14] What both women share is the dedication of their learning to the service of God, a dedication that results in their being singled out as *exempla*. While not every woman can indulge in martyrdom or victory on the battlefield, she can, on a more modestly domestic scale, use her reading to turn her husband to God.

Textually, then, women's reading is ringfenced by male voices and saintly models; is it similarly constrained visually? Do the woodcuts allow women greater freedom of interpretation and negotiation? Four will be considered here. The first depicts the Knight, the two clerics, and two scribes charged with compiling sources for the work (figure 9.1). Since it appears both on the title page and as the second in the book, women readers have, as it were,

Wie der Ritter vom Thurn wy-
der vß dem garten gieng vnd jm zwen ſchriber vnd zwen prieſter
begegneten den er beualch diß bůch zů machen/

Also vñ vff ſöllichs gieng ich vß dē garten da begegnetē mir
zwen prieſter vnderwegē/vñ zwen ſchriber / die ich deßhalb
beſchickt hatt/ Denen gab ich nun myn egemelte meynung
zů erkennē/vñ liess mir ſy jn der byblen/ ouch in den kronick
en vō Franckrich/von Egypten/von Engelland/vnnd vō
andern enden leſen/ Daruß die beſten exempel gezogen/
die in eyn bůch vergriffen/ Vnnd das vmb kurtz vnd beſſer
verſtentnyß willen nit in rymen/ Sonder in ſag wyße ſtellen/vñ dero zwey
machen laſſen/das eyn mynen döchtern/vnnd das ander mynen ſünen geben will/ Dann als ferr ſy ſich zů gůtem/zů lob vnnd zů eren wurden ſchick
en/ Wer mir ſondere fröd/Als ouch das eyn yeder getrüwer vatter/ vß na-
türlichem jnfluß ſynen kynden ſchuldig vnnd pflichtig iſt/

War eyn edel vnnd hüpſch meynung iſt/ſich zů ſpieglen in dem ſpie-
gel der alten hyſtorien/ Die vnnß von vnnßern fordern verlaſſenn
vnnd geſchriben ſynd/ Vnnß dar durch zů gůtem zů wenden/vnnd
das übel zů fliehen/daruff ich dann der Ritter vō thurn alſo ſprich/ Myne
A iiij

9.1 The Knight, two clerics, and two scribes. Marquard Vom Stein, *Der Ritter vom Turn* (Basel: Michael Furter für Johann Bergmann von Olpe, 1493), fol. 4r. Munich, Bayerische Staatsbibliothek.

to pass learned, authoritative males even to access the text. Male primacy is reinforced by the position of the woodcut: on the title page it occupies center-space; in the work itself it occupies the top half of its page, dominating the text beneath it, although framed and contained in its turn by the chapter heading and ornamental borders. The chapter heading reads, "How the Knight of the Tower left the garden and met two scribes and two priests whom he ordered to make this book." Thus the father, as embodiment of authority and the law, may leave the garden; visually and textually his daughters remain in it throughout, symbolically restricted and contained, not least by the code of conduct prescribed in the work: dedication to what is good, praiseworthy, and honorable [zů gůtem / zů lob vnnd zů eren] (89).

Thus the work is prefaced by an image of male authority and collusion that echoes the two prefaces. The open book in the scribe's hands indicates men's direct access to texts that women may access only through male mediation. The Knight's armor serves to identify him as father-narrator and as embodiment of "potency and the law"; however, it also associates the text with aggressive male violence.[15] The prominent gate and fence may, like the fence in the background of the previous woodcut of the Knight resting under the tree in the garden, be visual reminders of the *hortus conclusus* of the Song of Songs: "A garden enclosed *is* my sister, *my* spouse; a spring shut up, a fountain sealed."[16] In the Song of Songs this image describes the Shulammite maiden, whom the Middle Ages identified with Mary. Originally a metaphor for Mary's perpetual virginity, the *hortus conclusus* developed into a symbol for virginity in general. It also became the setting for representations of the Virgin—often reading—or of the Madonna and Child, signifying both the restoration of Paradise through the Passion, Death, and Resurrection of Christ and Mary's foreknowledge that her son was born to die. In the context of the *Ritter vom Turn* the visual allusion may serve as a reminder of the ideals of chastity, purity, and subservience to the dominant male will into which the work is meant to fence young women; the text itself becoming a garden productive of such virtues. In the final woodcut (figure 9.2) the wooden palisade has become a wall that unambiguously locks the two daughters—and by implication actual women readers—into the garden and hence into the expectations and patterns of behavior expounded in the work. The Knight's daughters are further locked in by the position of the woodcut in the center of the page, surrounded by text, chapter heading, and ornamental borders. Silent throughout the text, they become images of the model reader the Knight is trying to create through his text: the one who does not answer back and establish an alternative narrative of her own.

This final woodcut, in which the Knight hands his daughters the completed book, recalls manuscript miniatures of an author presenting a copy

verbergen/ſyns nechſten ſchand vnnd laſter/mag alles gůtt bekomen/ Wie dann das die ewangelia vnnd die bůcher der wyſen thůnt jnn halten vnnd bewyſen.

Wie der Ritter vom Thurn ſy-
nen döchtern dyß bůch zů jren handen über antwurt

Lſo vnnd hie mitt mynen lieben döchtern ſo ich dann dyß myn bůchlin üch jn exempel vnnd vorbyld wyße mit anzeigungen der gůten vnnd wolthůnden frowen/ Deßglich der bößen vnnd belümdeten/regimentz vnnd thaten / Wie die gůten zů eren / vnnd die bößen zů ſchanden vnnd laſter komen ſyent/mit mancherley andern meynungen/ Wie jr üch dann halten vnnd wo vor jr üch hůten ſöllenn / Alles mitt kurtz vergriffnen vßlegungen zů ſamen geleſen/vnd ſetzen laſſen hab/ So vil vnnd ich dero dyßer zyt nach kleyne myner verſtentnyß hab zů wegenn bryngen vnnd wyſſen mögen / Will ich abbrechen vnnd dyß bůchlyn alſo

9.2 The daughters in the garden. Marquard Vom Stein, *Der Ritter vom Turn* (Basel: Michael Furter für Johann Bergmann von Olpe, 1493), fol. 73r. Munich, Bayerische Staatsbibliothek.

of his work to a patron. Theoretically, therefore, the daughters occupy the position of patrons, in other words, the position of financial, social, and cultural power. However, there are differences. Such pictures usually show the author kneeling in supplication whereas the Knight is shown standing, in full armor, wearing a prominent sword. His stance and dress alter the dynamics of power since he is not supplicant but in control, asserting his authority through the donation of a work that will outlive him. The female reader, having finished the book, finds herself in the position of the Knight's daughters, presented with a work that she is meant to reread and internalize:

> Vß vatterlicher getrüwer lieb üch bytten / Dwil ich anders nichtz dann üwers heyls vnnd eren byn begeren / Das jr es offt vnnd vil lesen üch das lassen zů hertzen gon / vnnd deß all zyt jngedenck syn wőllent / Hab ich vngezwyuelte hoffnung / jr werdent dar durch hie jn dyser zyt der welt lob vnnd ere / vnd dort jn ewigkeyt selige belonung erlangen / Dar zů üch gott der almechtig syn gnad vnnd hilff all zyt wőll verlyhenn. (239)
>
> [Asking you out of true fatherly love, since I desire nothing more than your salvation and your honor, that you read it oft and at length and take it to heart and remember it at all times. I have the unshaken hope that by reading this book you will achieve here in this time the honor and praise of the world and there in eternity blessed reward. May Almighty God give you His grace and aid in this.]

The woman reader is thus left in no doubt as to the expected fruits of her reading and its impact on her own life: reading the *Ritter vom Turn* will lead to eternal salvation. It is in that sense an authoritatively redemptive text in the tradition of the Bible, its word—like the Bible's—a paternally sanctioned truth. Moreover, women readers have to pass an authoritative male to exit both garden and book, so are unable to "escape" without taking the work and its precepts with them.

Male figures frame the reading of the text visually but what of images of women readers? There is only one; it is within the text, so itself framed by the same authoritative males: the Virgin Mary, who is shown reading in the Annunciation woodcut (Luke 1.26–38) (figure 9.3). According to Saint Bernard, Mary is reading the very passage in Isaiah that foretells her conception and the birth of Christ: "Therefore the Lord himself shall give you a son; Behold, a virgin shall conceive, and bear a son, and shall call his name Immanuel" (Isaiah 7.14). In other words, Mary is reading the text that tells of her own salvational fertility at the moment she becomes fertile, so in a sense the Word itself becomes fertile and Mary becomes the fulfillment of her own reading, the incarnation of the meaning of the text.[17]

The Annunciation woodcut stands without chapter heading at the top of the verso, dominating its text. As is customary in northern European art in the later Middle Ages Mary is portrayed in a domestic interior,[18] a visual motif echoed by the text, which describes Mary herself as "eyn kamer vnnd tempel gotz" [a chamber and temple of God] (200).[19] Kneeling at a *prie-dieu*, she holds the open book in front of her. The iconographic motif of the open book was introduced in the twelfth century:

> Theologically this image of the Virgin Annunciate reading a book denoted Mary's foreknowledge that her child was born to die in her own lifetime,

FVrbaß so will ich reden von einer junckfrowen der gelichen
nie gewesen ist/noch nyemer würdt/das ist die heylige junck
frow Maria/die müter vnßers heyles / Welche so hoch ge-
würdiget/ vnnd mitt so vil alles güten erfüllet ist / das dz
nieman volschriben noch volsagen kan/Dañ sy von tag zů
tag jn der hochmechtikeit jrs thüren sons/yemer vnd yemer
würd erhöhet Dyße süsse junckfrow hatt ouch jren son mer
angebettet/vnnd geforchtet dann dheinen andern/ Dann sy wol wüßte/
wer vnnd von wannen er was/ Sy ist eyn kamer vnnd tempel gotz gewe-
sen/vnnd noch dar jnn die vermahelung gottes gehandlet ist / vnd trůg dz
leben deß behalters der welt/Da doch got wolte/dz sy dem heyligē Joseph
vmahelt/der da eyn frömer alter man wz/Dañ got der herr wolt geboren
werden/jn schyn der vermahelung/zů gehorsamen der gesatzt / der zyt vnd
da mitt erwenden die rede der welt / Vnnd jr ouch gesellschafft geben sy zů
regieren vnnd zů füren jn Egypten/Also kam es dar zů/da Joseph vnam
das sy schwanger was/meynt er sy zů verlassen/vnd sagt zů jr/er wüßte wol
das es nitt vō jm were/Deßhalb jn der selben nacht sandt jm gott der herr
gesichteklichen eynen engel/das er nit von jr gieng/Wañ sy were schwang
er durch göttliche würckung/mitt dem son gotz vmb behaltung willenn
welt/Dar ab er grosse fröd entpfieng/ vnnd jr füro hyn vil mer zucht

9.3 The Annunciation. Marquard Vom Stein, *Der Ritter vom Turn* (Basel: Michael Furter für Johann Bergmann von Olpe, 1493), fol. 54v. Munich, Bayerische Staatsbibliothek.

thereby making her acceptance of God's request that much greater and her sacrifice more meaningful.[20]

Thematically, the Annunciation woodcut is linked to the *hortus conclusus* image at the beginning and end of the *Ritter vom Turn*; it also, significantly, comes *after* one of the three Marys at Christ's tomb. Above Mary's womb hovers the dove; in the foreground is a vase of lilies-of-the-valley. Lilies symbolize Mary's purity; the tripartite shape of the vase recalls the Trinity but also, in its potbelliedness, Mary's function as the vessel for Christ. The Archangel Gabriel stands with his right hand raised in the traditional greeting, his left carrying a staff topped by his traditional symbol, the fleur-de-lys. He also bears the scroll on which the text of the "Ave Maria" normally appears, God's Word as it becomes flesh in the Virgin's womb.

What function would this woodcut have fulfilled in the context of the *Ritter vom Turn*? First, it serves simply to illustrate the text. Second, Mary represents the ultimate in model women readers, being the ultimate example of piety, chastity, and submission to a paternal Will. Third, she embodies a certain type of male desire. In her much-quoted article on the representation of women in film, "Visual Pleasure and Narrative Cinema," Laura Mulvey postulates a "determining male gaze" that "projects its fantasy onto the female figure which is styled accordingly."[21] Since Mulvey is writing about woman as an erotic spectacle who "holds the look, plays to and signifies male desire,"[22] her remarks may seem inapplicable to an image of the Virgin. However, while Mary does not "hold the look," she is the object not just of a female gaze but of a determining male gaze (that of the artist; that of male readers of the text) and she does "play to" a particular form of male desire: that of God for a chaste vessel for His son, that of husbands for a chaste vessel for theirs, that of fathers for chaste daughters. Fourth, the woodcut could—like other depictions of the Annunciation—have functioned as a devotional image, the object of meditation. In *Painting and Experience in Fifteenth-Century Italy*, Michael Baxandall stresses the active nature of the interior visualization of holy stories, images of such stories forming the basis of an active religious meditation, what Baxandall terms "a visualizing meditation."[23] Women readers of the *Ritter vom Turn* might actively have visualized the Annunciation, possibly with themselves as Mary. Fifth, then, the woodcut figures the function of the whole work: women reading the woodcut read an ideal image of themselves reading the ideal book, the Bible, original history, and repository of truth and moral guidance. We have seen that Mary's reading is linked to her fertility. Similarly, by reading the *Ritter vom Turn*, fifteenth-century women could also have become fertile with legitimate heirs, having been guided into socially acceptable—that is, chaste and malleable—conduct. Thus, like Isaiah, the *Ritter vom Turn* generates its own fulfillment.

The possibility of understanding the woodcut in this way is indirectly supported by two other very different images of women readers. The first is the miniature of Mary Duchess of Guelders in her *Hours* (1415), which depicts her as the Virgin Mary reading.[24] She stands in the *hortus conclusus*; on her left a figure resembling an annunciating angel bears a scroll with the words "Ave Maria." Hence the Duchess could, on reading her *Hours*, actively visualize herself as the Virgin reading and align herself with this image of female perfection. The second is the famous miniature of Mary of Burgundy in her Book of Hours. Robert Scribner, in "Ways of Seeing in the Age of Dürer," observes:

> Given that the Flemish princess was the most likely person to use the prayerbook and to behold this image, we are presented with a "Chinese boxes" notion of visualised reality, with the viewer seeing her represented self before a representation of herself in the presence of sacred persons. If we posit that the prayerbook held by Mary in the miniature is also a Book of Hours, perhaps the very book in which the miniature is reproduced, we see a vertiginous double-mirroring of reality: Mary able to see herself reading the book in the very book she is reading.[25]

A similar process of self-visualization and "double-mirroring of reality" may have been provoked for women readers by the woodcut in the *Ritter vom Turn*, all the more if this text assumes the redemptive role previously suggested.

Structures of male commentary and exegesis have been traced; verbally and visually a model female reader has been constructed and fenced into an authoritative paternal interpretation of the text. Is there any scope for women's reading to suit themselves? One story may *just* show a slight gap in the fence. It tells of the disruption of the liturgy by the congregation's gossip. St. Martin is celebrating Mass, assisted by the future St. Brictius, who starts laughing. After Mass St. Brictius reveals that he saw two devils recording all the congregation's words.[26] Just as the congregation's gossip forms an alternative text to the liturgy, so the text recorded by the devils on parchment becomes an alternative instruction manual for the Knight's daughters, a manual on how not to behave—or how to behave subversively—one which women readers could exploit to their own ends. However, St. Martin subsequently incorporates the incident into his sermon, stressing the sinfulness of inattentive gossip and the preferability of absence from Church altogether. Thus the disruption of the liturgy through the transgressive word is mitigated by the word's assimilation into the very process it is undermining. Disruption becomes *exemplum*, a process mirrored by the *Ritter vom Turn* itself, in which examples of transgressive female behavior are transformed into didactic tales that convey the lesson to be learnt from illicit conduct.

The woodcut illustrating the story correspondingly shows women as the sole transgressors (figure 9.4). The trinity of worshipful, devout men is set against the trinity of gossiping, impious women. The men are depicted as absorbed in the Mass; the women in their worldly affairs. Just as the wine is transformed into Christ's blood, so the women's speech is transformed into text, though the scrawled appearance of their writing conveys both the meaninglessness of their words when compared to the salvatory speech of

Schlüg er mit der hand vff das büch vñ vermeynt sy zü geschweigen/ aber etlich wolten es darumb nit myden/ Da batt er got das er sy schwygen machte/vnd jnen jr torheit zü erkennen geben wölte/ Also vff dz da fiengen frowen vnnd man an die also geschwatzt hetten/ vnnd gelachet/ mit kleglicher stymen zü schryen/wie dann lüt die tüfelhaftig synd/vnnd lyttent so grossen schmertzen das es ein erbermde was zü hören/ Da nun die meß geschehen was/sagt jnen der heilig man/wie er den tüfel vff jnen gesehenn hette/vmb jrs geschwetzs vnnd böser geberden wyllen/so sy hynder der meß gehandelt hetten/ Vnd sagt jnen dar by wz grossen schadens daruß keme/ Deß glich die gnad vnnd den lon so sy hyn wyder mit jrem andacht hynder der messe verdienen möchten/ Darumb sy sich fürbas flyssen vnd demütiklichen got bytten vnd lieb haben solten/ Darnach durch bytt vñ anrüffung deß heiligẽ mans/komen sy all wyder zü jren synnen/vnnd aller pyn vnd schmertzens entladen/vnnd hüten sich dar nach vor söllichem/ Darumb dyß eyn güts byspel/ist das nyeman hynder der meß söllich geschwetz vnd gelachter üben sonder ernsthaft vnnd andechtig syn sol/

Wie der tufel hynder der mesz die klapperig etlicher frowen vff schreib/vnd jm das berment zü kürtz wart/vnnd ers mit den zenen vß eynander zoch/

9.4 Gossiping women. Marquard Vom Stein, *Der Ritter vom Turn* (Basel: Michael Furter für Johann Bergmann von Olpe, 1493), fol. 18v. Munich, Bayerische Staatsbibliothek.

Christ at the Last Supper and the speed at which the devils must write to keep up with the sheer volume of gossip. Since the devils are recording their words on parchment, the gossiping women are arguably "dictating" an alternative text for female readers, albeit one that is diabolically rather than paternally sanctioned.[27] Text and woodcut collude, warning that the woman who reads against the Knight's exegesis fashions a transgressive text of her own, becoming the "one in a hundred" "wickeder" and "more evil" for it.

Notes

I am indebted to the Faculty of Arts Research Fund, University of Bristol, for grants that enabled me to carry out research on the woodcuts at the Bayerische Staatsbibliothek, Munich, the Newberry Library, Chicago, and the Österreichische Nationalbibliothek, Vienna; and to the DAAD for a grant that enabled me to carry out research on *Der Ritter vom Turn* at the Herzog August Bibliothek, Wolfenbüttel.

1. The English translations are my own and based on the text in Marquard vom Stein, *Der Ritter vom Turn*, ed. Ruth Harvey, Texte des späten Mittelalters und der frühen Neuzeit 32 (Berlin: Erich Schmidt Verlag, 1988), here p. 183. All subsequent page references will be given in parentheses in the text. Marquard's translation echoes one version of the French original: see Geoffroy de la Tour Landry, *Le Livre du Chevalier de la Tour Landry pour l'enseignement de ses filles*, ed. M. Anatole de Montaiglon (Paris: Jannet, 1854), p. 178. An English translation by William Caxton was published in 1484: see *The Book of the Knight of the Tower*, ed. M.Y. Offord, Early English Text Society, supplementary series 2 (London: Oxford University Press, 1971).
2. Ruth Harvey, "Prolegomena to an edition of 'Der Ritter vom Turn,'" in *Probleme mittelalterlicher Überlieferung und Textkritik: Oxforder Colloquium 1966*, ed. Peter F. Ganz and Werner Schröder (Berlin: Erich Schmidt Verlag, 1968), p. 163 [162–82], and Hans Joachim Kreutzer, "Marquart vom Stein," in *Die deutsche Literatur des Mittelalters: Verfasserlexikon*, ed. Wolfgang Stammler et al., 2nd edn., 10 vols. (Berlin: de Gruyter, 1987), vol. 6, col. 133 [129–35] suggest the daughters may have been a useful fiction. If so, their fictionality would open a different interpretation of the undeniably salacious aspects of the text since these would function more clearly as the means to sexual titillation. Indeed, a double readership may have been intended from the start: the male reader, who would have enjoyed the male authority stamped on and the risqué entertainment offered in the text; and the female reader, for whom the stories were meant to function as warnings or models, but for whom some of the stories may also have been sexually titillating. As Holt N. Parker states: "The woman is a fiction, a male-created mask, which authorizes and privileges a male-created text." In other words, the male reader may have been intended as the prime recipient, the daughters and female readers a vehicle for arousing material. See Holt N. Parker, "Love's Body Anatomized: The Ancient Erotic Handbooks and the Rhetoric of Sexuality," in *Pornography and Representation in Greece and Rome*, ed. Amy Richlin (Oxford: Oxford University Press, 1992), p. 92 [90–107]. My thanks to Heike Bartel of the Department of German, University of Nottingham, for this reference and her helpful comments on this essay.
3. For discussion of the authorship of the woodcuts see the following: Franz Bock, *Die Werke des Matthias Grünewald*, Studien zur deutschen Kunstgeschichte 54 (Strasbourg: Heitz and Mündel, 1904); Louis Poulain, "Der Ritter von Turn von Marquart von Stein" (unpublished diss., University of Basel, 1906); Rudolf Kautzsch, *Die Holzschnitte zum Ritter vom Turn (Basel 1493)*,

Studien zur deutschen Kunstgeschichte 44 (Strasbourg: Heitz and Mündel, 1903); Hans Koegler, "Die Basler Gebetholzschnitte vom Illustrator des Narrenschiffs und Ritters vom Turn," *Gutenberg-Jahrbuch* 1 (1926): 117–31; Werner Weisbach, *Der Meister der Bergmannschen Offizin und Albrecht Dürers Beziehungen zur Basler Buchillustration: Ein Beitrag zur Geschichte des deutschen Holzschnittes*, Studien zur deutschen Kunstgeschichte 6 (Strasbourg: Heitz and Mündel, 1896) and Weisbach, *Die Baseler Buchillustration des XV. Jahrhunderts*, Studien zur deutschen Kunstgeschichte 8 (Strasbourg: Heitz and Mündel, 1896); Wilhelm Worringer, *Die altdeutsche Buchillustration* (Munich: Piper, 1912), pp. 81–82; Erwin Panofsky, *The Life and Art of Albrecht Dürer* (Princeton: Princeton University Press, 1943; repr. 1955), pp. 28–29; Heinrich Röttinger, "Die Holzschnitte der Druckerei des Jacob Cammerlander in Straßburg," *Gutenberg-Jahrbuch* 11 (1936): 129 [125–40]; Friedrich Winkler, *Dürer und die Illustrationen zum Narrenschiff* (Berlin: Deutscher Verein für Kunstwissenschaft, 1951), p. 57. See also Harvey, "Prolegomena," p. 180; and Theodor Brüggemann in Zusammenarbeit mit Otto Brunken et al., *Handbuch zur Kinder-und Jugendliteratur*, vol. 1, *Vom Beginn des Buchdrucks bis 1570* (Stuttgart: Metzler, 1987), col. 755 [739–78].

4. Peter Strieder, *Dürer: Paintings, Prints, Drawings*, trans. Nancy M. Gordon and Walter L. Strauss (London: Frederick Muller, 1982), for example, attributes the woodcuts unequivocally to Dürer and his assistants (p. 93).
5. J.L. Grigsby has identified the collection as the *Miroir des bonnes femmes*. Grigsby shows that the French original of the *Livre* adapts from the *Miroir* the sequence of stories about good and bad women taken from the Bible. See J.L. Grigsby, "Miroir des bonnes femmes," *Romania* 82 (1961): 458–81; and Grigsby, "A New Source of the *Livre du Chevalier de la Tour Landry*," *Romania* 84 (1963): 171–208.
6. For the French original see *Livre du chevalier de la Tour Landry*, p. 1.
7. Diane Bornstein cites Marguerite and Blanche of Burgundy, daughters-in-law of Philip the Fair, who were suspected of adultery because they had each given a knight a purse of cloth-of-gold. The women were thrown into prison; the young knights were flayed alive. See Diane Bornstein, *The Lady in the Tower: Medieval Courtesy Literature for Women* (Hamden: Archon, 1983), p. 120.
8. For the French see *Livre du chevalier de la Tour Landry*, p. 8.
9. Indeed, should the daughters be a convenient narrative fiction, the force and immediacy of the father-narrator's strictures on the actual (female) reader are increased since s/he becomes the prime recipient. Writing about Middle English devotional literature, Anne Clark Bartlett argues the following: "The conventional goal of promoting devotion by 'reforming' the identity of the readers helps explain why devotional texts regularly address their audiences directly, calling them, for example, 'dear friend.' " See Bartlett, *Male Authors, Female Readers: Representation and Subjectivity in Middle English Devotional Literature* (Cornell: Cornell University Press, 1995), p. 19. Similarly, in the *Ritter vom Turn* this strategy helps to draw both the assumed daughters and the actual female readers into the logic of the father-narrator's exegesis of the stories and closes down potential escape routes into independent exegesis by female readers. The question remains as to whether the female reader is

equally drawn into identification of herself with the visual representations of the daughters and feels constrained by them or whether she is able to resist.

10. Kaja Silverman, "Dis-Embodying the Female Voice," in *Re-Vision: Essays in Feminist Film Criticism*, ed. Mary Ann Doane, Patricia Mellencamp, and Linda Williams, The American Film Institute Monograph Series 3 (Los Angeles: University Publications of America, 1984), p. 132 [131–49].
11. Silverman, "Dis-Embodying the Female Voice," p. 134.
12. Silverman also comments: "The participation of the male subject in the production of discourse may be limited, and contingent upon his 'willingness' to identify with the existing cultural order, but the participation of the female subject in the production of discourse is nonexistent" (p. 132). This is precisely the case in the *Ritter vom Turn*, where the lack of female participation in the discourse also serves to reinforce the father-narrator's authority. The role of the dialogue between the Knight and his wife lies outside the scope of this chapter.
13. "Lappidoth" means "torches" and only occurs as a proper name in this context. For a commentary on Judges see James D. Martin, *The Book of Judges* (Cambridge, UK: Cambridge University Press, 1975); and J. Alberto Soggin, *Judges: A Commentary*, trans. John Bowden, Old Testament Library (London: SCM Press, 1981).
14. For St. Katherine and her iconography see Diane Apostolos-Cappadona, *The Dictionary of Women in Religious Art* (Oxford: Oxford University Press, 1998), pp. 66–68; Sally Fisher, *The Square Halo and Other Mysteries of Western Art Images and the Stories that Inspired Them* (New York: Harry N. Abrams, 1995), pp. 40–42; *Dictionary of Subjects and Symbols in Art*, ed. James Hall (London: John Murray, 1974; repr. 2000), pp. 58–59; and Peter and Linda Murray, *The Oxford Companion to Christian Art and Architecture* (Oxford: Oxford University Press, 1996), p. 95.
15. The armor might also indicate the Knight's role as protector of his daughters' virtue: just as the book is intended to help them protect their own reputation through "correct" behavior, so the Knight's physical strength is protection against the sort of assault described by him in his preface. However, male violence toward women is frequently described in the text so the armor may be a reminder of the force available to men as the ultimate control mechanism.
16. Song of Songs 4.12.
17. This is supported by Lesley Smith's argument that the book held by Mary "represents the Christ that Gabriel is sent to announce. Lest we think that Christ did not exist before the birth of Jesus, this already-present book reminds us of the doctrine of the eternity of the Word. The Word made flesh (so graphically evident in the parchment pages of a manuscript book) in Mary's book is symbolically present at the very moment of his conception." See Smith, "Scriba, Femina: Medieval Depictions of Women Writing," in *Women and the Book*, ed. Lesley Smith and Jane H.M. Taylor (London: British Library, 1997), p. 22 [21–44]. For the significance of representations of the Virgin reading and their relationship to women's literacy in the Middle

Ages see Pamela Sheingorn, " 'The Wise Mother': The Image of St. Anne Teaching the Virgin Mary," *Gesta* 32.1 (1993): 69–80. My thanks to Diane Wolfthal for this reference.

18. See *Dictionary of Women in Religious Art*, p. 20. An ecclesiastical interior was also common.
19. This echoes the widespread metaphor of Mary's womb as the vessel for Christ.
20. *Dictionary of Women in Religious Art*, p. 18.
21. Laura Mulvey, "Visual Pleasure and Narrative Cinema," *Screen* 16.3 (1975): 11 [6–18]; repr. in *Feminism and Film Theory*, ed. Constance Penley (London: BFI Publishing, 1988) p. 62 [57–68].
22. Mulvey, "Visual Pleasure," p. 11.
23. Michael Baxandall, *Painting and Experience in Fifteenth-Century Italy* (Oxford: Oxford University Press, 1972), pp. 45–46.
24. Berlin, Staatsbibliothek, MS. Germ. Quart. 42, fol. 119v.
25. Robert Scribner, "Ways of Seeing in the Age of Dürer," in *Dürer and His Culture*, ed. Dagmar Eichberger and Charles Zika (Cambridge, UK: Cambridge University Press, 1998), pp. 104–105 [93–117].
26. This is the legend of the demon Tutivillus, whose task it was to record the idle gossip of people in church and read it out at Judgement Day. Tellingly, in this version two devils are needed to keep up with the flow.
27. If the book in the Annunciation woodcut represents Christ, the Word made Flesh, then what sort of word-made-flesh does the devils' record of the women's gossip represent? Moreover, gossiping women represent a conventional misogynist stereotype in both art and literature, a tradition that closes down the space for a subversive reading. The woodcut also presents a visual contrast between Mary, who as the model of piety is passive, and transgressive women, who are active.

CHAPTER 10

VISUALIZING THE FEMININE IN THE *ROMAN DE PERCEFOREST*: THE EPISODE OF THE "CONTE DE LA ROSE"

Sylvia Huot

This chapter looks at an episode in the fourteenth-century Roman de Perceforest with particular visual significance: the representation of feminine constancy by a magical rose. Courtly and misogynistic readings of this image are pitted against each other in the ensuing intrigue.

This chapter focuses on an episode from the *Roman de Perceforest* known as the "conte de la rose."[1] The *Perceforest*, an anonymous prose romance set in a mythical British antiquity, was written for Guillaume I, count of Hainault and father-in-law of King Edward III of England; it is thought to have been completed ca. 1340. The "conte de la rose" episode, one of numerous set pieces incorporated into this vast romance, was doubtless adapted from oral or written sources; Gaston Paris has identified several analogous tales in various languages.[2] If the basic narrative was not original with the author, however, he nonetheless manipulated his material to fit it into the overall narrative program and ideological framework of the *Perceforest*. A central theme of this vast romance is the conflict in pre-Arthurian Britain between a Greek monarchy installed by Alexander the Great and an indigenous clan, known as *le lignaige Darnant*, descended from the Trojan Brutus. The rival cultures struggling for dominance are distinguished in large part through their respective identification of women as autonomous subjects governed by their own desire or as passive objects of a predatory male sexuality. These competing models of gender and sexuality, and in particular the very different readings of the feminine inherent to each, are brought into sharp focus in the "conte de la rose" episode.

The "conte de la rose" tells the story of the couple Margon and Lisane of the kingdom of Gorre. Margon, a poor knight, goes to seek his fortune at the court of Perceforest, king of England. To assure him of her fidelity, Lisane gives her husband an ivory box containing a magical rose: as long as she remains faithful to him, it will preserve its scent and freshness. Margon consoles himself during his time at court by withdrawing to a private spot and peeking at his rose several times a day. Eventually this behavior is observed, and two wicked and envious knights, Melean and Nabon, pressure the king into asking Margon what he carries in his box. Thinking the affair to be completely harmless, the king tells the two envious ones what he has learned. Once Melean and Nabon know the secret of the rose, they force Margon into a wager: if they succeed in seducing his wife and thus withering the rose, he must spend a year carrying a shield with an image of a woman riding astride a knight on all fours, and if they fail they will forfeit their lands to him. Not only do they fail, but the clever Lisane imprisons them and makes them spin and wind wool to earn their keep. The truth comes out when Margon, accompanied by no fewer than eight of the king's highest-ranking knights, returns home and is invited to view the activities of the now very chastened Nabon and Melean. This is a humiliation from which the two never recover; they ask only to be allowed to flee to a place so remote that no one will ever know who they are. Back at court, Margon is invested with the lands of the two villains, while Lisane is fêted by the ladies. The story gives rise to the "Lai de la rose a la dame lealle," which, according to the narrator, is particularly loved by women.[3]

The narrative is clearly modeled on the familiar pattern of the medieval "wager" romances, such as Jean Renart's *Roman de la rose ou de Guillaume de Dole* and Gerbert de Montreuil's *Roman de la violette*, though without the misunderstandings and false claims that lead in those texts to the punishment of the innocent woman. The choice of the rose as the central emblem for the lady may perhaps have been suggested by the similar role of the rose-shaped birthmark in Renart's poem. The rose also alludes unmistakably to the *Roman de la rose* of Guillaume de Lorris and Jean de Meun, which lurks in the background of more than one episode of this lengthy romance.

In the "conte de la rose" episode, the rose and the shield are alternative visual emblems for the autonomous woman, subject to different readings. The tale pits an antifeminist reading against one that is more pro-feminine or anti-misogynist, using visual signs and coding as a primary means of expression. First the rose is shown to be subject to two different readings, one of which foregrounds feminine honor and sexual self-governance while the other rejects such notions. The misogynist reading of the rose, in turn, gives rise to the negative image of feminine autonomy as a form of male humiliation. Since spinning is the quintessential "women's work" of the Middle Ages, the enforced labor of Melean and Nabon offers a third image of femininity, or more accurately of effeminacy: the imposition of emblematic femininity onto a male body results in a shameful emasculation. The punishment of the two would-be seducers thus offers a kind of riposte to the shield, by constructing this feminine power of emasculation in quite different terms.

The rose enters the narrative as a closely guarded secret; even the reader does not know why the knight constantly withdraws to a private spot in order to peer inside the little box that he always carries on his person. We learn its story when he explains it to Perceforest. Since this conversation takes place on the first of February, when no rose could be in bloom, Margon's treasured possession can only be viewed as a marvel. It is, in fact, "tant belle et tant odourante qu'il fist grant bien au roy de la veoir" [so beautiful and so fragrant that it did the king great good to see it] (4:339–40). The rose is portrayed in this initial description as an emblem of the loyal and virtuous wife: precious, steadfast, unchanging. Her love and her fidelity are as beautiful as a rose in bloom, and have the same power to refresh the spirits of the beholder. Her strength of mind is so strong that she can withstand any amount of temptation or separation from her husband, as represented in the rose's miraculous power to retain its freshness indefinitely, even through the winter months.

The villainous Melean and Nabon, however, have a different perspective on the rose. For them, it represents the woman's vulnerability: her fidelity is as ephemeral as a rose about to wilt and wither away, and her virtue can be overcome as easily as a rose can be plucked and dried. In Margon's explanation to Perceforest, the purpose of the rose is primarily to dispel his own (ungrounded) fears by providing him with a sure sign of his wife's fidelity. He explains that is was she who persuaded him to go and seek his fortune at court:

> Quant je entendis le proupos de ma femme, je lui respondy qu'elle disoit mout bien, mais consideré l'amour que j'avoie a elle pour sa grant bonté, beaulté et jennesse, je ne la pourroie nullement laissier et que puet estre elle avroit trop de requerans dont je seroie impacient. Adont elle me respondy que de ce elle me asseuroit franchement. (4:341)
>
> [When I heard my wife's suggestion, I replied that she spoke very well, but considering the love that I had for her because of her great goodness, beauty, and youth, I could in no way leave her and that perhaps she would have all

> too many suitors, which would upset me. Then she replied that she could freely/openly set my fears to rest on that count.]

When Nabon and Melean speak to Margon about the rose, however, they subtly recast it not as a transparent sign of Lisane's intrinsic fidelity but as a disciplinary device that enables him to keep watch over her at a distance. As one of them states:

> Margon, je ne sache chevalier si eureux de vous, car vous estes tant asseur de vostre femme qu'elle ne puet de son corps faire courtoisie a homme qui vive sans vostre sceu. Et elle, qui de ce se doubte, come saige s'en garde. (4:344)
>
> [Margon, I know of no other knight as fortunate as you, for you are so certain of your wife that she cannot grant any bodily favor to any man alive without your knowledge. And, knowing that, she conducts herself with propriety.]

The wicked knight then stakes his claim that, if given the chance to see Lisane in person, "je suis certain que je m'y conduiroie tellement que la rose appaliroit et seche devendroit" [I am certain that I would conduct myself such that the rose would fade and wither] (4:344).

The very specialness of the rose, which assumed a kind of miraculous power in the husband's eyes, now emerges as emblematic of the unnaturalness of a woman loyal in love: such a creature would be as rare as a rose blooming in midwinter, and about as likely to endure. Thus, as long as it remained a secret visual token shared only by husband and wife, or even by others who adhere to the courtly code of values promoted at Perceforest's court, the rose was indeed a representation of feminine love, loyalty, and virtue; but as soon as it is seen by the uncourtly and envious villains, it becomes a sign of feminine weakness. Moreover, the rose moves from being a private sign of the husband's sense of self-worth as object of his wife's love, to being a public sign of the honor or shame of the man who succeeds or fails at possessing the lady in question. Depending on the perspective from which it is read, the rose implies a view of the lady either as empowered subject, or as the object of male rivalry and predation.

Melean and Nabon in turn propose a new emblem for the powerful woman in control of her own desires: the image on the shield that her husband will be forced to bear for a year following their seduction of his wife. There is no question that Lisane does in fact value her own autonomy and that she has resisted being defined as an object of male exchange. We are told that the marriage is one of mutual love, contracted on the couple's own initiative. The husband won her love through his chivalric valiance, but he is a poor knight socially beneath her family and for this reason her parents opposed the marriage. That the marriage took place anyway does show a certain willfulness on Lisane's part. Margon explains that the couple chose to legitimize their mutual love through marriage rather than entering into an unsanctioned, extramarital affair, stating, "en ce point amour nous demena tant que oultre le vouloir de son pere et de sa mere nous nous mariasmes pour eviter toute villonie" [at this point we were so swept away by love that, against the wishes of her father and her mother, we got married in order to avoid any base behavior] (4:340). Unfortunately, this privately contracted marriage served not to establish an alliance between Margon and his father-in-law, but only to sever all ties with Lisane's family: "ce fait despleut tant a son pere que du sien il ne nous donna comme rien" [this fact so displeased her father that he did not give us any of his wealth] (4:341).

The positive reading, then, suggests that Lisane's self-possession and genuine love for her husband will guarantee her fidelity; but the negative reading of a willful woman holds that she is primarily interested in sexual adventuring, and that she will subjugate her husband like a cruel dominatrix. In this latter view the entire marriage takes on a different meaning: just as Margon was socially inferior and thus unable to receive Lisane as an object binding him to her family, so now he will suffer for this inferiority and for the lack of institutionalized approval accorded the marriage. She will turn out to have used him as a means of guaranteeing her own freedom, knowing that a weak and poor man like him would not be able to control her and that his possession of her is not entirely legitimate anyway.

Thus the two wicked knights on the one hand reinterpret the miraculous rose, transforming this sign of feminine strength into one of feminine weakness and vulnerability; and they also propose a new visual representation of feminine strength, one that is imbued not with beauty and vitality but with a vulgar comedy. Another way of stating this is that they transfer the concept of the self-possessed woman from the courtly register to that of the *fabliaux*. In that world, having a wife who knows her own mind and acts accordingly can never be a token of power, joy, or comfort for her husband, but only one of shame; nor can a marriage between a high-born lady and a lower-born man result in anything other than domestic discord and cuckoldry. As for the rose itself, they have clearly imposed a reading that derives not from traditional associations of the rose with purity and virtue, but from the *Roman de la rose* and in particular the portion by Jean de Meun, in which the rose is increasingly reduced to a sexual prize that is there for the taking.

The ultimate visual spectacle offered by the narrative is, of course, quite different from what these two knights had expected: not one of their own sexual pleasure with the lady and the ensuing humiliation of her husband, but rather, one of their own humiliation. The room in which the knights are kept is equipped with a peep-hole through which the lady and her servants or guests can view the unfortunate prisoners, monitoring their behavior and subjecting them to her disciplinary regime. When Melean first realizes his situation, for example, he begins to lament his misfortune, and then finds that his behavior has not gone unobserved:

> Endementiers que le chevalier se dementoit, la bonne dame l'escouttoit. Adont elle ouvry un petit trou quarré qui estoit en l'huis de la tour, puis commença a dire: "Sire chevalier, folie faittes de blasmer les dames et damoiselles . . . Sy ne dittes chose dont vous soiés reprins, ains mettés la main a l'oeuvre et fillés debonnairement, s'en avrés mieulx vitaile." (4:356–57)
>
> [While the knight was lamenting, the good lady was listening. Then she opened a little square window that was in the door to the tower, and began to speak: "Sir knight, you are foolish to put the blame on ladies and damsels . . . So don't say things that will get you in trouble, but set to work and spin, so you can be better fed."]

If the husband has his rose that he peeks at in private moments, the wife now has her own private source of entertainment. The two wicked knights forced the husband to make his rose public, and hoped to humiliate him still further with the public display of the shaming shield. Similarly, the wife chooses the moment for a public revelation of her two prisoners. Having learned the importance and status of the guests that Margon has brought to their castle, she reveals to the assembled company that she has been visited during the past year by two knights from court, and then takes everyone for a viewing.

A major part of the knights' punishment and subjugation is precisely this inability to control their public image: they will be the object of either a curious and mocking gaze, or of complete oblivion, according to the whim of the woman who now keeps them. The fear of being seen in such an ignominious state gripped Melean from the beginning, when he retreated with his distaff into a corner despite the fact that he was alone in a locked room: "jasoit ce qu'il pensa que personne ne le veoit, toutesvoies lui signiffioit Honte que trop secretement ne le pouoit faire" [even though he didn't think anyone could see him, Shame still made him feel that he couldn't be too secretive about it] (4:358). The implements of their work, like the cuckold's shield, are signs that strip Melean and Nabon of masculinity and of aristocratic status all in one stroke. When Lisane tells her husband that she is making his two adversaries earn their living, he is amazed:

> Quant Margon entendy ce, il eut grant merveilles a quoy ilz pouoient gaingnier leur pain. Si commença a rire, puis dist: "Madame, ouvraige de chevalier est de pou de valeur quant au gaingnaige, car aidier ne s'en scevent." (4:377)

> [When Margon heard that, he wondered greatly how they could earn their keep. He began to laugh, then he said: "Lady, a knight's work is of little value when it comes to earning a living, for he doesn't know how to do that."]

And when the revelation is described in the "Lai de la rose," one of the knights witnessing the event comments, "Par foi, je croi qu'en cest païs n'a gent / Qu'aient veü. . ./ Chevaliers nul qui filast pour argent" [By my faith, I don't think that there is anyone in this land who has seen a knight spinning for money].[4] Lisane's treatment of Melean and Nabon is thus doubly shaming: it robs them of both class and gender status. When Melean realizes that he has no means of escape, in fact, he is so horrified that "la sueur lui encommença venir au front de doleur et de vergoingne" [sweat began to break out on his forehead from sorrow and shame] (4:357); and catching sight of the spindle and spools, "il dist qu'il amoit mieulx mourir que faire tel ouvraige" [he said that he would rather die than do such work] (4:356). Being seen in that state by a group of knights from the royal court effectively destroys the two. There is nothing left but to flee, destitute and shamed, "en telle terre ou puis ne furent congneus" [to a land where they would not be known] (4:379).

The image of the knights spinning imprints itself on the collective consciousness of Perceforest's Britain in the form of an expression that, we are told, became widespread:

> Et touteffois sus ce vint de nouvel une galerie en la Grant Bretaigne de dames aux chevaliers, ausquelz il desplaisoit. Car quant un chevalier requeroit a une dame aucune chose qu'elle ne voulsist pas ottroier, fust a gas ou a certes, elle respondoit en disant: "Sire chevalier, depourtés vous de celle requeste qu'on ne vous apprende a filler!"; dont pluiseurs chevaliers se deportoient, vergoingneux et confus, et maudissoient les deux chevaliers dont celle maudite reprouche venoit. (4:385)
>
> [And from this there arose a new way for ladies in Great Britain to make fun of knights, to their displeasure. For when a knight would ask a lady for anything that she didn't want to grant him, whether jokingly or seriously, she would reply by saying: "Sir knight, drop your request lest you be taught to spin!"; whereby many a knight gave up, ashamed and disconcerted, and cursed the two knights from whom this horrid reproach had come.]

The image that spreads throughout the kingdom, then, is not that of cuckoldry as the inevitable supplement to marriage, but that of emasculation as the result of sexual predation. The feminine power that is represented here is not the power to oppress the men who foolishly trust in them, but that of resisting the men who prey on them. This emblematic image, and the story behind it, further suggest that men are emasculated not by committing themselves to the love of one woman, but precisely by not being able to do so: it is the arrogance of what we might now call sexual harassment perpetrated by men, that will lead to their downfall. The true violation of courtly gender codes is revealed to be not the autonomous woman who marries a poor but worthy knight out of true love against her father's wishes, but the predatory man who seeks to exploit women for personal pleasure and gain.

The different visual images of the story work as part of the romance's overall program of cultural ideology, one thread of which is the regulation of heterosexuality and the definition of British culture as a civilization that is founded on the suppression of rape.[5] Before the advent of King Perceforest, we are told, Britain was terrorized by the clan of Darnant.[6] These knights recognized no central authority or rule of law, and they took it as their fundamental right to rape every woman they found. In a debate within the clan over whether or not to submit to the authority of the new king, Gelinant du Glat is the only one of the clan leaders who argues that they need to mend their ways and that their treatment of women goes against God and Nature, who had always intended that a woman should be "dame de son corps" [mistress of her own body] (1:400). Gelinant condemns the clan's sexual practices in the strongest of terms:

> Et nous, qui avions ou devions avoir sens et raison, avons exurpé et tollu aux dames et aux damoiselles et abusé contre la franchise que le Dieu de Nature leur avoit donnee, car le plus de nous se delectent en elles efforcer et tollir ce que homme ne doibt avoir s'il ne leur plaist que quant ilz le peuent avoir de gré, et en ce mesfaisons nous encontre le Dieu de Nature. (1:401)
>
> [And we, who had or should have had sense and reason, have usurped and ravished ladies and damsels and abused them in violation of the freedom that the God of Nature had granted them, for the majority of us delight in forcing them and in taking from them what no man should have if they do not wish it, but only if they can have it by consent, and in this we sin against the God of Nature.]

Gelinant's characterization of his kinsmen's behavior is no exaggeration; the narrator provides numerous examples of their proclivity for rape at every opportunity.

Gelinant's plea is rejected out of hand by another leader who speaks for the overwhelming majority of the clan:

> Et selon ce que je puis concepvoir en ses parolles, il m'est advis qu'il entend a estre des chevaliers recreans qui entrent en hermitaige par couardise, car selon ce qu'il monstre il n'y a fors que nous renonçons au droit qui nous vient de noz ancestres et que nous avons usé toutes noz vies et devenons serfz aux femmes qui ne sont faittes fors pour noz voulentez acomplir. (1:401)

> [And from what I understand of his words, it seems to me that he means to be one of those lazy knights who go into a hermitage out of cowardice, for he claims that there is nothing for it but for us to renounce the right that comes to us from our ancestors and that we have exercised all our lives, and that we should become the slaves of women who were created only to fulfill our desires.]

Although the lineage of Darnant is eventually subjugated, the fear of a return to that regime of rape haunts Perceforest's Britain. Numerous monuments and inscriptions mark the spots where members of the clan were killed by Perceforest's knights while in the act of raping a damsel or lady. Several of these flagrant rapists are even magically preserved—variously headless, impaled on swords or spears, or engulfed in flames—as visual reminders of the wickedness of their crime and the power of Perceforest's regime in suppressing it. These monuments, inscriptions, and "undead" bodies are described repeatedly, as the many knights who populate Perceforest's kingdom encounter them in the course of their travels. The story of rape and its containment within a larger hierarchy of male homosocial violence is thus written, both textually and visually, across the British landscape as the realm is brought under the rule of law and order.

Women in particular refer constantly to that reign of sexual terror, invoking that era as a kind of absolute or ultimate evil to be avoided at all costs. After the Roman invasion has devastated the kingdom and left it virtually bereft of knights or rulers, for example, the women gather in the forest,

> pour consoler l'un l'autre et parlerent du tamps advenir que trop pouoit estre divers a elles et a leurs filles, car sy net estoit le noble sang destruit que le lignaige Darnant si pourroit aincoires bien revenir en regne, dont elles seroient pis que mortes. (4:955)
>
> [to console one another, and they spoke of the time to come which might be very difficult for them and for their daughters, for the nobility was so utterly destroyed that the lineage of Darnant might well return to power, which for them would be a fate worse than death.]

One woman even considers putting her two young daughters to death in order to spare them from falling into the "vilté et servaige" [degradation and servitude] (4:955) that she fears may be coming. Fortunately, her powers of divination reveal that a new king will soon be installed, making such drastic measures unnecessary. At another point Perceforest's queen invokes those dark days in a debate with her husband, who is annoyed that a group of recently married knights have left court in order to establish their new households. The king expresses the wish that the "hunt" of love should go on forever, since it inspires young men to deeds of chivalry, and he curses the "capture" that allows them to relax and enjoy the fruits of their labors. He wishes that the damsels had remained aloof and forced the knights to keep vying for their love indefinitely. The queen points out that in fact young ladies must eventually give in to their suitors:

> Car s'en tamps et en lieu les chassans n'avoient le guerredon de prise, les chassans se deporteroyent de chassier, ou par annuyance ou par viellune. Et quant ce seroit sceu, jamais ne seroit aucune emprinse, ains se maintendroyent a guise de bestes . . . Aussy en est entre homme et femme la chasse deshonneste qui jadis regna es mauvais et pervers du lignaige Dernant l'enchanteur, qui ne usoient de chasse ne d'amour, ains ravissoyent les fammes sans chasse, sans raison et sans avoir regard a honneur, mais comme les bestes mues. (4:149)
>
> [For if the time and place never came for the hunters to have the reward of capture, they would give up on the hunt, through annoyance or old age. And when that was known, no hunt would ever be undertaken, and everyone would behave like beasts . . . For it was an immoral hunt of man and woman that once prevailed among the evil and perverse lineage of Darnant the Enchanter, who made no use of hunt nor of love, but ravished women without any pursuit, without reason and without any regard for honor, like dumb animals.]

In a culture so preoccupied with sexual violence and its suppression, this adventure, in which the two villains are of the lineage of Darnant, takes on a particularly important meaning.

As Nabon and Melean hatch their plan, in fact, they tell each other that if they do not succeed, "nous ne sommes pas dignes d'estre du lignaige Darnant, le vaillant prince auquel femme ne peut oncques resister qu'il n'en feist son voloir" [we are not worthy of being of the lineage of Darnant, the valiant prince whom no woman could ever resist but that he had his will with her] (4:344). Yet their subsequent misadventure forces them to reevaluate the entire concept of feminine resistance and acquiescence. Darnant's ability to have his will with any woman might mean that he was so attractive that no woman *would* refuse him, or it might mean that he was so violent that no woman *could* refuse him, however much she might want to. The knights' image of their ancestral heritage, in fact—that they, like Darnant, must be irresistible to women—is countered by Perceforest's characterization of Darnant's sexuality as destructive and shameful. Upon learning of the wager, he exclaims: "Et en verité le fait demoustre bien que vous estes du lignaige de Darnant l'enchanteur qui oncques ne fist honneur a femme" [and in truth, this matter shows clearly that you are of the lineage of Darnant the enchanter, who never behaved honorably toward women] (4:347).

This very distinction, resting as it does on the concept of feminine desire and self-determination, is one that dawns on Nabon and Melean only after their failure with Lisane. When Nabon, the second to be imprisoned, learns that Melean has failed to seduce Lisane he expresses surprise, protesting, "oncques de femme ne vous veis redargué" [I've never seen you spurned by any woman] (4:363). Melean ruefully explains the lesson he has learned:

> Ainsi est il de moy, Nabon, qui ay eut la grace de mettre toutes femmes au dessoubz ou j'ay mis ma cure; mais j'ay par ci devant esté heureux de adressier a femmes a qui pesoit qu'elles n'estoient requises. Or ay maintenant trouvé mon maistre, car il m'a dompté et mon malice mis a neant. (4:364)
>
> [So it is with me, Nabon, who have had the gift of overcoming all women that have caught my fancy; but up to now I have been lucky enough to have accosted women who were annoyed at not being asked. Now I have found my master, for he has conquered me and reduced my machinations to nothing.]

Rather then imposing his will on women, Melean now sees that he was never more than a tool of feminine desire anyway: his sexual exploits succeeded only because they corresponded to the wishes of the women in question. His use of a masculine term for the victorious Lisane, whom he now terms "mon maistre" and whom he designates with the masculine pronoun "il," further underscores his sense of role-reversal: as he is the feminized culprit, guilty of malice and cupidity, so she is the masculinized victor, endowed with wisdom and correctional powers. Perhaps the ultimate punishment of Melean and Nabon is that their own misogyny produces and determines the very form of their disgrace. In their feminized state they are reduced to the helpless servitude that they had previously attributed to women, and they live out the nightmare scenario evoked by the clan leaders when they rallied the troops against Perceforest: the fear that they might "devenir serfz aux femmes" [become the slaves of women] (1:401).

If the demise of Nabon and Melean is a tale of misogyny punished and exposed, traditional misogynist views of women and of marriage are further discredited in an interesting passage when Margon is en route to check up on Lisane after Nabon and Melean have failed to return to court. When he is nearly home, Margon is gripped by an irrational fit of jealousy, in which he imagines "les deux mauvais gloutons joyssans de sa femme" [the two wicked louts taking their pleasure with his wife] (4:368) and is afraid to go any further. Taking refuge at a fountain, he launches into a lengthy diatribe against marriage, portraying the bachelor condition as one of idyllic freedom, a metaphoric Golden Age:

> En verité, devant celle mauvaise obligation, j'estoie en grant paix et deduit, en grant soulas at franchise. Tous esbatemens m'estoient presens. Par tout ou j'aloie, plaisances infinies me venoient au devant. En tous lieux ou j'aloie, je trouvoie ma vyande preste, atournee a point de tant noble queux comme de

> nature qui le m'avoit pendue. Par tous les arbres ou j'aloie ne m'en convenoit ja baissier, mais tout en chevauchant prendoye laquelle que je vouloye, fussent ou poires, ou pommes, noys, autres fruis, nettoyé et espammés de doulce rousee qui par-dessus couloit sans atouchement de vilain. Haa! homme marié, regarde comme francq j'estoie! (4:369)
>
> [In truth, before this evil obligation, I was in great peace and delight, in great solace and freedom. All enjoyments were available to me. Everywhere I went, infinite pleasures came before me. In all places I went to, I found my meat prepared, done to perfection by the noble cook nature, who had hung it there for me. I never had to bend down when going through the trees, but while riding I would take whatever I wanted, be it pears, apples, nuts, or other fruits, washed clean by the sweet dew that flows from on high, untouched by vile hands. Ha! married man, look how free I was!]

Since the reader is aware of Lisane's fidelity and of her treatment of Nabon and Melean, Margon's lament can only be seen as misguided and self-indulgent. His antimarital delusions are further undermined by the reaction of the eight royal knights who, unbeknownst to him, are camped nearby and who listen with bemusement to his words, "car tous huit estoient mariés, mais ne s'en sçavoient encores plaindre" [for all eight of them were married, but they hadn't yet had any cause to complain] (4:372). The episode suggests that just as the reading of the rose as unnatural or vulnerable was a serious misperception arising from male delusions of sexual prowess, so also the view of marriage as painful servitude reveals less about the behavior of women than about the bad faith and unfounded suspicions of men.

Margon's sentiments and his use of imagery reminiscent of the Golden Age echo Jean de Meun's *Rose*, in particular the discourse of Ami with its juxtaposition of the virulent diatribe of the Jaloux and the nostalgic evocation of a Golden Age of natural pleasures and sexual freedom.[7] The entire story effects a subtle recasting of key elements of the *Rose*, highlighting courtly and chivalric values of love, fidelity, marriage, and the honor of ladies. The marvelous rose, as we have seen, rewrites the erotic rose of Guillaume de Lorris and (especially) Jean de Meun into an emblem of feminine virtue and invulnerability. Rather than storming into the castle to ravish the lady and her rose, Nabon and Melean find that it is they who are locked up in a tower of enforced chastity, and they who are "bad mouthed"—quite justly—through the endless repetition of the story. And the manifestly inaccurate assumptions underlying the outburst of a jealous husband are exposed as nothing short of silliness: as the happily married knight Lionnel tells Margon during the encounter at the fountain, "folie fait plourer avant que on soit batu" [it is folly to weep when you haven't yet been beaten] (4:373).

The two visual images that emerge from this story, the eternally blooming rose and the knightly spinners, are embedded in the language of Perceforest's Britain through the *lai* and the locution they give rise to. As part of the cultural iconography they reinforce the central preoccupation with sexual violence that pervades the kingdom. But unlike the monuments that visually inscribe the violent force of law onto the landscape, this particular set of images adopts a more woman-centered perspective, showing how the sexual predations of two clan members were foiled not through male violence but through the stratagems of a woman. The queen's words already imply that if women wish to retain mastery over their own bodies, they must recognize both the extent and the limitations to their power. They have the right to resist unwanted advances and to hold out until their suitors prove themselves worthy, but they must also accept the necessity of giving in eventually, since it is only by granting their favors to the one man who truly deserves it that they can avoid being abused by all men. The "Conte de la rose" in turn alerts men to the necessity of regulating their own sexuality, since their very insistence on sexual omnipotence entails the greatest risk of emasculation; and holds out the promise that if they give their love to one lady, they will be richly rewarded.

Notes

1. *Perceforest: Quatrième partie*, ed. Gilles Roussineau, 2 vols., TLF 343 (Geneva: Droz, 1987), vol. 1, pp. 332–85. All citations of Part 4 of the *Perceforest* are from this edition. Citations of Part 1 are from Jane H.M. Taylor, ed., *Roman de Perceforest: Première partie*, TLF 279 (Geneva: Droz, 1979). Translations are my own.
2. See Gaston Paris, "Le Conte de la Rose dans le Roman de *Perceforest*," *Romania* 23 (1894): 78–140.
3. The composition of the "Lai de la rose" is mentioned at the end of the episode (p. 385). However the text of the *lai* does not appear until a subsequent performance in Part 5 of the *Perceforest* (Paris, Bibl. Nat. fr. 348, fols. 328r–335r). This portion of the text is unedited, but the *lai* was printed by Paris, "Conte de la rose," pp. 116–40, and by Jeanne Lods, (ed.), *Les Pièces lyriques du Roman de Perceforest*, Société de publications romanes et françaises 36 (Geneva: Droz; and Lille: Giard, 1953), pp. 69–81. When the *lai* is performed, the narrator comments: "Quant Ponchonnet eult le lai harpé et chanté de la bouche, vous ne pourriez croire coment il fu voulentiers ouy et entendu des dames et des damoiselles qui la estoient" [When Ponchonnet had played and sung the *lai*, you would not believe how readily it was heard and attended to by the ladies and maidens who were there] (fol. 335r).
4. Lods, (ed.), *Les Pièces lyriques*, ll. 535–37.
5. The didactic value of the romance is announced at the beginning with reference to the Greek chronicle of which the romance is supposed to be

a translation: "elle est tresaventureuse en chevalerie ne il n'est chevalier nulz s'il l'a leue qu'il n'en vaille mieulx" [it is packed with chivalric adventure, and there is no knight who would not be more worthy for having read it] (1:122). The romance's status as a virtual "manual of chivalry" is discussed at length by Jeanne Lods, *Le "Roman de Perceforest": Origines, composition, caractères, valeur et influence*, Société de publications romanes et françaises 32 (Geneva: Droz; and Lille: Giard, 1951).

6. The most detailed portrayal of the "lignaige Darnant" and their ethos appears in Part 1 of the *Perceforest*, which describes the clan's way of life, the suffering they inflict on women, and the violent struggle whereby the clan is finally defeated and exiled by Alexander, Perceforest, and Perceforest's brother Gadifer, aided by various local knights and a large contingent of local women.
7. The discourse of the Jaloux and the ensuing description of the violence and discord that typifies marriage (ll. 8425–9462) follows directly after the description of the idyllic Golden Age (ll. 8325–424) and is immediately followed by the account of how this idyll was destroyed by the advent of civilization, characterized by greed, violence, and power struggle (ll. 9463–634); see Guillaume de Lorris and Jean de Meun, *Roman de la rose*, ed. Félix Lecoy, CFMA, 3 vols. (Paris: Champion, 1973–75).

CHAPTER 11

TOO MANY WOMEN: READING FREUD, DERRIDA, AND *LANCELOT*

Miranda Griffin

This chapter explores the Prose Lancelot *in the light of Derrida's reading of resistance in psychoanalysis. Griffin suggests that the text's characters and critics, as well as Freud, veer between scrutinizing women for visible signs of their identity and constructing them as blind spots to the process of reading.*

Reading can be seen as a practice that invites and stages processes of visualization by the readers and characters of a text. This chapter will explore these processes as they are invited and staged by the Vulgate Cycle, especially by its longest component text, the *Lancelot*.[1] I shall argue that the scrutiny enacted by such processes in this text does not necessarily lead to clarity of focus, but rather, that an insistence on visibility can result in confusion, specifically, between various female characters: a confusion that is recurrently couched in visual terms. In the Vulgate Cycle, as I shall demonstrate, women often function as blind spots, troubling a gaze that desires distinction and definition, but which ends up finding and producing fusion and confusion.

The *Lancelot*, and the Vulgate Cycle in general, are texts preoccupied with origins, reiterating and revisiting narratives of etiology and genealogy throughout. In my discussion, I shall focus on two points in the *Lancelot* at which the means of determining these crucial origins are couched in terms of vision and reading, and depend upon the distinction between women who resemble one another, a distinction that is magnified rather than resolved when the gaze of characters and critics is brought to bear on the women in question. At these points in the *Lancelot*, two things coincide: first, the manuscript tradition becomes irreconcilably variable (in other words, there are so many different versions of these sections that it is impossible to resolve them to one version from which they all must have originated); and second, female characters are revealed as multiple, doubled, too alike for comfort and irresolvable to one figure. I shall look at these episodes in the light of Derrida's reading of Freud; my argument will therefore negotiate between multiple levels of reading and interpretation, which will also reflect on the processes of reading that happen in the encounter between medieval literature and modern theory.

In *Résistances de la psychanalyse*, Derrida produces one of his close readings of Freud, to ponder the nature of analysis, and, more specifically, the nature of what cannot be analyzed, what is seen as resisting analysis.[2] He focuses on the second chapter of *The Interpretation of Dreams*, in which Freud outlines the method of interpreting dreams by giving an analysis of his own dream, which involves one of his female patients, Irma.[3] During the course of his analysis of this dream, Freud realizes that the woman he took to be Irma in his dream is a conflation of her and two other women who also had been, or would have been, resistant to Freud's interpretation of their complaints. Another of Irma's symptoms reminds Freud of his wife. As he explains these connections, Freud indicates in a note that a lot more could be said about this conflation, but that he would get distracted and wander off track were he to pursue this line of enquiry.

> Ich ahne, daß die Deutung dieses Stücks nicht weit genug geführt ist, um allem verborgenen Sinn zu folgen. Wollte ich die Vergleichung der drei Frauen fortsetzen, so käme ich weit ab.—Jeder Traum hat mindestens eine Stelle, am welcher er unergründlich ist, gleichsam einen Nabel, durch den er mit dem Unerkannten zusammenhängt.[4]
>
> [I had a feeling that the interpretation of this part of the dream was not carried far enough to make it possible to follow the whole of its concealed meaning. If I had pursued my comparison between the three women, it would have taken me far afield.—There is at least one spot in every dream at which it is unplumbable—a navel, as it were, that is the point of contact with the unknown.][5]

Derrida's readings of Freud frequently and willingly privilege the marginal, and it is this footnote that Derrida picks up on to analyze the nature of the resistance of analysis. Put simply, he argues that the analysis proposed and enacted by psychoanalysis is bound to fail because, by its very nature, it will hit something that will not be analyzed—something that the processes of analysis construct and place at the heart of the strategies of interpretation. Derrida wants to reveal this point of unreadability as crucial to psychoanalysis, and to show, in contrast, that his way of reading never privileges a certain point that cannot be read, but sees and pursues the endless possibilities in each part and at each stage of the reading process. This formulation of reading resonates with the experience of modern critics reading the *Lancelot*: the variants of certain points in this case can appear to offer a formidable proliferation of readings, but can also seem to propose an impossibility of interpretation. I want now to turn to the *Lancelot* to examine, in the light of Derrida's reading of Freud's reading, the first point at which reading invites and troubles a visualization of individual women, only to conflate these women into an unreadable mass of resemblance.

My first point in the *Lancelot* where the manuscript culture becomes almost impossible to reconcile into one edited version provides a reflection of Derrida's focus on Freud's unsuccessful attempts to separate or distinguish between a number of women. A passage of the *Lancelot* that Ferdinand Lot called "une contradiction interne de l'œuvre,"[6] describes Guenevere, whom Arthur has recently married at this point in the text.

> Si avoit pris la roine Genievre n'avoit pas plus de .VII. mois et demi. Et che estoit la plus bele feme dont nus eust onques oï parler el pooir le roi Artu. Et saciés que onques a son tans el roialme de Logres n'en ot une qui s'aparellast a lui de grant biauté fors que .II. seulement, si fu l'une dame du chastel qui siet en la marche de Norgales et des Frans, si a non li chastiax Gazevilte et a dame ot non Heliene sans peir, et chis contes en parlera en avant; et l'autre fu fille au Roi Mahaignié, che fu li rois Pellés qui fu peires a Amite, meire Galaat, chelui qui vit apertement les grans mervelles del Graal et acompli le siege perillous de la Table Reonde et mena a fin les aventures del roialme perelleus et aventureus, che fu li roialmes de Logres. Cele fu sa meire, si fu de si grant biauté que nus des contes ne dist que nule qui a son tans fust ne se peust de biauté a lui apparellier et si avoit non Amite en sornon et en son droit non Helizabel. (*Lancelot*, 7:59–60)
>
> [He had been married to Queen Guenevere not more than seven and a half months. She was the most beautiful woman that anyone had ever heard tell of in Arthur's domain. And you should know that at that time in the kingdom of Logres there was none who equaled her in beauty, with only two exceptions. One was the lady of a castle which lies on the border of Norgales and the land of the Franks, which is called Gazevilte, and the lady's name is Hélène sans pair, and this tale will speak of her further on. The other was the daughter of the Maimed King, that was king Pellés, who was father to Amide, the mother of Galaad, he who clearly saw the great wonders of the Grail and sat in the Perilous Seat at the Round Table and brought to an end the adventures of the perilous and adventurous kingdom, the kingdom of Logres. She was his mother, and was of such great beauty that none of the

> tales say that any woman of her time could equal her in beauty. Her nickname was Amide and her real name was Helizabel.]

This, however, is the version that the modern editor Alexandre Micha gives in his edition: as a good editor should, Micha offers a resolution of all the variants, and the reading that we should have at this part of the text, in accordance with what will happen later in the text. However, manuscript evidence shows a great deal of confusion about the name of the Grail hero at this point of the Vulgate Cycle, a result of too many variants, and, as I shall show, too many women.

In the tradition of Grail literature leading up to the Vulgate Cycle, from the Grail's first appearance in French literature in Chrétien de Troyes's late twelfth-century *Le Conte du Graal*, through its Continuations and Robert de Boron's Grail Cycle in the thirteenth century, the name of the chosen Grail knight has always been Perceval (or variants of it, such as *Perlesvaus*, in a prose romance more or less contemporaneous with the Vulgate Cycle). The *Lancelot*, and subsequently, *La Queste del Saint Graal*, change this, relegating Perceval to the role of companion to the true Grail knight, Galaad; Perceval is never quite equal to Galaad in prowess or purity, but nonetheless attains some degree of communion with and knowledge of the Grail. In the Vulgate Cycle, Galaad is the son of Lancelot and the daughter of the maimed Grail King, *le Roi Mehaignié*. Perceval, on the other hand, has traditionally been portrayed as the son of the Grail King, rather than his grandson, so the entry of a completely new protagonist into the tradition of Grail literature leads to problems of consistency and coherence.[7] This is very graphically demonstrated in the variants of the passage just quoted. From the appendix in which Micha gives all the variants of this extract, it is clear that this passage is a site of confusion about the identity and genealogy of the Grail knight.[8] In other words, this is a passage that scribes, readers, and critics have scrutinized for the Grail knight's origins, only to produce more confusion, rather than any clarity of vision.

I shall cite just one example here, the first quoted by Micha, to give an idea of the genealogical and nominal tangles in which some scribes found themselves. The scribe of MS Paris, Bibliothèque Nationale, fonds français 96, a fifteenth-century manuscript of the *Lancelot*, simply appears to forget that the Grail knight will be Galaad, making the Grail knight Perceval and Amide his sister.

> Et l'autre fut fille au roy mahagnié, ce fu le roi Perlés qui(t) fu pere Perceval, a celui qui vit appertement les merveilles de Graal et acomplit le siege perilleux de la Table Ronde et mena a fin les aventures du royaume perilleux, ce fut le royaume de Logres. Celle fut sa seur et fut de grant beaulté, que li

> contes dit que nulle qui a son temps fust ne se peust a elle appareiller de beauté, si avoit non Amide en sournon, et en son droit nom Helizabel.[9]
>
> [The other was the daughter of the Maimed King, that was king Pellés, who was father to Perceval, he who clearly saw the great wonders of the Grail and sat in the Perilous Seat at the Round Table and brought to an end the adventures of the perilous kingdom, the kingdom of Logres. She was his sister, and was of such great beauty that the tale says that no woman of her time could equal her in beauty. Her nickname was Amide and her real name was Helizabel.]

Of the thirty manuscripts that transmit this passage, seventeen name the Grail knight Perceval or Perlesvaus, and six call him Galaad. The rest fudge the issue or do not name the Grail knight at all. Other manuscripts show signs of scribal hesitation or confusion; genealogical details are crossed out, or written over. The overall effect of this passage in the *Lancelot* is one of baffled desperation on the part of the scribes, who seek to iron out inconsistencies that they encounter in the text they copy, but which they are unable to eliminate completely.[10]

For critics, this point in the *Lancelot* offers tantalizing clues to the evolution, and even the origin, of this text. Does the confusion evident here indicate, as Elspeth Kennedy argues it does, the original *Lancelot* anticipating at this point a quest narrative in which Perceval will win the Grail?[11] Is the *Lancelot*'s source an Arthurian tale in which Perceval is the Grail knight? Such questions are liable to take the present study far afield: what is at stake here is that this is a passage that hints at the origin of the *Lancelot*, while giving very mixed messages about the origin of the Grail knight.

While the confusion surrounding the name of the Grail hero in this passage is an important focus for critical attention, what has been marginalized in the debate about the "contradiction interne" is the context for the mention of the knight who is to accomplish the quest for the Grail later in the Vulgate Cycle: the hierarchy of beauty into which Guenevere, Hélène sans pair and Amide appear to be so neatly fitted. It is this part of the passage that resonates with Derrida's citation of Freud's unwillingness to pursue the comparison and conflation of the three women called to mind by his dream. Initially, it may appear that this is a specious similarity: whereas Freud has difficulty separating the three or four women whose comparability may, if he does not pay attention, lead him off course, Guenevere, Hélène sans pair, and Amide are categorized nicely into gold, silver, and bronze positions by this passage from the *Lancelot*. However, any distinction between these three women is undermined by their representation as split and duplicated. The language that attempts to visualize them as distinct ends up, through hyperbolic overdetermination, conflating them.

All three are described as peerless in their beauty; the articulation that Micha has chosen as the best reading of the introduction of the two other beauties who outshine Guenevere, "n'en ot une qui s'aparellast a lui de grant biauté fors que .II. seulement" [there was none who equaled her in beauty, with only two exceptions], demonstrates the way that this passage both insists upon, yet elides, the difference between these women, as it privileges first Guenevere's unrivalled beauty and then the women who, precisely, embody that rivalry.

Although she is allotted first place in the hierarchy of beauty, Amide/Helizabel is not at all a singular creature. First, and most obviously, she is split by her doubled name: this splitting, in turn, doubles her with Lancelot, Galaad's father, who also, we are told on the first page of the *Lancelot*, has two names.

> Li rois Bans estoit viex hom et sa feme jovene et molt estoit bele et boine dame et amee de boines gens; ne onques de lui n'avoit eu enfant que .I. tout seul qui valés estoit et avoit non Lancelos en sournon, mais il avoit non en baptesme Galaaz. (*Lancelot*, 7:1)
>
> [King Ban was an old man and his wife was a young, very beautiful and good lady, loved by good people. He had no child by her apart from one, a boy, called Lancelot as a nickname, but his baptismal name was Galaad.][12]

Amide therefore becomes both the mother and the lover of a character called Galaad, and, because of the overlapping and entangled genealogies proposed by the various variants of this passage, Amide is designated as both mother and sister to the Grail hero, thereby doubling her in name and in nature. Elsewhere in the *Lancelot*, Amide also functions as a double for Guenevere, in order for Galaad to be conceived. Lancelot is given a potion that makes him think he is at Camelot; he enters Amide's room, "il li faisoit tel joie et tel feste com il faisoit a sa dame la roine" [He made as much joy and merriment with her as he did with his lady the Queen] (*Lancelot*, 4:209), and Galaad is the result.

In second place, Hélène sans pair is indeed mentioned later in the text, her beauty having condemned her to imprisonment until either a woman more beautiful than her, or a man who is a better knight than her husband, can be found (*Lancelot*, 8:398–99). However, as only the penultimate in the hierarchy of beauty, and initially mentioned as a specific point of comparison between Amide and Guenevere, her peerlessness is troubled. Hélène sans pair is also doubled in the *Lancelot*. Her name is shared by Lancelot's mother, also called Hélène, and anglicized by Malory, who calls Galahad's mother Elaine.[13] Hélène's putative peerless status thus draws attention to the dual nature of all three of the most beautiful women in Arthur's kingdom.

In third position in the ranking of beauty—last, but very much not least—Guenevere is a figure who is always a focus of anxiety, because of her double role as the first lady of the kingdom and adulteress. In this way, despite—and because of—attempts to organize them into a hierarchy that distinguishes them one from the other, Amide, Hélène sans pair, and Guenevere all end up looking very similar indeed, each one standing for and referring to the other two. We may, at this point in a reading of the *Lancelot*, very well recall Freud's warning against the pursuit of comparison between women, lest it lead one astray.

When reading *Résistances de la psychanalyse*, it is striking that Freud and Derrida are seemingly so reluctant to articulate the connection between the inscrutability, the obscurity of the three women in Freud's dream, on the one hand, and their gender on the other. It is surely worth dwelling at least a little on the fact that the feminine, the woman, whose desire Freud famously spoke of in terms of a "dark continent," should stand, at this point in Freud's writing, for that which resists the analysis Freud wishes to perform. Not only, then, do Irma and the women with whom she is conflated stand for that which resists analysis, they also represent a blind spot in both Freud's and Derrida's readings of this dream. In a similar way, it could be argued, the overwhelming resemblance between the ostensibly hierarchized beauties in the passage just discussed functions as a blind spot for those critics intent on discerning in this passage the key to the origins of the Grail knight.

In his reading of Freud, Derrida focuses on the notion of the "navel" of the dream as a figure for that which is inimical to analysis: the navel is a figure that combines the notions of a cut and of a knot, both of which, Derrida suggests, indicate different ideas about what resistance to analysis entails. A knot implies an entanglement of meanings, one that could be teased out in time, temporarily remaining obscure, whereas a cut suggests a severance from any means of analysis.

> . . .comme il s'agit d'un empêchement externe en quelque sorte, on peut supposer qu'il y a du sens au-delà, qu'il y a du sens à aller au-delà, même si en fait on ne le peut pas. Dans le second cas, il s'agit d'une limite structurelle qui nous interdit d'aller au-delà et laisse donc indécidée la présomption de sens.[14]
>
> [Since it concerns an external prevention of some sort, one may assume that there is meaning beyond, that there is a sense in going beyond, even if one cannot do it. In the second case, a structural limit prohibits us from going beyond and thus leaves the presumption of sense undecided].[15]

In fact, this duality of a confusing overproduction of meaning on the one hand and a refusal of interpretation on the other can be detected in Freud's footnote itself, the two elements separated by the ".—" combination to which Derrida draws our attention. "If I had pursued my comparison between the three women, it would have taken me far afield," implies that there is more to pursue, more meaning to be perceived, and in fact a rather dangerous amount of new meaning, which would lead Freud, and his readers, off course. After the full stop dash combination, however, "There is at least one spot in every dream at which it is unplumbable—a navel, as it were, that is the point of contact with the unknown," suggests that no more meaning could be pursued, that the dream here becomes not just unknown but unknowable.

This image of the navel indicates that the point of resistance to analysis is also the point that marks the origin of the dream, and the point that marks the severance from this origin. In the Vulgate Cycle, and criticism written on it, much of this anxiety about perceiving, reading, and interpreting origins is concentrated in the figure of the feminine, and specifically the essentially duplicitous and duplicated Guenevere.

The second very complex part of the *Lancelot*'s manuscript tradition that I want to examine here, and the section of the text that Micha tackles first in his edition, is the episode known as that of the "false Guenevere," in which a young woman arrives at court claiming that she is the true queen, and that the present queen is an impostor, substituted for the real Guenevere on the night of her wedding to Arthur. This episode is found in manuscript form in two distinct versions. Much ink has been spilled in the pursuit of the answer to the question that Micha says is "d'importance primordiale": "de ces deux versions, quelle est celle qui revient à l'auteur, et donc laquelle est antérieure à l'autre?" [The question is of the greatest importance: of these two versions, which is the one which stems from the author, and therefore which one predates the other?].[16]

This question has preoccupied both Micha and Kennedy, and resulted in two opposing theories, and two sets of corresponding terminology.[17] In his *Étude*, Lot compares the long and short versions of this part of the *Lancelot*, and concludes that the shorter false Guenevere story was a rough draft by the same author who later produced the longer version, as well as the whole of the Vulgate Cycle, excluding *Merlin* and its Continuation.[18] Micha refutes this claim and argues that the literary quality of the shorter version is so inferior to its longer counterpart that it must be the product of a later, second-rate, *remanieur* who wished to condense this part of the *Lancelot*.[19] In response to Micha's thesis, Kennedy robustly defends scenes and themes that the French critic condemns as unconvincing, and contends that the shorter version represents an earlier form of the *Lancelot*: it is, she argues, not a rough draft by the same author, as Lot claimed, but an independent, coherent text that was developed by the creators of the Vulgate

Cycle.[20] She therefore dubs this version, which she has edited and presented as an autonomous romance, "non-cyclic," since it does not play a part in a Grail cycle, but is, Kennedy argues, later absorbed into one, becoming the first part of a much longer romance, with the effect that the events portrayed in the non-cyclic *Lancelot* are reinterpreted in the light of the newer Grail material.[21]

Both versions of the false Guenevere episode occur in the *Lancelot* just after Lancelot and Guenevere have first slept together; we could, then, read Guenevere's split and doubling as being occasioned by the initiation of her adultery.[22] In the longer version, the two Gueneveres are half sisters: the "true" Guenevere is the legitimate daughter of King Leodagan and his queen, and the "false" one is the daughter of the king and his seneschal's wife, so they have the same father and different mothers. They are born on the same day, both called Guenevere, and are so alike as to look like twins: "si estoient ansdeus si d'une samblance que la ou eles furent norries connoisoit l'en a paine l'une de l'autre" [And they both looked so alike that, as they were growing up, it was almost impossible to tell them one from the other] (*Lancelot*, 1:95). In the shorter version, the identity of the false Guenevere is unknown, and her lack of family resemblance to Queen Guenevere is overcome by the use of a potion, which causes Arthur to fall for the false Guenevere (*Lancelot*, 3:33–34); she also possesses a wedding ring that is identical to the real Guenevere's (*Lancelot*, 3:26).[23]

In both cases Arthur and his court are baffled, and Arthur is temporarily convinced that the new arrival is his true wife. The question asked by the text is formulated by Burns as "Which Queen?,"[24] but could just as well be expressed in Micha's terms: "De ces deux [Guenièvres], quelle est celle qui revient [au père/à la mère], et donc laquelle est antérieure à l'autre?" [Of these two [Gueneveres], which is the one that stems from the [father/the mother], and therefore which one predates the other?]. Both the critics of this episode, and the characters in it, are thus intent on identifying the original, the true Guenevere—and the true false Guenevere.

Characters and critics are faced with the same problem: neither Guenevere is immune from being called false. The means of distinguishing the two women is the status of their respective relationships with Arthur. It is here that the label "fausse" as applied to the Guenevere who is the daughter of the seneschal's wife, begins to look problematic. It is the "false" Guenevere, after all, who is the most "true" to Arthur, and his "true" wife who has been "false" toward him by conducting her affair with Lancelot. One could go so far as to say that readers are able to identify the "true" Guenevere by the fact that she has slept with Arthur and Lancelot, and the "false" Guenevere by the fact that she has only slept with Arthur. It is evident, then, that the distinction between truth and falsehood relies here upon a narrative that foregrounds origin and visibility, and yet is troubled by that narrative.

The *Merlin* Continuation is the last part of the Vulgate Cycle to be composed, although in manuscripts and in Arthurian chronology it precedes the *Lancelot*. This text offers an apparently straightforward resolution to the problem. The half-twin sisters are only distinguishable by "vne ensenge petite autre tel comme corone de roy" [a little sign like a king's crown] on the real Guenevere's "rains" [flank].[25] This comes in useful after the foiled attempt of the false Guenevere's cohorts to abduct the real Guenevere. King Leodagan questions his daughter, "& ele li conte la uerite si comme ele estoit alee de cief en chief" [and she tells him the truth just as it had happened from beginning to end].[26] Leodagan is not content, however, until Guenevere has been put to bed, and her father inspects her body for a sign that her speech was truthful:

> Lors sen part li rois leodegans & sen uient en la chambre ou genieure sa fille estoit. si enmaine .iij. puceles auoec li por lui aidier a colcier. & quant ele le uoit si commenche a plorer molt durement. & li rois le prent par la main & le trait a vne part si parole a lo seul a seul. & ele li conte la uerite si comme ele estoit alee de cief en chief. & li rois li dist quele ne sesmait de rien car ele naura mais garde. & li rois commanda as .iij. damoiseles quil la couchassent & eles fisent son commandement. ne li rois leodegans ne se vaut partir de la chambre tant quil laient couchie. puis en uint al lit sa fille & haucha le couuertoir & le reborse tort aual tant quil uit lensenge de la coroune sor ses rains. & lors sot il tout vraiement que ce estoit sa fille quil auoit eu de sa feme.[27]
>
> [Then King Leodagan leaves and comes to the room where Guenevere his daughter was, taking three maidens with him to help him to put her to bed. And when she sees him she begins to cry very hard and the King takes her by the hand and takes her to one side and speaks to her alone. She tells him the truth just as it had happened from beginning to end and the King says that she should not upset herself about anything, for she will not be afraid any more. The king ordered that the three maidens put her to bed and they carried out his order. King Leodagan did not want to leave the chamber until they had put her to bed, then he came to his daughter's bed and lifted the cover and pulled it all the way back until he saw the sign of the crown on her flank. And then he knew truly that this was his daughter by his wife.]

Although he has heard "la uerite" from his daughter, Leodagan's subsequent action suggests that her word could be separated from her body, that there is at least the possibility and potential that Guenevere's verbal protests could belie a deceptive body. Rather than relying on possibly deceptive words, Leodagan prefers to locate epistemological certainty in the realm of the visible. He studies Guenevere's body for the sign that she is "true": that she is of pure royal blood and thus worthy of wearing the crown on her head as she already has it inscribed onto her body. His investigation, like that of the critics who examine the variants of the false Guenevere episode, is bent on discovering the truth of Guenevere's origins. Like Freud, Leodagan appears worried that the duplicity of the female might lead him astray. Although, unlike Freud, he does pursue his investigation in order to arrive at a definitive truth, Leodagan's rather sinister inspection of his daughter's body indicates that the feminine, personified here by Guenevere, maintains the threat of inscrutability, just as the variants of the false Guenevere episode propose conflicting narratives of the true origin of the *Lancelot*.

We could perhaps see in the true Guenevere's birthmark a prefiguring of the navel to which Derrida draws our attention: it is a point that marks the origin and the original, and yet also suggests a radical unreadability, indicating that it is impossible to reduce the feminine to one, that it will always be plural. Women, for Freud, Derrida, and the Vulgate Cycle, are at once blind spots in processes of interpretation, and points at which too much meaning is generated: they represent both a cut and a knot. The threat these women embody lies in the way in which they simultaneously refuse and multiply any interpretation the reader, scribe, analyst, or editor may attempt to impose upon them.

For Freud, Derrida, and the *Lancelot*, then, the unreadable, that which resists reading and that which threatens univocal reading, is implicitly gendered feminine. The feminine is unreadable because it invites a visualization in which too much is seen, within which it is difficult, if not impossible, to distinguish between all the women offered to the gaze of the character, reader, or critic. The false Guenevere episode and the passage enumerating the most beautiful women in the kingdom are both places at which the text itself reveals its status as polyvalent, multiform entity, which, like Guenevere and the other beauties, cannot be confined to one corpus. Consequently, they are places at which the text is divided and scrutinized by critics and editors, anxious to present the text closest to the "original," "celle qui revient à l'auteur." As Micha's appendix to the seventh volume of his edition of the *Lancelot* shows, as well as the separate presentation of the two versions of the false Guenevere episode, the Vulgate Cycle is not a body of work that can be confined to a unique original, but is, conversely, a multiple text that teasingly hints that such an original can be extrapolated from the narrative of its evolution, but refuses to reveal it. As readers, then, critics become avatars of Leodagan, inspecting the body of work for signs of its origins. The repeated and replicated female bodies, which, under the scrutiny of the critical gaze of scholars, and of Guenevere's father, are revealed as indiscernible one from another, generate too much interpretation, and yet refuse to be read.

Derrida's reading suggests that the most desirable reading practice is that which continues, undaunted, to perceive and produce as many readings as possible, but he does not articulate the notion that the blind spots, the women who populate the Vulgate Cycle, and Freud's dreams, are generated by, and generate, such interpretative strategies. The less legible these women are, the more textual interpretation they provoke. While Derrida attempts to differentiate between the impossibility of reading and the endless possibility of reading, we can see, reading back through Freud to the Vulgate Cycle, that an obstacle to reading can itself signal and produce multiple readings. It is not, then, a question of a choice between not reading or reading too much, or between not seeing and seeing too much; it may be more useful to see the sentences on either side of Freud's ".—" as equivalents, rather than opposites. My point in using *Lancelot* to read Derrida reading Freud is to highlight this: that the obstacles encountered by reading are as productive of readings as the endless permutation of variants. The multiple women in the Vulgate Cycle and in Freud's dream, then, can be read as standing both for the multiple obstacles to reading and the multiple possibilities of reading that are suggested and mobilized in a medieval text that exists in multiple versions.

Notes

1. The Vulgate Cycle is a long narrative prose text, which was composed in the first half of the thirteenth century and which is divided, in its manuscript tradition and in modern publication, into five different *branches*, or individual texts: *L'Estoire del Saint Graal, L'Estoire de Merlin, Lancelot, La Queste del Saint Graal, La Mort le roi Artu.* Although this is the order in which the texts appear in the manuscript tradition, *L'Estoire del Saint Graal* and the *Merlin* are usually thought of as later additions to the corpus. The only modern edition that gives all five complete texts is *The Vulgate Version of the Arthurian Romances, Edited from Manuscripts in the British Museum*, ed. H. Oskar Sommer, 8 vols. (Washington DC: Carnegie Institution, 1908–16; repr. New York: AMS, 1969). More modern editions of the various texts that comprise the Vulgate Cycle (some of which I will use in this chapter) are: *L'Estoire del Saint Graal*, ed. Jean-Paul Ponceau (Paris: Champion, 1997); *L'Estoire de Merlin*, ed. Alexandre Micha (Geneva: Droz, 1979); *Lancelot*, ed. Alexandre Micha, 9 vols. (Geneva: Droz, 1978–83); *La Queste del Saint Graal*, ed. Albert Pauphilet, 2nd edn. (Paris: Champion, 1984); *La Mort le roi Artu*, ed. Jean Frappier, 3rd edn. (Geneva: Droz, 1964). The second, much longer part of the *Merlin*, known as the Vulgate Continuation, is to this date the only part of the Cycle not to have been reedited, and is therefore quoted in this chapter from Sommer's edition. Translations from the Vulgate Cycle are my own.
2. Jacques Derrida, *Résistances de la psychanalyse* (Paris: Gallilée, 1996). Translations of this work are taken from *Resistances of Psychoanalysis*, trans.

Peggy Kamuf, Pascale-Anne Brault, and Michael Naas (Stanford: Stanford University Press, 1998).

3. Derrida, *Résistances*, pp. 180–99.
4. Sigmund Freud, *Die Traumdeutung*, Studienausgabe, Band 2 (Frankfurt: Fischer, 1982), p. 130n.
5. Sigmund Freud, *The Interpretation of Dreams*, The Penguin Freud Library, ed. Angela Richards and Albert Dickson, 15 vols. (London: Penguin, 1976), 4:186n.
6. Ferdinand Lot, *Étude sur le "Lancelot en prose"* (Paris: Champion, 1918), p. 108.
7. See Grace Armstrong Savage, "Father and Son in the *Queste del Saint Graal*," *Romance Philology* 31 (1977): 1–16.
8. *Lancelot*, 7:462–76. See also Alexandre Micha, "La Tradition manuscrite du *Lancelot en prose*," *Romania* 85 (1964): 297–98 [293–318], and Micha, *Essais sur le cycle "Lancelot-Graal"* (Geneva: Droz, 1987), pp. 19–20.
9. Cited in *Lancelot*, 7:462.
10. See Elspeth Kennedy, "The Scribe as Editor," in *Mélanges de langue et de littérature du Moyen Âge et de la Renaissance offerts à J. Frappier*, 2 vols. (Geneva: Droz, 1970), 1:523–31.
11. Elspeth Kennedy, *Lancelot and the Grail* (Oxford: Clarendon Press, 1986), pp. 143–55.
12. The syntax of this description also resonates with that, discussed earlier, of the introduction of the women who are more beautiful than Guenevere, perhaps marking yet another point of doubling between Lancelot and Amide.
13. Emmanuèle Baumgartner, "Sainte(s) Hélène(s)," in his *De l'histoire de Troie au livre du Graal* (Orleans: Paradigme, 1994), pp. 347–57—first published in *Femmes Mariages-Lignages XIIe–XIVe siècle: Mélanges offerts à Georges Duby*, ed. Jean Dufournet (Brussels: De Boeck University, 1992), pp. 43–54—traces the literary genealogy of women with this name from classical allusions in Wace. Other critics have difficulty separating Hélène and Amide: writing specifically on the Vulgate Cycle, Howard Bloch and Alison Stones both call Galaad's mother Elaine. R. Howard Bloch, *Etymologies and Genealogies: A Literary Anthropology of the French Middle Ages* (Chicago: University of Chicago Press, 1983), p. 211; Alison Stones, "Images of Temptation, Seduction and Discovery in the Prose *Lancelot*: A Preliminary Note," *Wiener Jahrbuch für Kunstgeschichte* 47 (1994): 733 [725–35].
14. Derrida, *Résistances*, p. 27.
15. Derrida, *Resistances*, p. 14.
16. Micha, *Essais*, p. 57.
17. On this debate, see Carol R. Dover, "From Non-Cyclic to Cyclic *Lancelot*: Recycling the Heart," in *Transtextualities: Of Cycles and Cyclicity in Medieval French Literature*, ed. Sara Sturm-Maddox and Donald Maddox (Birmingham, NY: SUNY, 1996), p. 55 [53–70].
18. Lot, *Étude*, pp. 359–77.
19. Alexandre Micha, "Les épisodes du Voyage en Sorelois et de la Fausse Guenièvre," *Romania* 76 (1955): 334–41, and *Essais*, pp. 57–83.

20. Elspeth Kennedy, "The Two Versions of the False Guinevere Episode in the Old French Prose *Lancelot*," *Romania* 77 (1956): 94–104 and *Lancelot and the Grail.*
21. Elspeth Kennedy, "The Re-writing and the Re-reading of a Text: The Evolution of the *Prose Lancelot*," in *The Changing Face of Arthurian Romance: Essays on Arthurian Prose Romances in Memory of Cedric E. Pickford*, ed. Alison Adams et al. (Cambridge, UK: D.S. Brewer, 1986), pp. 1–9.
22. See Charles Méla, *La Reine et le graal: La conjointure dans les romans du Graal de Chrétien de Troyes au Livre de Lancelot* (Paris: Seuil, 1984), p. 360, and Laurence Harf-Lancner, "Les deux Guenièvre dans le *Lancelot* en prose," in *Lancelot: Actes du colloque des 14 et 15 janvier 1984*, ed. Danielle Buschinger (Goppingen: Kummerle, 1984), p. 70 [63–73].
23. For an excellent discussion of this part of the *Lancelot*, see Paul Vincent Rockwell, *Rewriting Resemblance in Medieval French Romance: Ceci n'est pas un graal* (New York: Garland, 1995), pp. 43–60.
24. E. Jane Burns, "Which Queen? Guinevere's Transvestism in the French Prose *Lancelot*," in *Lancelot and Guinevere: A Casebook*, ed. Lori J. Walters (New York: Garland, 1996), pp. 249–50 [247–65].
25. *Vulgate Version of the Arthurian Romances*, ed. Sommer, 2:149.
26. *Vulgate Version of the Arthurian Romances*, ed. Sommer, 2:310.
27. *Vulgate Version of the Arthurian Romances*, ed. Sommer, 2:310.

RESPONSE

CHAPTER 12

THE MEDIEVAL LOOKS BACK: A RESPONSE TO *TROUBLED VISION*

Sarah Salih

Salih's response considers the reciprocity of visions of the medieval and objectifications of the Middle Ages in modern discourse; she engages with some of the concerns of the collection by discussing an example from an illustrated manuscript of Mandeville's Travels.

In British newspapers of May 9, 2003, Charles Clarke, the UK Secretary of State for Education, was reported to have remarked: "I don't mind there being some medievalists around for ornamental purposes, but there is no reason for the state to pay for them."[1] Although it emerged that the minister was misquoted (he had intended to disparage humanities research in general, rather than medieval studies in particular), the idea that the period and its students might be regarded as ornamental is strangely resonant. An ornamental Middle Ages is an unthreatening object: under the gaze of modernity, it sits meek and static on its shelf, representing all that is not modern and therefore to be disavowed. As Arthur Lindley argues, "the dominant mode of medieval film. . .is fabular. . .we automatically privilege the current signified over the medieval signifier."[2] In popular discourse, the medieval is thus an object that is never allowed to represent itself, as we see also in the use of "medieval" to refer to such distinctly modern phenomena as radical Islam. Thinking we know what the medieval is, we fail to look at it, and so the most effective medieval films are, for me, those exceptions to Lindley's analysis such as *Monty Python and the Holy*

Grail or *A Knight's Tale*, which disrupt the comfort of gazing at an unproblematic notion of the medieval.[3] It is a pleasure to respond here to a collection of essays that presents to our sight a "medieval" that is not ornamental, a medieval that looks back at its observers and has the potential to disrupt our ways of seeing. Our own vision of the medieval is thus troubled as it is brought into dialogue with the contemporary.

The medievalist enthusiasm for discourses such as film theory, though it tends to surprise non-medievalists (including some film theorists), indicates a perception that medieval culture was intensely visual, as much if not more so than contemporary culture. Narratives such as romance and hagiography were multimedia; documents were authenticated with seals and illuminated initials; history could be presented in visual form in objects such as the Bayeux Tapestry; artworks were cult-objects, which could inform visionary experiences. Text itself could be used for primarily visual effect, as, for instance, in Holy Trinity Church, Long Melford, where John Lydgate's devotional lyrics were used as up-market wallpaper.[4] This collection explores various aspects of that visuality. It is aware of both the connections and the differences between visual and verbal cultures: viewing an image may be a very different experience from reading a narrative that invites us to form mental images. It emphasizes the importance of the circumstances of viewing—whether it is shared or solitary, public or private—an interest shared by current film theory, which proposes that spectatorship itself is as much contextual and experiential as it is psychological or phenomenological.[5] It examines a range of objects: contributors look not only at medieval material, but also at the medieval's scrutiny of itself, and at both medieval and modern theories of gender and vision.

The great strength of this collection is the complication of both the concepts of vision and gender and of their mutually constitutive relations. The crude polarity of the masculine gaze on the feminine object, itself no longer current in film theory, was always qualified in its usefulness for medievalists, given the prominence of masculine objects of vision—Christ on the cross, arming scenes, priests at the altar, and kings enthroned—in medieval life, literature, and art. Thinking, indeed, of the extreme violence of some women's Passion visions, I would suggest that the position of the witness could easily slip into that of the torturer. In this collection, the gendering of spectators and sights is subject to explicit and implicit interrogations, as the contributors place the medieval into a position from which it can look back at us. The collection explores the multiplicity of the relations between vision and gender, starting from the editors' emphasis on the visuality of performative gender, which calls attention to the production of gender as a communal and relational process. It is usual practice to refuse gender an essence and to insist on its instability and contingency, but this collection's scrutiny of gender is so intense that there are moments when gender itself disappears into the blind spots identified by the editors in their introduction. We are presented with a series of gazes that finally fail to secure gender but expose instead the attempt to do so; gazes that confuse rather than clarify the difference of subject and object, neither guaranteeing the subjectivity of the gazer nor the objectification of the gazed-upon. While being brought into visibility may be an uncomfortable situation for the sodomite, there are also instances here when to see can be not to have, not to enter, not to control. Medieval objects and discussions of vision offer multiple gazes, with multiple dynamics.

I should like to take advantage of the position in which the editors of this volume have placed me to close with one example of some of the complexities of medieval gendered vision and of the relations between the visual and the verbal. I shall concentrate on a visual image that troubled and enriched my understanding of gender in its associated text, revealing unexpected intersections between gender and other categories. I encountered this in the course of my current work on a fifteenth-century illustrated manuscript of *Mandeville's Travels*: London, British Library MS Harley 3954. The illustrative cycle is in active dialogue with the popular text, and is quite different in its emphases from two other near-contemporary sets of illustrations of Mandeville: London, British Library MS Royal 17.c. 38 and Wynken de Worde's 1499 printed edition. The Harley manuscript has some blank spaces for illustrations, indicating that their layout was carefully planned during the copying of the text; on the four folios where there are three images, the text is reduced to a minimum to act as captions for the illustrations. One such folio is a particularly rich example of what can be gained from the analysis of image and words together: fol. 42r illustrates in detail a brief description of cyclops and two forms of headless men:

> And in one of hem beþ haueþ but on iȝe, and þat is in þe myddel of here frount. And þei etiþ noȝt but fleisch and fysch rawȝ.
> And in anoþer yle dwelliþ men þat haueþ noon heedis and here iȝen beþ in here schuldris and here mowþis vpon here breestis.
> And in anoþer yle beþ men þat haueþ noon heedis noþer iȝen and here mowþis beþ bihynde in here schuldris.[6]

The pictures, like a film adaptation of a novel, necessarily add concreteness and specificity to the fantastic world of the text (figure 12.1). They illustrate not only the text, but also the process of producing the text: in the lowest image the figure of Mandeville, in pilgrim's dress, stands in the left-hard margin, gesturing to the monsters with hand and staff, while in the central one he sits unobserved in the same position, gazing thoughtfully at them

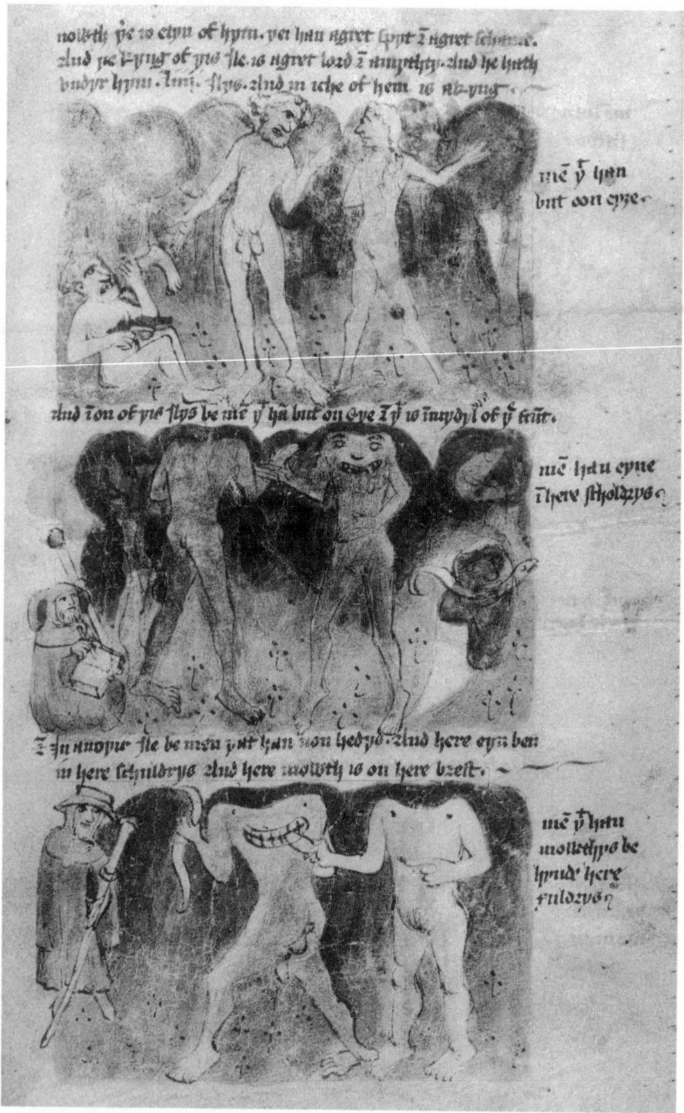

12.1 Cannibalistic giants and blemmyes. Manuscript of *Mandeville's Travels*, ca. 1430. London, British Library, MS 3954, fol. 42r.

while preparing to record his observations in a bound manuscript volume; its folios are still blank, so there is no way of knowing whether he is about to write or draw what he sees. In a textual and in this case, visual equivalent to "*gadlibiriens*," (p. 122, l. 23) the professional deflowerers who expose themselves to the dangers of snake-infested virginal vaginas, the figure of Mandeville mediates between the viewer and the desirable but dangerous sights of the world. The illustrations in this manuscript are thus self-consciously mediated; that the other two cycles I know do not make such use of the figure of Mandeville indicates that medieval visual material has varying degrees of self-awareness. Even in the Harley manuscript, however, Mandeville has his limits. In another chapter of the *Travels*, Mandeville is told of an island inhabited by fifty-foot giants, but remarks, "Y sauȝ neuer hem" (p. 122, l. 11). Given that the current critical consensus is that Mandeville is a fictive identity and that the author probably never traveled, the distinction between thirty-foot giants that Mandeville had seen and fifty-foot ones that he had not is a witty authenticity-effect, for nor had Mandeville seen any other of the dangerous and marvelous sights he describes. The illustrator is unlikely to have known this, but was alert enough to the text's construction of the Mandeville-persona to omit the figure of Mandeville from the uppermost image, where the cyclops eat human flesh. By contrast with the lower two, this provides a frisson of danger for the viewer of the image: these particular monsters are not as safely mediated as the rest.

By comparison with the minimalist text, the illustrations are also intensely gendered and sexualized. One cyclops and one blemmy have large and prominent male genitalia: their companions may be females, but are drawn less distinctly. This is consistent with the rest of the illustrations: male nudes appear with some regularity throughout the manuscript. Kathleen Scott's survey of the manuscript suggests on stylistic grounds that there were two illustrators, A and B, and the distribution of nudes confirms this assessment: A has one only when the text specifies "it is so hote þare in þat yle þat men [ballokez] hongiþ doun to here shankis" (p. 72, ll. 18–19), but B gives us naked men on several occasions when they are not required by the text. Such detailed depictions of nude men are not common in surviving medieval art: Christ has his loincloth, Adam his fig leaf, while illustrations of erotic scenes in romance are generally politely indirect. Their presence here is thus troubling.

Traditionally, sexuality in Mandeville is considered to be subject to an ethic of restraint; more recently Linda Lomperis has argued for a subtle strain of, if not homoeroticism, at least homosociality in the text.[7] There are certainly some very anxious representations of female sexuality, such as the virgin in dragon's shape who both desires and threatens knights, and beautiful boys are added to the maidens in the false Paradise. I do not mean to "out" Mandeville: there seems little point in attaching an identity to so nebulous and tricky a figure, but the text does give an interested reader the opportunity of developing homoerotic themes. There is, however, nothing subtle or restrained about the naked giants: the illustrator has made an emphatic and not entirely predictable reading of the text.

It is not possible to be certain why this illustrator made this reading. One suggestion that comes to mind is that the illustrator, for his, or indeed her, own personal reasons, found male nudes aesthetically interesting: while this may well be true, it does not explain the cultural work that the illustrations perform. I would suggest, in addition, that this illustrator's choices highlight the place of Mandeville in the recently discovered postcolonial Middle Ages: his visual response to the text is to wonder how gender intersects with other categories of culture and ethnicity. One possibility here might be that the illustrator is finding a way of coping with the huge array of difference—differences of culture, religion, physiology—in Mandeville's world. He cannot take the option of the illustrator of the near-contemporary Royal manuscript, which largely ignores the more exotic parts of the text to draw pictures of more familiar things, such as saints, relics, and mountains, because the spaces left for illustration in this manuscript have already made the choice to emphasize the exotic. In this analysis, he could be read as reassuring himself, faced with all this diversity, that there are at least some constants in the world, and one of them—perhaps the most important—is masculine anatomy. However odd their forms and their behavior, at least the giants are men, for we can see the naked truth of their anatomies, underlying their cultural differences.

There are, however, some problems with this interpretation: in particular, that the naked body is not necessarily the primary sign of masculinity. The illustrator has other ways of marking the difference between men and women, which are more generally familiar in medieval art; men have reddish skin, short hair, and sometimes beards; women have white skin and long hair (and sometimes beards, this being Mandeville, but that is a one-off, with an explanatory rubric to prevent confusion). There is also one fascinating drawing where the illustrator seems to be experimenting with new ways of indicating sexual difference; a very brief description of horned men is elaborated into what looks to me like an image of males with one horn and a female with three.

Collating the nudes back against the text they illustrate, a further pattern becomes apparent, not entirely consistent with the idea that they represent the constancy of masculinity. They tend to appear at moments that are quite heavily marked with otherness. The two folios with the heaviest concentration of male nudes illustrate the brief passage describing the Plinian races, all quite as strange as the cyclops and blemmyes. This being so, it is by no means obvious that drawing them with large penises makes them any less strange, and there are other visual indications that what we are seeing is a parade of otherness. This illustrator generally has a liking for architectural backgrounds, but the naked monstrous races are shown against wooded backgrounds, suggesting they are dwellers in the wilderness. Meanwhile, people whose differences are purely intellectual or religious are depicted clothed and in cities. I have discussed elsewhere a folio that illustrates an account of pagan practices, which include worshipping snakes, idols, and the first thing they see in the morning.[8] Although this is, by the standards of Western Christianity, distinctly alien behavior, the illustrator follows up the text's apologia for such worships by depicting them as happening in a civilized space; they may be other, but at least they are another *culture*, coherent on its own terms. The text imagines them as rational and articulate, able to explain their beliefs and practices, and the illustrations respond to that emphasis. The naked people in wooded settings, however, don't *do* anything much except engage in another sign of culturelessness, eating raw bits of human flesh. Otherwise, they just *are*: that is, they are objects for the attention of narrator and illustrator that cannot answer back. In the absence of the kinds of cultural similarity that enable Mandeville to converse with Muslims and admire cynocephali, the bodily strangeness of the monstrous races is rather emphasized than minimized by their hyper-masculinity. The illustrator does not conceive of ethnic difference in terms of skin color, and difference of bodily shape can be accommodated if the monsters in question, such as the cynocephali, exhibit signs of social order; this leaves nudity to signify ethnic difference. In this picture cycle, we don't know what the narrator, or the Sultan and his lords, would look like naked, because we are never shown them naked; clothed and marked by culture is their natural state; Mandeville in pilgrim's clothing is in visual contrast here to the naked monsters. Cultured males—Mandeville, the Sultan, the cynocephali—have swords, spears, and pilgrim's staffs; bearing the phallic symbols, they don't need the thing itself. So in the pictures of the giants and blemmyes, we are not seeing a phallus, but just a penis, a sign of monstrosity not of power. When we see it, we know that it belongs to a creature that is inarticulate, uncultured, and probably other than human; a creature comparable to the wild man or satyr, whose sexual potency must be disavowed and mastered by civilized men.

The picture cycle, then, responds to Mandeville's concerns about gender, and adds emphasis to his reticence about sexuality. A proper masculinity is one that is only minimally sexualized, whose sexuality is controlled and concealed. The very presence of quite so many male nudes suggests that there is also a pleasure involved in contemplating them—the figure of Mandeville certainly appears to enjoy gazing upon them—but the contexts suggest that it is not a narcissistic pleasure, but the pleasure of contemplating the other. If there is an erotic impulse here, it is heteroerotic, enjoying the contemplation of the culturally other, as much as it is homoerotic in enjoying the contemplation of the gendered same. However, the whole sexual economy of the text together with the illustrations is, from another perspective, homosocial; proper masculinity is produced by the control and disavowal of both the feminine and the hyper-masculine. We can recognize people as others when they have not produced this controlled masculinity, and recognize their similarity, despite all kinds of strange behaviors, if they do. Not every reader seems to have thought that Mandeville was a text with much to say about gender; the Royal illustrations more or less ignore it as a theme, and the 1499 woodcut illustrations only emphasize gender when the text calls for it. In the Harley illustrator, however, we can see one medieval reader of Mandeville who responded and elaborated on the idea that gender can be used as a marker for other forms of difference. Investigating the visuality of gender in this manuscript leads to unexpected conclusions. Skin color does not indicate ethnic but sexual difference; a man with a dog's head is less alien than a man with a large penis; masculine identity is located in cultural behavior, not bodily essentialism.

Whether in aesthetic or other terms, Mandeville's monsters are other than ornamental. To look at them is to see gender in a complex set of interactions with other processes of categorization. The medieval text and image look back at and trouble modernity, de-naturalizing our own terms. Though there is pleasure in the exploration of this "touch," I cannot be certain how my gaze on this image differs from those of its medieval viewers, or whether they found it more comforting than perplexing. Looking at the medieval remains a troubling pleasure; this process of disrupting difference and similarity by gazing upon them is an unclassifiable erotic.

Notes

I am grateful to the editors of this volume for many things: for organizing the original conference; for inviting me to contribute this response; and especially for their patience. Special thanks too to Scott MacKenzie for encouragement, conversation, and information about film theory.

1. "Clarke Dismisses Medieval Historians," *The Guardian* (May 9, 2003), p. 7, available online at <http://education.guardian.co.uk/higher/artsandhumanities/story/0,12241,952356,00.html>.
2. Arthur Lindley, "The Ahistoricism of Medieval Film," *Screening the Past* 3 (1998), published online at <http://www.latrobe.edu.au/screeningthepast/firstrelease/fir598/ALfr3a.htm>.
3. *Monty Python and the Holy Grail*, dir. Terry Gilliam and Terry Jones (1975); *A Knight's Tale*, dir. Brian Helgeland (2001).
4. Gail McMurray Gibson, *Theater of Devotion: East Anglian Drama and Society in the Late Middle Ages* (Chicago: University of Chicago Press, 1989), pp. 86–87.

5. See, for example, Miriam Hansen, *Babel and Babylon: Spectatorship in American Silent Film* (Cambridge, MA: Harvard University Press, 1991).
6. The folio is reproduced in color in Alixe Bovey, *Monsters and Grotesques in Medieval Manuscripts* (London: British Library, 2002), fig. 16. Text from *The Defective Version of Mandeville's Travels*, ed. M.C. Seymour, Early English Text Society, original series 319 (Oxford: Oxford University Press, 2002), p. 87, ll. 6–12. Further references will be included in parentheses in the text.
7. Iain Macleod Higgins, *Writing East: The "Travels" of Sir John Mandeville* (Philadelphia: University of Pennsylvania Press, 1997), pp. 192–93; Linda Lomperis, "Medieval Travel Writing and the Question of Race," *Journal of Medieval and Early Modern Studies* 31.1 (2001): 147–64.
8. Sarah Salih, "Idols and Simulacra: Paganity, Hybridity and Representation in *Mandeville's Travels*," in *The Monstrous Middle Ages*, ed. Bettina Bildhauer and Robert Mills (Cardiff: University of Wales Press, 2003), p. 123 and fig. 13 (pp. 113–33).

CONTRIBUTORS

William Burgwinkle teaches French and Occitan literature at the University of Cambridge and directs studies in Modern and Medieval Languages at King's College Cambridge. He is the author of *Razos and Troubadour Songs, Love for Sale: Materialist Readings of the Troubadour Razos*, and the recently completed *Knight Out: Sodomy and Masculinity, 1120–1220.* He is currently working on visual memory, concentrating on the intersection of torture and the sublime in medieval hagiography and early photography.

Emma Campbell recently completed a Ph.D. on Old French saints' lives at King's College London. She has articles in *French Studies* and *Comparative Literature*, and has translated into English an interview with Jean-Luc Nancy for a special edition of *Angelaki*. She was winner in 2002 of the Gapper Prize for the best graduate essay in French Studies.

Miranda Griffin was until recently Tutorial Fellow in Medieval French at St. Hilda's College, Oxford. She completed her doctorate at Cambridge University where she submitted a thesis on the Vulgate Cycle. She has published articles on Marie de France and the *fabliaux*, and her book, *The Object and the Cause in the Vulgate Cycle*, is forthcoming. Her current research interests include ideas of transformation in medieval literature, and the figure and function of Merlin in thirteenth-century prose romance.

Simon Gaunt is Professor of French Language and Literature at King's College London. He is the author of *Troubadours and Irony, Gender and Genre in Medieval French Literature* and *Retelling the Tale: An Introduction to Medieval French Literature*. He is the editor (with Sarah Kay) of *The Troubadours: An Introduction* and (with Ruth Harvey and Linda Paterson) of *Marcabru: A Critical Edition*. He is currently working on a book on love and death in medieval literature, *Martyrs to Love*.

Cary Howie is a postdoctoral fellow in Romance Studies at Cornell University. He recently completed a Ph.D. in Comparative Literature at Stanford University, with a dissertation entitled *Claustrophilia: Readings in the Erotics of Enclosure*.

Sylvia Huot is Reader in Medieval French Literature and a Fellow of Pembroke College at Cambridge University. Her publications include *From Song to Book, The Romance of the Rose and Its Medieval Readers, Allegorical Play in the Old French Motet*, and the forthcoming *Madness in Medieval French Literature: Identities Found and Lost*. She is currently working on a study of cultural ideologies in the *Roman de Perceforest*.

Catherine M. Keen is Lecturer in Italian at the University of Leeds. Her research interests include medieval Italian literature, especially Dante, and the political thought and civic culture of the medieval Italian city-states. Her publications include a forthcoming book on Dante and the City, and articles on Dante, Cino da Pistoia, and other early Italian lyricists. Her current research explores the representation of exile in Italian lyric verse of the thirteenth and fourteenth centuries.

Robert Mills is Lecturer in English at King's College London. To date, his research has mainly been concerned with representations of the punished body in the late Middle Ages and, within that broad theme, constructions of pain, pleasure, gender, and sexual identity. He has published several articles on these topics and edited (with Bettina Bildhauer) *The Monstrous Middle Ages*. His book on medieval punishment iconography is forthcoming.

Francesca Nicholson recently completed her doctoral thesis on the women troubadours at the University of Cambridge. Her research interests include medieval Occitan and French literature, gender theories, psychoanalysis, and phenomenology. She has several articles on these topics forthcoming.

Anne Simon is Senior Lecturer in the Department of German at the University of Bristol. She is author of *Sigmund Feyerabend's Das Reyßbuch deß heyligen Lands*, and editor (with Elizabeth Andersen, Jens Haustein, and Peter Strohschneider) of *Autor und Autorschaft im Mittelalter*, and (with Helen Watanabe-O'Kelly) of *Festivals and Ceremonies: A Bibliography of Works Relating to Court, Civic and Religious Festivals in Europe 1500–1800*. Her current research interests are the relationship between text and image in the Middle Ages; the history of the book; writing for women; pilgrimage and travel literature.

Sarah Salih is Lecturer in English and American Studies, University of East Anglia. Her research is mainly concerned with later medieval writing in England, specializing on the topics of sexuality, virginity, and gender. Her recent publications include *Versions of Virginity in Late Medieval England*

(2001), *Gender and Holiness: Men, Women and Saints in Late Medieval Europe*, coedited with Samantha J.E. Riches (2002), and *Medieval Virginities*, coedited with Anke Bernau and Ruth Evans (2003). She is now planning a large-scale survey of representations of paganity.

Diane Wolfthal is Associate Professor of Art History at Arizona State University. She is author of *The Beginnings of Netherlandish Canvas Painting* and *Images of Rape: The "Heroic" Tradition and Its Alternative*, and editor of books on peace and (with Rosalynn Voaden) on the family. Her book on images in Yiddish books produced in sixteenth-century Italy is forthcoming.

INDEX